THE LEARNING OF DEMOCRACY IN LATIN AMERICA:
SOCIAL ACTORS AND CULTURAL CHANGE

THE LEARNING OF DEMOCRACY IN LATIN AMERICA:
SOCIAL ACTORS AND CULTURAL CHANGE

PAULO J. KRISCHKE

Nova Science Publishers, Inc.
New York

Senior Editors: Susan Boriotti and Donna Dennis
Coordinating Editor: Tatiana Shohov
Office Manager: Annette Hellinger
Graphics: Wanda Serrano
Book Production: Matthew Kozlowski, Jonathan Rose and Jennifer Vogt
Circulation: Cathy DeGregory, Ave Maria Gonzalez and Raheem Miller
Communications and Acquisitions: Serge P. Shohov

Library of Congress Cataloging-in-Publication Data

Krischke, Paulo J. (Paulo José)
    The learning of democracy in Latin America: social actors and cultural change / Paulo J.
Krischke.
      p. cm.
    Includes bibliographical references and index.
    ISBN 1-59033-062-5.
    1. Democracy—Latin America. 2. Democratization—Latin America. 3. Political
participation—Latin America. 4. Social change—Political aspects—Latin America. I. Title

JL966 .K75 2001
320.98—dc21

                            2001054697

ABOUT THE AUTHOR

Paulo J. Krischke holds a Ph.D. in political science from York University, Canada (1983) and teaches in the area of political theory and comparative studies in the Interdisciplinary Graduate Program in the Humanities, Universidade Federal de Santa Catarina, Brazil. He has been a visiting scholar at the following universities: Universidad Nacional Autónoma de México, Notre Dame University, USA and Temple University, USA. He is also a senior researcher in the areas of political science, sociology and anthropology at the Conselho Nacional de Desenvolvimento Científico e Tecnológico (CNPQ), and has written extensively on social movements, the political role of the church in Latin America, political culture, social and political democratization, and related processes and theories.

Address: Caixa Postal 5147, Florianópolis, SC 88040-970, Brazil. [email: krischke@cfh.ufsc.br or pjk@ativanet.com.br]

CONTENTS

ACKNOWLEDGEMENTS

This book would never be finished without the steady support, encouragement, and loving kindness of my wife Dulce and our daughter Vitoria. Many people contributed to the book, and no list of their names could possibly acknowledge all their contributions. Some of the colleagues who read parts of the text are mentioned at the beginning of each chapter. Philip Evanson, Judith Hellman and Jeffrey Hoff read most of the typescript and offered valuable suggestions. Stephen Chilton kindly accepted to write the Preface, and made many important comments to improve the structure of the book. I am very grateful for their suggestions, which actually influenced the revision of the text - though I doubt that I was able to meet all their expectations. I must also express my appreciation for the academic environment where the research for this book was undertaken: the Center for Studies in Contemporary Culture (CEDEC, São Paulo) and the Graduate Program in the Humanities, Universidade Federal de Santa Catarina (Florianópolis, Brazil). Early drafts for the chapters of the book were presented for discussion in meetings of: the World Congress of Sociology (ISA), (Chapters 4 and 7); the Latin American Sociological Association (ALAS), (Chapter 5); the Brazilian Association of Graduate Study in the Social Sciences (ANPOCS), (Chapters 1, 2, 3 and 6); and a FLACSO seminar on "Scenarios of Political Democratization in Latin America." Previous versions of these chapters were published by the following journals: **International Sociology**: Chapter 1; the **Canadian Journal of Development Studies**: Chapter 2; **Ciências Sociais Hoje (*ANPOCS*)**: Chapter 3; **Revista Crítica de Ciências Sociais (*Universidade de Coimbra*)**: Chapter 4; **Revista Venezolana de Sociología y Antropología (*Universidad de Merida*)**: Chapter 5; **Comparative Political Studies**: Chapter 6; **Revista dos Municípios (*Instituto Brasileiro de Administração Municipal*)**: Chapter 7; **Latin American Research Review**: Chapter 8. All chapters were reformulated for this book, and the comments from anonymous referees of the above journals were very helpful for the revision.

Florianópolis, March 31, 2001.
Paulo J. Krischke

PREFACE

Stephen Chilton

This book is the first overview in English of Professor Krischke's work over the past decade or so. It makes accessible research that unilingual researchers (like this writer) have heard about only indirectly: work whose theoretical ground is simultaneously multilayered, cross-national, and accepting – not detached, quite the opposite, but generous. The purpose of this Preface is to indicate the fundamental coherence of Krischke's approach, a coherence that the very diversity of his work may obscure.

Krischke's central concern is to understand, clarify, and advance the process of democratization in Latin America.[1] This concern might be of only theoretical, utopian interest in other times and places, but the last twenty years have seen a remarkable opening of democratic possibilities in Latin America. That opening comes out of a decline in the power and legitimacy of entrenched, traditional forces: the landowning / extractive and local industrial/financial elites, the political parties representing them, and the civil-military bureaucracy enforcing their authority. These actors continue to have formidable power, but their monopoly on it has been effectively challenged by two new social forces. First, there is a rising technological-commercial and dependent industrial/financial class, with their strength based on international corporate ties and international political support. That strength can be opposed by traditional elites, but it is not controllable by them. Second, there is the power of local communities, where "community" might be constructed around a common culture, residence, and/or employment.[2] Previously, such organization could not arise independent of the traditional elite, whose power was precisely their ability to control the local communities in their domains. Now, however, local communities have independent sources of power: the support of the technological-commercial and dependent industrial/financial class in pursuit of allies in its own struggle against the traditional elites; the support of the national and international NGOs committed to norms of democratic rule and human rights,[3] including the right to organize; and the support of the new norms themselves, in the sense that they are widely understood and even agreed-to, so that communities seeking to organize have a language for participating in the public discourse and a constituency of sympathizers. The balance among these three forces and the fact that each has power resources independent of the others means that no one of them can have a monopoly on power; none can crush the others.[4]

Within such a context, ideas and movements can transform politics and society in ways that are not ordinarily possible, because to gain and retain power, one must find new answers to several fundamental questions for oneself and one's supporters:

A. What are our claims, precisely, and by what normative standard do we justify them, not only to ourselves but also to others?
B. Who is the "we" in these questions, exactly?
C. How does one organize that "we" in practice: how does one appeal effectively to supporters; how does one organize them for political action; and can that organization survive in political struggle?

These questions are correlative; the answer to any can potentially alter or undercut answers to the others. When society is in flux, when the old configurations of power no longer dominate, then the previous answers to these questions become problematic, and new ideas and new forms of organization and political action become much more important than usual. Those who find ways to answer these questions will define the shape of politics. For these reasons, Krischke's work takes on a particular relevance and indeed urgency. In Latin America, in this period of history, his normative concerns are met by an immediate need to understand the ideas and political configurations that flow from them or might still do so.

So what is Krischke's orientation? Even cursory examination of his work reveals that he shares a "preferential option for the poor" – one common characterization of liberation theology, shared by many NGOs and other groups in society –, meaning that the concerns of the poor, the powerless, the voiceless are most important and should be addressed first. In all his work Krischke treats these disenfranchised and silenced groups as subjects of history; he does not dismiss their actions and choices as mere annoyances to the real business of governing.

Reading at that cursory level, one could take Krischke's position as an ordinary choice of sides, his preference to be accepted tolerantly as one aspect of the general competition among interests, as in, "Your commitment is to the poor; I have my own, different commitments." However, Krischke's commitment (in contrast to liberation theology) is to the existence of free discourse, not to any predefined set of institutions, procedures, groups, or interests. Open discourse is thus a criterion for judging these things, and his commitment is to that criterion, even while he considers some specific situation, proposal, or group.

As Krischke understands it, discourse is about people recognizing and defining their interests, organizing, bargaining, forming coalitions, and coming to terms with others' views and interests, all of this taking place within fundamental conditions approximating an ideal speech situation.[5] All of these activities constitute what U.S. political science terms the political party / interest group system, and the present work should be viewed as a contribution to its theory. The major difference between Krischke's work and the traditional (U.S.) political party / interest group research is that Krischke has to consider explicitly whether those "more fundamental conditions approximating an ideal speech situation" exist, while U.S. scholars can (or at any rate do) take them for granted.[6] If Krischke's research rings strange to the ears of those within the traditional field of political party and interest group scholarship, they should consider what their field would look like if it were applied to a society in which the fundamental assumptions of political discourse were consistently violated.

It is for these reasons that Krischke's "preferential option for the poor" arises not from a belief that the poor's claims are inherently superior but instead from the rather ordinary observation that they are the most excluded from discourse and thus those whose treatment most violates the norms of democracy. Anatole France (1894:Ch. 7) once wrote in sorrow and anger that "The law, in its majestic equality, forbids rich and poor alike to sleep under bridges, beg in the streets or steal bread." Krischke's perspective is the contrapositive of this: he seeks open discourse for all, a democratic society whose members both speak and listen to the legitimate interests of all, rich and poor alike, as they decide the norms to regulate their common life – a society where no one's voice could be so lost as to make them sleep under bridges.

May 29, 2001

REFERENCES

Fahrenbach, Helmut, ed. (1973). *Wirklichkeit und Reflexion: Walter Schulz zum 60. Geburtstag*. Pfüllingen, Germany: Günther Neske.

France, Anatole (1894). *Red Lily*.

Gaventa, John (1982). *Power and Powerlessness*. Urbana, IL: University of Illinois.

Habermas, Jürgen (1983/1990). *Moral Consciousness and Communicative Action*. Cambridge, MA: MIT.

Habermas, Jürgen (1973). Wahrheitstheorien. In Fahrenbach, ed. (1973:211-265).

Risse-Kappen, Thomas, Steve C. Ropp, and Kathryn Sikkink, eds. (1999). *The Power of Human Rights: International Norms and Democratic Change*. NY: Cambridge.

ENDNOTES

[1] His work is situated within Latin American history, social structure, and institutions, but the lessons apply to any society in normative flux. Krischke does not generalize his findings, nor shall this Preface, but the reader should find their broader implications clear.

[2] The emphasis here is on organization for political action, not on the natural, pre-existing, "organic" ties among people. The two are obviously related, but organization is necessarily a social construction.

[3] This would include the liberation theology movement within the Roman Catholic Church and, of course, similar support from a variety of NGOs. See the discussion of these groups' power, both its nature and its dynamics, in Risse-Kappen, Ropp & Sikkink, eds. (1999).

[4] This is not meant to imply that they possess equal power.

[5] This was originally Habermas's term, on which he tried to ground discourse ethics: norms were justified if people agreed or would agree to them under the conditions of the ideal speech situation (Habermas 1973). Unfortunately, once any specific characterization of the ideal speech situation is advanced (by him or anyone else), it is vulnerable to postmodernists' objections that it is either inaccurate or incomplete, so that some are advantaged by it and thus exercise an unjust power, even if they are not conscious of it. Habermas (1983/1990) reconstructed his argument to meet this objection, so my characterization of Krischke's position does not do him (or Habermas) full justice. However, these philosophical issues are not of immediate concern in the context of democratizing Latin America, where the most rudimentary conditions of open discourse have been quite openly violated.

[6] Many exceptions can be found in the community power literature, of course. See, for one good example, Gaventa (1982).

INTRODUCTION

"(...A) public understanding could arise consistent with the historical conditions and constraints of our social world. Until we bring ourselves to conceive how this could happen, it can't happen."
(John Rawls, 1985)

In the year 2000 the Brazilian government organized the country's Fifth Centennial Celebration in Porto Seguro, Bahia, where the first Portuguese arrived on April 22, 1500. The official celebration was widely publicized by the media, and in every major city of the country there were shows and popular events related to the Centennial Celebration. However, there were also protests and demonstrations, especially by the native peoples, Afro-Brazilians, other minority groups and sectors of the opposition, who felt excluded from (and/or victimized by) the official history of this country.

For instance, some groups managed to organize a protest demonstration, which attempted to march during the official celebration in Porto Seguro. The TV variety show *'Fantástico'* - which is sub-titled 'The show of life' (*'O Show da Vida'*) and has the widest national audience Sunday nights - presented a two-hour program on the centennial celebration that week. Five minutes of these two hours presented flashes of the images of the protest demonstration in Porto Seguro, mainly focusing on the arrest of a half-naked youngster, who stood with open arms in front of the police, trying to block its attack on the protestors. The young man was Gildo Jorge Roberto, 18 years old, a member of the Terena ethnic group.

The images of his action appeared nationwide and worldwide in the news coverage of the repression on the march against the official celebration. On the same show of *'Fantástico'* there were several other scenes focusing on the native peoples, usually showing their dances for tourists, or their survival conditions in the Amazon rainforest. This approach to the native cultures thus seemed to emphasize their 'exotic and primitive' character, as part of the 'landscape' that surrounded the official centennial celebration. This prejudiced depiction of native cultures supported *'Fantástico''s* presentation of the march against the official celebration as a failed protest by isolated individuals who wanted to disturb the official event – as if the protestors were not able to understand and cherish the importance of our Brazilian heritage.

But this interpretation of the protest could not be farther from the truth. The march had been carefully organized several months in advance, by various social movements that acted as a network, under the demand 'For Another Fifth Centennial Celebration'. Gildo, the Terena youngster whose action had been highlighted by the TV program, was later interviewed by a newspaper on April 25.[1] He told the reporter that he had travelled more than 2,000 miles, from his village in central Brazil, in order to reach Porto Seguro. On April 22 he marched six miles, with more than 3,000 people, representing 140 native, Afro-Brazilians and other groups. Describing the state military police's attack on the protesters he said:

We were prepared to participate in a peaceful demonstration. I carried a poster that said 'We Want Another Fifth Centennial Celebration'. This means we want to rebuild what has been lost. We already have had too much repression, pain, violence.

This was the ambitious strategic project of the movement: nothing less than to rebuild what has been lost in 500 years of Brazilian life. The point however is that this aim was not seen by the participants as an irrational drive: it was rather seen as a specific historical demand for self-respect and recognition. Gildo thus specified the immediate aim of the demonstration:

We did not intend to spoil anybody's party. If we could have only seen the President, that would have been good enough for me. For then he would have known that we were there, present and alive, protesting against neglect.

The strategic dimension of the demonstration was thus clearly defined, both in the long run and in the short term, as a non-violent action of popular protest, against historical oppression and neglect by government officials.

On the symbolic-identity level, the demonstration revealed a movement defined by a sense of pluralism and respect for difference. In a previous report, the newspaper stressed the fact that the 'Landless Rural Workers Movement' (*MST*) had tried to join the demonstration, but was stopped by police barriers on the road. In any case, several other popular groups, such as those of slum dwellers, church communities, neighborhood organizations, union members, local sections of political parties, etc. joined the march (a handful of priests, one Catholic bishop and one national MP of the Workers' Party, *PT*, marched also as 'a personal testimony'). The different native peoples and Afro-Brazilian groups marched adorned with their various colors and clothes. Gildo said that *'We were marching happily and were singing when hell fell on our heads'.*

Another striking aspect of Gildo's identity, which also characterizes other social movements, is a sense of ambiguity toward the mass media. Gildo said in the interview that he approached a police officer during the repression, grabbed a walkie-talkie from his belt and threw it away: *'This was a protest, because I wanted to forget the humiliation I had just suffered. Perhaps that radio had recorded everything, and I was ashamed, and started to cry again.'*

Then Gildo was hit by a club on his head, blacked out, and was taken away by his friends. One can understand Gildo's revolt and shame, in facing a public record of his humiliation. Various students of native cultures have noticed their fear of the power of the media, even of its ability to record the normal events of daily life, because it might reveal their weakenesses to strangers, in a debasing and undignified way. Imagine then Gildo's terrible situation, a young warrior portrayed as falling under repression with his bare hands... However, three days later Gildo agreed to a newspaper interview, and this may be seen as part of his aim of 'rebuilding what has been lost', his self -respect and self-esteem.

On the other hand, the political-cultural dimension of the movement 'For Another Fifth Centennial Celebration' is a common thread throughout Gildo's interview:

> *We were marching when the police started to throw bombs at us. I did not know what it was, I did not understand what was happening, for (where I live) I have almost no contact with the city. It was horrible, lots of noise, women weeping, children crying, I did not understand anything. I had never before taken a close look at a firearm or a bomb...*

The riot squad randomly launched teargas grenades and shot rubber bullets into the crowd; at the end of the day, 150 demonstrators had been arrested, and several others were injured (luckly not seriously). In the beginning Gildo had confronted the attackers with his open arms, trying to stop them. He said:

> *... 'Don't kill my people; we are already so few and you want to finish us'. I knelt before them, begged, cried, shouted. I asked them why were they doing that and they answered 'we're just following orders, you have to go back; you're not going to spoil the celebration'. I insisted, and begged them to kill me. 'You may kill me but let the native people demonstrate. We're poor and humble, but we also have rights' ... One of them pushed his gun into my chest and I fell to the ground.*

A political culture based on civic rights pervades Gildo's discourse. It sounds like a textbook case of the 'civic culture', with its participatory emphasis, and personal commitment to justice, peace and plurality, against government arbitrariness and violence. Gildo was reaffirming his traditional identity as a Terena, in cooperation with various other identity groups, in a common struggle for 'Another Fifth Centennial Celebration'- for *'we are poor and humble, but we also have rights'*. Gildo's 'rank-and-file' testimony shows a competent and persuasive coordination among the (apparently fragmentary and diverse) identities and strategic and political-cultural dimensions of the movement's action.

This action carefully combines and articulates the modern cultural foundations of Western civilization with traditional (apparently pre-modern) aspects of community life, in a way which some would perhaps call 'postmodern'. (A similar combination can be seen in the much more radical example of the current *'Zapatista'* movement of Chiapas in Mexico; see Yúdice, 1998). Such a combination is not a random *'bricolage'* of circumstantial elements, a burlesque farse of the official history - e.g. as we are used to seeing in the Brazilian carnival. Rather, it was a serious dramatic action, an intelligent, acute and satiric denunciation of the official Fifth Centennial Celebration. In fact, the official celebration was revealed, by this very action, as a political disaster and a tragic parody of Brazilian history, from its beginning up to the present. At the end of the interview, Gildo stated:

'I wish the President would reconsider what happened (to us) in Porto Seguro. It looks like the beginning of our history, when the Portuguese and the colonists (Bandeirantes) finished us off'.

We hope to demonstrate throughout this book that new social movements in Brazil, and in Latin America as a whole, articulate their priorities within the identity, strategic and political-cultural repertory of the processes of democratization – and that the fate of democracy in Latin America will mainly depend on this fact. This means that democratization is a historical process of learning new values, identities and political strategies, that enables groups and individuals to create and sustain a new way of life and new institutions in order to organize this lifeworld. Our own history tells us that this can be done in the midst of outrageous social inequity and authoritarian political-cultural traditions. For current processes of democratization share everywhere the reflexive and intersubjective character of the present global stage of Western civilization.

Certainly, a process of democratization may be blocked or reversed at any time, by local structural, cultural, psychological and other factors such as prejudice, impatience, sectarianism, stupidity, laziness... But the worldwide success of the new movements such as feminism, environmentalism and pacifism testifies to their intersubjective ability to articulate identity and strategic and political-cultural priorities, in their individual and collective actions, attracting growing alliances and supporters among the public (even when there are very few active members within each movement). This ability was tested in Brazil during and after the establishment of formal democratic rights in the new constitutional regime (1988). The new context allowed an expansion of the public sphere, whereby social actors and movements acquired (and developed) new strategies, identities and a 'civic culture'- albeit incipient and limited by the political transition from authoritarian rule.

This institutional change facilitated the emergence of many new actors, such as the 'new unionism' independent of state control (there are now four central union organizations, with different political orientations); various popular neighbourhood confederations in the main cities; the Movement of Landless Rural Workers (*MST*), and other diverse groups of rural workers. Many of these groups were first organized during the previous military regime, and their actions influenced the process of transition to formal democracy. There were others that vanished after the transition, or else adopted new aims and strategies *vis à vis* both the government and their social allies or adversaries. The convergence and cooperation of these popular groups with other movements empowers their capacity for intervention in the public arena, to influence the political system and public opinion as a whole.

Brazil is undergoing a process of democratization that remains unfinished, because the 'incomplete tasks of modernity' in the country are paramount. The legacy of Western culture and institutions arrived in Brazil through biased and discriminatory means.[2] One of the results is that Brazil's economy is the world's 11th largest, but its income distribution is among the most unfair. This is a society that may be called 'hierarchical', in comparison with Western liberal societies, according to the categories proposed by John Rawls.[3] Rawls maintains that hierarchical societies do not uphold the liberal doctrines of individualism, and therefore do not consider most of their nationals as citizens - i.e, as 'free and equal moral persons'. But hierarchical societies may be considered 'well ordered societies' - and as such accepted by the Western world - as far as they respect the human rights of their members, represented by groups, movements and institutions organized through a 'decent hierarchical consultation', based on a religious worldview and/or other forms of tradition such as natural law.

For instance, a study has maintained that the 'Landless Rural Workers Movement' (*MST*) can be seen as a democratizing force within a hierarchical society, both because of its joint appeal to formal constitutional rights and natural law on the one hand, and for its challenges to landowners and government through a 'decent hierarchical consultation' - within the movement itself and *vis à vis* the party system and state agencies - on the other hand.[4] The success of this movement in the political-cultural dimension is shown by the support it has received from public opinion (nationally and internationally), despite the enormous obstacles it faces in confronting the ruling elites.

Its strategic aim of land occupation for farm production has skillfully attracted alliances with other movements, NGOs, and opposition political parties - while simultaneously maintaining its independence as an autonomous movement. Moreover, the identity of its members, as peasants or rural workers, has expanded throughout the process, to include a sense of self-reliance, civic courage and cooperation in daily life, as well as a recognition of the right to difference, in constant dialogue with other sectors of society.[5] Certainly, all these conquests may be suppressed or reversed in the future, but they show that a popular movement can raise and achieve progress for its cause, despite the enormous obstacles it faces, in a society with undemocratic traditions.

Various similar examples of popular movements in Brazil exist. Thus, it is necessary to recognize that many contemporary Brazilian movements are 'new' movements, distinguished from the 'old' ones, which only defended particularist special interests or a traditional worldview - such as the 'anti-modern' peasant movements from the early 1900s, or even the 'old unionism' controlled by the state since the 1930s. However, it is important to note that many of the new movements still maintain, but with a different meaning, certain communitary emphases of the old ones. For instance, it has been argued - since the 1988 constitution formally established civil and political rights - that the 'grassrootism' prevailing among many popular movements (i.e., their refusal to occupy positions in the political arena, or even to interact with formal politics) is no longer a traditional anti-authoritarian defense mechanism. It may be seen rather as the beginning of a difficult process of social democratization of the lifeworld, similar to others that previously took place in countries which earlier established a fuller democratic regime, and a participatory political culture.[6]

This is why it is so important to compare the Brazilian process of democratization to similar processes in the Southern Cone countries. For this can help us to understand the enormous challenges faced by new union and social movements in Brazil, connected with the heavy load of tradition in Brazilian political culture and institutions. For instance, the central line of studies on Latin American democratization, known as 'regime analysis'[7], posits Brazil as an extreme case of 'party underdevelopment'.[8] Brazilian political parties are weak and unstable, with weak roots within society, and their political representatives enjoy complete autonomy *vis à vis* their constituency, which facilitates an extremely high interparty mobility. For this very reason, parties and politicians suffer from a vast deficit of credibility among the electorate, who show the highest degree of apathy and scepticism in Latin America.

Other studies have stressed some important changes in the last decade, in Brazil and Uruguay (and to some extent also in Argentina), resulting in the electoral growth of leftist and opposition parties. For instance, Constanza Moreira (2000) argued that Brazil and Uruguay *'are the only Latin American countries that have relatively autonomous and active labour unions, that have organic links with leftist parties'*.[9] In both countries the Left has consolidated an electoral base, even to the point of reaching the run-offs in national presidential elections. This is not by chance: *'both countries experience a similar legacy from the previous authoritarian regimes: the introduction of 'liberalizing' economic models which continue up to this day'*. The study recognizes differences between the Brazilian Workers' Party (*PT*) and the Uruguayan *'Frente Amplia'*, but insists on the similarities, which challenge the established political order:

> *a) In both countries the consolidation of an autonomous labor union movement was decisive for the emergence of a leftist political party able to overcome its origins, as a small 'ideological' party, to the point of becoming a 'massive' popular party; b) these processes occurred after the crisis of industrial developmentalism, influenced by the Latin American movements of the 1960s, 'Terceiristas', etc. This accounts for their pacifism, their trying to gain access to power through elections, and their engendering of a specific political culture (egalitarian, grassrootist, state-orienting, and movement-appealing) disinterested in the traditional monopoly of political representation; c) in both cases, an alliance between the suport of the unions and that of the middle classes seems to determine the chances of electoral victory for the Left .*[10]

Most certainly, the growth of the Left in Brazil and Uruguay are important processes that bear some similarities. However, the differences are perhaps much greater than Moreira's study seems to recognize. For instance: Uruguayan mainstream parties are very stable, and were formed in the 19th century; Uruguay's political system established liberal institutions in the early 20th century, as well as a welfare system considered for a long time to be the most successful in Latin America. One of the results of this democratic tradition is that the country's income distribution is one of the most equitable in the region, in spite of the fact that most of the electorate considers it now to be unjust, with immediate consequences in the political arena. We have seen above that Brazilian institutions and traditions are at the opposite pole of this liberal historical legacy.

Moreover, as long as the Brazilian *PT* continues to remain strongly linked to social and union movements, it will probably continue to suffer from a certain 'schizophrenia' between political and social action (contrary to what happens in Uruguay). One example is *'the gap which often exists between union and parliamentary struggles, or between the struggles of the popular movements and the need for the party to formulate a clear cluster of proposals, to be presented within and outside the Parliament, to induce government to solve those problems.'* [11]

A recent example of this gap was the *PT*'s lack of success in mediating between the government and the movement 'For Another Fifth Centennial Celebration', in Porto Seguro. Newspapers reported that *PT*'s national chairman José Dirceu met with the leadership of the movement, on the eve of the demonstration, trying to convince them to open negotiations with the government, but that he was not successful (which apparently justified police repression of the demonstration). Another important difference is that in Brazil there are four Central Union organizations, whereas in Uruguay there is only one, which is closely related to the *Frente Amplia*. The Brazilian union organizations may at times jointly oppose certain government policies, but they have different political orientations and only one is in line with the *PT*.

Notwithstanding the many contrasts between Brazil and Uruguay, it is certain that their leftist parties have similar electoral profiles: they recruit their constituencies from among the youthful, better-educated, urban voters who live in the large cities, and among organized workers. Research indicates that party identification is higher among these constituencies than in the electorate at large. Thus, Moreira's study explains party growth of the Left in Brazil and Uruguay (and to some extent also the growth of the Radicals in Argentina) as a phenomenon opposed to current regional integration through neoliberal policies. Also, it emphasizes at the end some of the crossroads faced by the Left, as it becomes the main alternative to the *status quo* in Brazil and Uruguay:

> *They lost the 1998 Presidential elections, but increased their representation in parliament; they conquered new ground at the municipal level, and started the new century with two decisive challenges: a) to conquer votes in the countryside, in less modernized, less urbanized, and especially in less politicized towns; b) to create an alternative program of government, not only to continue to mobilize discontent against current processes of economic reform, but also to achieve a higher consciousness about the risks of opposition to a model of development each day less 'domestically controllable'.* [12]

In any case, the growth of the opposition is related both to unsolved problems inherited from the authoritarian regime and to new circumstances generated during the transition governments. For instance, many scholars have emphasized the contradictory effects of current state adjustment policies in Latin America: they promoted short-term economic stability but this caused immediate political problems. In fact so-called neoliberalism reinforced income concentration and exacerbated social inequities, which in turn stimulated social protest and organization against the authoritarian regimes and the liberal transitions that adopted such policies. [13] However, current studies also emphasize that the processes of democratization cannot focus only on the basic issues of income distribution and social equity. In fact, the processes of democratic institutionalization have to reorganize economic productivity to face the challenges of world economic integration - at the national, regional and international levels - as well as the urgent needs and growing expectations of the electorate, which may reach well beyond the issue of income distribution.[14]

The point here is that political democratization requires mature and accountable political actors, among leaders as well as in the various segments of society who are capable of creating and supporting representative institutions to settle and negotiate divergent orientations and interests around a common aim and a balanced view of the future. This ideal of democratic institution-building is in itself a compelling demand, that has helped to unify oppositions to authoritarian oligarchic rule, and to organize coalitions in Latin America's new democratic regimes. Important as it is, the demand for coalitional institution-building is not sufficient, for it raises the question it is supposed to answer: How can mature political leaders and citizens emerge – ones who will abide by the rules of democratic life and institutions?[15]

This is a question that no 'institutional engineering' may resolve - in spite of the obvious need for institutional and legal reforms during democratic transitions. The Peruvian presidential 'self-coup' of 1992 (and its consequences until Fujimori's recent resignation) offered a radical example of the potential for setbacks and political regressions in Latin America, in spite of previous democratic institutionalization. (See Mauceri, 1995). The emphasis on coalitional institution-building devises and attempts to implement a legal and institutional framework for political democracy - establishing the rules and procedures for public interest representation. But it cannot answer the question about who are the actors capable of playing this crucial political role (and what their capabilities are to support interest representation).

The controversy around the candidacy of Luis Inacio Lula da Silva for the Presidency in Brazil was a case in point during the 1989, 1994 and 1998 electoral campaigns, among Brazilians and foreigners alike - and it may be raised again if he runs for the fourth time in 2002. Is a union leader with only elementary and technical schooling able to administer the huge political and economic problems of this country? In fact, the debate should consider the flawed process of institution-building which characterized Brazilian constitutionalization - and which could eventually result in a political stalemate between Congress and the Presidency, regardless of the electoral results. Moreover, one should also consider the capabilities of **other** political interlocutors, and their willingness to abide unconditionally by the rule of law- especially in facing the (real or imagined) threat of Lula's candidacy. In short, the question remains: how can **social** actors become **political** actors, who are capable of creating and developing effective democratic institutions?

This book highlights democratic learning and experience as an ongoing process, both in the social and political arenas. This process depends on the innovations and flexibility introduced by social and political actors, in their learning interactions towards the expansion and consolidation of a public sphere. For instance, Chile, Uruguay and Costa Rica are not noted in Latin America for the strenght and affluence of their economy, but rather for their ability to adapt and restructure their democratic traditions and institutions to new national and international challenges.

It is certain that other countries, which did not have a democratic tradition or long-standing democratic institutions to rely upon and update, are facing much greater difficulties, both in coalitional institution-building and in the learning of a democratic culture. However, this is not to say that institutional changes and cultural innovations are not occurring in these countries - but rather that they face stronger undemocratic opponents and larger 'authoritarian enclaves' in the oligarchic traditions and institutions.

This book underscores these changes in the behavior and orientations of social and political actors in Latin America, as they start to build up a new democratic political culture. However, political culture is a much debated topic in the literature, and we are bound to take sides in the controversy.[16] Instead of applying a ready-made set of typologies about what political culture is (or should be) in Latin America, we adopted an actor-oriented approach. This approach looks at what sociopolitical actors say and do about themselves - their shared, **common** and **public** actions and orientations, and the normative evaluations they make about the conditions of their daily life **vis à vis** the polity.

This sounds very general indeed as a research approach, and it is intended to be that way. For this is a line of study which is very recent in Latin America, and which intentionally participates in the open-ended character of the ongoing processes of democratization - maintaining also that such openness is constitutive of all historical events. Thus, a basic assumption which runs as a threadline throughout the book is that the paradigm-change of Latin American social sciences is part of an intellectual reorientation that accompanies (and tries to explain) the processes of cultural and political democratization.[17] In short, social scientists are also sociopolitical actors and as such they may participate in the democratization of political culture, as the building and consolidation of democracy begins.

This book also proposes a different and general approach to political culture, because it combines various methods of empirical analysis, in order to test conceptual reformulations in an ongoing research program. For instance, Chapters 2, 4, 6 and 7 rely on local case studies to clarify some trends in the study of political culture among social actors at the grassroots of Brazilian society. Other Chapters (1, 3, 5 and 8) review the literature on specific topics of conceptual reformulation, in order to achieve a comparative outlook on Latin American cultural and political democratization. This outlook is still in the making,[18] and in all chapters the variety of research techniques and conceptual reformulations underscores the need for a reflexive evaluation on the study of political culture, in order to overcome the present state of overgeneralization that characterizes the studies on this topic in Latin America. This is why this book is organized as a collection of independent essays rather than as a finished work on political learning. The aim, therefore, is to raise questions and provisional interpretations that are seldom raised, rather than to offer definitive conclusions, about how social actors may become political actors during democratization. The remainder of this introduction describes the content of each chapter of the book.

Chapter 1 offers an example of the already-mentioned intellectual reorientation among social scientists, and debates the limitations and interfaces of two of the main approaches to democratization in Latin America. The contributions of these studies underlay the institutional and cultural blockages that hinder democratization, both among the elites and the populations of Latin America. Their different emphases on either culture or institution serve as mutual corrections for a more balanced appraisal of democratization. But neither of the two approaches looks at these problems as challenges to political learning. This suggests that a new approach must be taken in order to understand what individuals and social actors are learning to say about their needs and their capabilities to satisfy them. The point here is that the study of democratization should provide a comprehensive account of political learning, among polities, societies and individuals which are embedded in the authoritarian traditions of the background culture of Latin American oligarchic legitimacy. Social scientists as well as other sociopolitical actors are acting reflexively on this tradition in order to overcome its legacies, in Brazil and elsewhere in Latin America.[19]

Social and political leaders have to be (and are being) studied in Latin America, because changes in their actions and orientations have been decisive in initiating the liberal transitions, and are even more fundamental in the current attempts at democratic consolidation. New individual and collective political actors emerged from changes within society, when individuals started to organize as **social** actors, attempting to change their daily life in order to influence the polity. Therefore, changes of political culture are shown to relate to social demands, electoral trends and other forms of representation, which in turn help to expand and consolidate the public sphere.

Chapter 2 introduces this topic through a discussion of the contributions of grassroots participation in democratic political change. It compares data and analyses on social actors in Mexico and Brazil, and suggests that in contrast to the Mexican cases, the participatory practices and orientations of Brazilian low income groups had a more permanent significance in the process of political democratization. These changes are related to two points in particular: local transformations in the political culture confirmed by electoral results at the municipal level, and the cumulative influence of social demands on public policies. This change of social actors into political actors depends also on an expansion of the public sphere (considered in Chapters 4, 6, and 7 for the case of Brazil, and in Chapter 8 for the case of Chile). Apparently, this expansion of the public sphere is also taking place now in Mexico (especially in the aftermath of the *Zapatista* rebellion, and the Presidential elections of 2000).

Thus, Chapters 2 and 3 take the theoretical debate of the first Chapter (culture vs. institutions) showing how grassroots organizational activities interact with institutional democratization. The need to study the emergence of social actors during the Brazilian transition, and their influence in the political arena, has been crucial during the 1980s and 1990s. Such actors as the labor unions, neighborhood and consumer groups, as well as feminist, ecological, cultural and ethnic minorities, became juridically recognized during the process of constitutionalization. The third chapter conducts an overview of studies on this topic and proposes a general interpretation of their findings for political democratization.

Social actors and demands are considered from the perspective of a 'needs-based' approach. Political competence is assessed through categories of Habermas's communicative action. The conclusions indicate some reasons for the incompleteness of political democracy in Brazil. Thus, in spite of the increasing diffusion of participatory demands within society, many important social and political actors have great difficulty in achieving the communicative competence (in terms of decentered orientations) to represent and negotiate their goals within the polity.

Moreover, a juridification of social relations (for instance, the regulation of the right of the unions to strike) was still in the making, despite the fact that general civil and political rights were formally established by the 1988 Constitution. Therefore, the unfinished process of political democratization in Brazil is seen to depend basically on the ongoing changes in the political culture, and on the exercise and regulation of constitutional rights by social and political actors. Only cultural change may lead to responsible and active citizenship, effective legal guarantees, a representative party system, and the consolidation of political democracy. Therefore, Chapter 3 develops the contrast proposed earlier with Mexico (Chapter 2), to show that within Brazilian democratization there are also traditional political actors and institutions which oppose the participatory trends that emerge in society.

The fourth chapter presents an empirical analysis of changes in political culture and social organization conducted in the city of Florianópolis (Southern Brazil), and focuses on the development of neighborhood groups which emerged during the transition to civilian rule. This chapter analyzes changes and continuity in the actions and orientations of these neighborhood organizations after they were released from a tight political control under the military regime (and the local oligarchy).

The study shows that these groups engaged in alternative forms of interaction among themselves and the polity. They created a 'parallel' public sphere along the lines of representative, participatory and neoclientelist policies. These outcomes related in turn with the expansion and consolidation of the local polity (municipal institutions, government agencies and the party system). The results are analyzed through Habermas's categories concerning the dynamics and stages of cultural competence. This chapter provides details of the political process, showing how the grassroots and institutional tendencies opposed the traditional forces that attempted to hinder political democratization.

Chapter 5 presents a broad review of sociopolitical changes in Latin America during the last decade, focusing on the evolving capabilities of social and political actors in achieving democratic institutionalization. This is mainly seen as an intersubjective process of communicative action - deployed into strategic interest representation, forms of symbolic expression (identities), and normative rules and orientations embedded in the emerging democratic culture. The overview illustrates these changes through the ongoing debates and research results among the various approaches in the literature, studying the role of social and political actors in the processes of democratization This chapter highlights the growing presence in other Latin American countries of the same trends and conflicts that have emerged in Brazilian democratization – i.e. the confrontation among the grassroots and institutional trends, on the one hand, and the traditional forces of the establishment, which resist and oppose such changes, on the other hand.

Chapter 6 looks more closely at the processes of social and cultural reorientation among the leadership of low income groups in Brazilian society. It focuses on the changes introduced by the church 'Base Communities' (local 'CEBs' of the Catholic church) within their constituency, and among the leadership of popular groups and movements in which their members participate. The basic point here is that *CEB* influence relates to motivational effects in the daily life of the participants, rather than to a direct politicization in the public sphere. These effects are very important to political democratization when they interact with local changes in the political culture and institutions. For they help low income groups (peasants and workers) to overcome submissiveness to authoritarian traditions and to work out new orientations for social action and political participation. Nevertheless, the formation and development of democratic institutions and ideologies depends on other historical conditions and political actors beyond the influence of the *CEB*s.

This study was inspired by Jürgen Habermas's distinction between the motivational and the legitimation spheres of contemporary societies, as well as by his 'communicative action' theory - as a test case to assess this and other approaches to cultural change during the Brazilian transition. The point here is that the *CEBs* of the Catholic Church are able to state truthfully that they are not taking partisan sides in elections, and other public institutional actions in the polity. However, the whole *CEB* approach embodies the democratic values of respect, tolerance, discourse, etc. – which provide necessary foundations for political institutionalization. Both this chapter and the next (Chapter 7) look at the details of the political processes resulting in democratization, with the former using a case study approach and the latter using a quantitative approach.

The seventh chapter is the report of a research survey on local changes in the political culture of low income neighborhood groups in three cities of Santa Catarina state in Southern Brazil. It introduces a discussion of current empirical research on the national political culture in Brazil, emphasizing the interactions between sociopolitical participation at the municipal level and the party system at all levels of representation. The diversity of social situations and political outcomes (government policies and electoral results) underlines the central role of the party leadership and the local administrations in stimulating the learning of a democratic culture by the electorate.

The report compares the usual typological findings of survey research on national political culture with local studies of the shared (**common** and **public**) actions and orientations of local social actors. The comparison relies on Habermas' categories of the dynamics of cultural change to evaluate the competence of social actors in accessing the public arena. (See Chilton, 1991, for a similar approach). In these cases as elsewhere, historical change has roots in the economic and political structures, but it is culturally implemented through the interactions between government policies (here, low-income housing policies) and the demands/orientations of the citizens. Citizens may further elaborate, clarify, and normatively ground their orientations, as their array of choices is sharpened and instituted within the polity.

The foregoing conclusions may sound idealistic but they are supported by historical events in Latin America: The 'Chilean pathway to democracy' is the subject of Chapter 8, providing a benchmark for the assessment of the delayed processes of political democratization in other Latin American countries. This chapter is a review of five *FLACSO* studies published in Chile during the country's political transition to democracy. Among other important contributions, these studies portray the crucial role of the intellectuals as sociopolitical actors during the debate of political alternatives, for they helped to systematize and clarify the actions and orientations that emerged in society.

These studies carefully distinguish between social and political democratization, highlighting the problems and opportunities existing in the daily life and in the polity - and which had to be faced in the pathway to democracy in Chile. The authors adopt different approaches to the theme, all of them rigorously grounded on empirical analysis. They jointly underscore the decisive changes in the political culture that social and political actors have achieved, among most segments and tendencies of society, during the restructuring of a competitive political arena.

This cultural reorientation of social and political actors in Chile presents a showcase for Latin America, demonstrating the possibility of overcoming the legacy of submissiveness, particularism and patronage inherited from authoritarian and oligarchic rule. Certainly, the arrest of Pinochet in London and his later prosecution in Chile raised a new test for Chilean democratization, to see whether the country's institutions (and a majority of the population) will be able to 'lift the veil' of a traumatic history that remained concealed. Incidentally, the same problem of 'settling accounts' with the military leaders of the previous dictatorship in Uruguay, on the issue of human rights violations, was ruled out by a referendum in 1989. (See Bielous, 1991).

This is the learning process of a democratic culture, relatively independent of formal education and other conventional correlates of cultural democratization (such as occupation or income). In short, this is an open-ended process whereby the communicative interactions among politicians and the electorate may reorient public policies, within the gradual democratization of political culture.

The point of this hopeful conclusion is to stress the fact that social and political actors are already communicating among themselves in Latin America (perhaps as actively as never before) in their increasing attempts to construct and expand a new democratic polity. In this context, social scientists are also democratizing sociopolitical actors, who are listening and responding to what is being said. Social scientists are actively participating in the learning of democracy, in order to surpass the legacy of intolerance and authoritarianism that pervades Latin American history.

REFERENCES

Alencastro, L.F. 2000. **O Trato dos Viventes**, São Paulo: Cia. das Letras.

Bermeo, N. 1992. "Democracy and the Lessons of Dictatorship", *Comparative Politics*, April: 273-291.

Bielous, S.D. 1991. "Por qué la Ciudadania Uruguaya Decidió Oponerse al Princípio de Igualdad Ante la Ley?", *Argumentos,* 14:120-131.

Chilton, S. 1991. **Grounding Political Development**. Boulder, CO: Lynne Rienner Publishers.

Habermas, J. 1984-7. **Theory of Communicative Action**, 2 vols. Boston: Beacon Press.

Inglehart, R. 1997. **Modernization and Postmodernization: Cultural, Economic and Political Change in 43 Societies**, New Jersey: Princeton University Press.

Krischke, P.J. 1998. "A Cultura Política Pública em John Rawls: Contribuições e Desafios à Democratização", *Filosofia Política*, Nova Série, 2: 85-98.

Krischke, P. J. 1999. "Contextos de Socialização, Desigualdade e Diferenças na Democratização: Revisando a Teoria de Ronald Inglehart sobre a Mudança Cultural", in **Anais do Seminário Internacional "Por uma Cultura da Paz"**, Curitiba: UNESCO/Editora da UFPR.

Laurell, A.C. 2000. "Structural Adjustments and the Globalization of Social Policy in Latin America", *International Sociology*, 15 (2): 306-325.

Lipset, S.M.; Seong, K-R; Torres, C.A. 1993. "A Comparative Analysis of the Social Requisites of Democracy", *International Social Science Journal*, 136: 155-175.

Mainwaring, S. and Scully, T. 1995. **Building Democratic Institutions: Party Systems in Latin America**, Stanford, CA: Stanford University Press.

Mauceri, P. 1995. "State Reform, Coalitions, and the Neoliberal '*Autogolpe*' in Peru", *Latin American Research Review*, 30 (1): 7-38.

McCoy, J. (Ed.). 2000. **Political Learning and Redemocratization in Latin America: Do Politicians Learn from Crisis?** Coral Gables,MI: North-South Center.

Moisés, J. A. 1986. **E Agora PT? Caráter e Identidade**, São Paulo: Brasiliense.

Moreira, C. 2000. "La Izquierda en Uruguay y Brasil: Cultura Política y Desarrollo Político-partidário", in Mallo, S. and Moreira, C.(Eds.), **La Larga Espera: Itinerarios de la Izquierda en Argentina, Brasil y Uruguay**, Montevideo: Ed. Banda Oriental.

Paulilo, M. I. 2000. "MST: O Julgamento das Vítimas", *Revista Lugar Comum*, 9/10, UFRJ.

Phillips, L. (Ed.). 1998. **The Third Wave of Modernization in Latin America: Cultural Perspectives on Neoliberalism**, Wilmington, DE: Scholarly Resources, Inc.

Rawls, J. 1985. "Justice as Fairness: Political not Metaphysical", **Philosophy and Public Affairs**, 14 (3): 203-225.

Rawls, J. 1999. **The Law of Peoples**, Cambridge, MA: Harvard University Press.

Sheanan, J. 1997. "Effects of Liberalization Programs on Poverty and Inequality: Chile, México, and Peru", *Latin American Research Review*, 32 (3): 7-38.

Yúdice, G. 1998. "The Globalization of Culture and the New Civil Society", in Alvarez, S.; Dagnino, E.; and Escobar, A. (Eds.), **Cultures of Politics and Politics of Cultures. Re-visioning Social Movements in Latin America**, Boulder, CO: Westview Press.

ENDNOTES

[1] Interview with Celso Bajarano Jr., (*'Terena queria morer'*,'Terena wanted to die'), *Folha de São Paulo*, April 26, 2000, 1/6.

[2] See Alencastro, Luis Felipe. *O Trato dos Viventes*, (São Paulo: Cia. das Letras, 2000) for a historical account of 330 years of slave traffic and its lasting effects on Brazilian society and polity.

[3] Rawls, John. *The Law of Peoples* Cambridge, MA: Harvard University Press, 1999.

[4] Krischke, Paulo. 'A Cultura Política Pública em John Rawls: Contribuições e Desafios à Democratização', *Filosofia Política*, Nova Série, 2:85-98. 1998.

[5] See Paulilo, Maria Ines.'MST: O Julgamento das Vítimas', *Revista Lugar Comum*, 9/10, UFRJ, 2000.

[6] See Chapter 2 of this book.

[7] See Chapter 1 of this book.

[8] See Mainwaring, Scott and Scully, Timothy, *Building Democratic Institutions: Party Systems in Latin America*, Stanford, CA: Stanford University Press, 1995.

[9] Moreira, Constanza, 'La Izquierda en Uruguay y Brasil: Cultura Política y Desarrollo Político-Partidário', in Mallo, Suzana, and Moreira, Constanza. 2000. *La Larga Espera: Itinerarios de la Izquierda en Argentina, Brasil y Uruguay*, Montevideo: Ed. Banda Oriental (p. 4 of the original typescript).

[10] Moreira, 2000: 7.

[11] Moisés, José Alvaro, *E Agora PT? Caráter e Identidade*, São Paulo: Brasiliense, 1986.

[12] Moreira, 2000:11.

[13] See on this topic especially Chapters 5 and 8 of this book. See also Shenan, 1997; Phillips (ed.),1998 and Laurell, 2000.

[14] See the references on economic restructuring in Chapter 5. Chapter 3 also discusses the relevance of non-economic ('radical') needs among the trends for democratization.

[15] I thank Stephen Hellman and Phillip Evanson for sharp comments on this point.

[16] Inglehart (1997) attempts to overcome the economic determinism of modernization/ development theories (e.g. Lipset et al. 1993) but recognizes that development leads to democracy *when it affects political culture and the social structure* (Inglehart, 1997: 161). See Chapter 1 of this book for a discussion of competitive approaches to democratization. Chilton (1991) proposes that political development should be assessed through an interpretation of political culture in terms of "moral/cognitive deleopment".

[17] See Chapter 8 of this book for an account of this process in Chile. See also Bermeo (1992) for a seminal analysis of the "lessons of dictatorship"on political learning. The book edited by Jennifer McCoy (2000) analyses four national cases of political learning among the elites, during the transition to democracy (Chile, Uruguay, Argentina and Venezuela). It presents a valuable comparative analysis of elite behavior during democratic institutionalization, and recognizes the need for further research on changes in mass political culture. One should also add the need for a more comprehensive approach to the study of individual, social and political democratization. (See Chapter 1 of this book).

[18] See especially Chapter 5 of this book.

[19] Again, Chapter 8 on the Chilean transition also offers a specific review on this topic, showing how the reorientation of of intellectuals plays a role in national democratization. On the issue of paradigm change in the social sciences see especially Chapters 1 and 3.

Chapter 1

REGIME ANALYSIS VS. CULTURAL STUDIES: PROBLEMS OF DEMOCRATIZATION[*]

The aim of this chapter is to examine two of the main approaches to the study of democratization in Latin America—namely, regime analysis and cultural studies— assessing some of their interfaces (different contributions on common issues) and conceptual problems and limitations left open for future systematization. Our main concern here is to assess these approaches` contributions to the understanding of the precise nature of sociopolitical change during the processes of democratization. It will be seen that they make important contributions, both to the interpretation of elite behavior during institutional changes (regime analyses) and to the evaluation of cultural changes among the population at large (cultural studies). They even converge around central issues, presenting alternative explanations for theoretical and historical problems of Latin American democratization. Such are the issues of clientelism and of the normative concept of democracy, the relevant sociopolitical actors, the level and unit of analysis, etc. – which both approaches face differently. These approaches criticize each other vigorously, and I suggest that they both fail to present a comprehensive interpretation of democratization—or one, at least, capable of articulating political, social and personal changes.

After two decades of studies on the political transition from authoritarian rule, the study of Latin American democratization should lead social scientists to become more democratic, at least from two practical standpoints of our professional activity. The first is that we should be learning to tolerate dissent and to appreciate the differences among competing explanations, as we receive the contributions that others have to offer to our common issues of study. The second stance goes hand in hand with the first: we learn to relativize our own point of view, as we try to render it more precise, to avoid the trends of

---

[*] This chapter was written with the support of a scholarship of the *Conselho Nacional de Desenvolvimento Científico e Tecnológico (CNPq)*. The author thanks the helpful comments of Sergio Cunha, Hector Leis, Leonardo Avritzer, Elisa Reis, Gerardo Munck, Vicente Palermo and Stephen Chilton.

overgeneralization and "conceptual stretching" — all of this in order to contribute more effectively to our ongoing dialogue.

Nevertheless, this dialogue among competing approaches to the study of democratization may often sound like a heated dispute, in which circumstancial blockages and fundamental theoretical disagreements blend together and come to the fore. But there is no surprise in the fact that democracy is controversial even on theoretical grounds. For it is in this very way that debates help to clarify the competition among alternative theoretical approaches: they offer specific contributions (interfaces) from each approach to our common issues of study, and thus reveal each approach's unsolved conceptual and practical problems, which in turn expose the internal limits of that approach. Our understanding of democratization is enhanced by these controversies, which show political learning in LatinAmerica as an open-ended process that goes far beyond the present state of our theories.

This chapter examines some interfaces and limitations of two of the most influential approaches to the study of democratization in Latin America. These approaches criticize each other vigorously, offering significant alternative explanations to this area of study. The first approach was termed "regime analysis" by Gerardo Munck (1998), and the second was named "cultural studies" by Sonia Alvarez, Evelina Dagnino, and Arturo Escobar (1998). These two books are among the most recent and relevant accounts of Latin American democratization wtitten by leading practitioners of these two approaches.

Some of the contributions and limitations of regime analyses are emphasized, relying on Munck's (1996) acute review of these studies – to which I refer the reader for a thorough account of the literature. Using the book edited by Alvarez et al. to exemplify the cultural studies approach, the chapter describes the unique features of this approach and the nature of its dissent from the regime analysis approach. Finally, the conclusions outline some of the interfaces between both approaches to common issues of study in Latin American democratization. They also suggest some of the limitations or unsolved conceptual and practical problems of both approaches. But these interfaces and limitations are not conceived here as the only possible outcome of this debate. Others will have to risk their own conclusions as challenges for future research in this area.

THE REGIME ANALYSIS APPROACH

The 'minimalist' definition of democracy advanced by Joseph Schumpeter (1942: 269) — as 'the democratic method (or) institutional arrangement for arriving at political decisions in which individuals acquire the power to decide via a competitive struggle for the people's vote' — has formed the core of the elite model of democracy ever since. Certainly, the minimalist or elite approach includes also a number of other procedural specifications (following Dahl's [1971] idea of polyarchy) that render the democratization of the political regime amenable to empirical research. Gerardo Munck (1996) reviews a number of studies on political democratization, in Latin America and elsewhere, and maintains that the procedural emphasis held by regime analysts has become dominant in the literature:

> There is an overall consensus that part of what defines a political regime are the procedural rules that determine: 1) the number and type of actors who are allowed to gain access to the principal government positions, 2) the methods of access to such positions, and 3) the rules that are followed in the making of publicly binding decisions.
> *(Munck, 1996: 3-4)*

The influence of regime analysis on the study of Latin American democratization is certainly justified, for its procedural and institutional emphasis on elite replacement converged with the historical processes of political transition and constitutional reform that institutionalized the new democratic regimes all over the continent during the 1980s. Nevertheless, this literature recognizes that there are severe constraints on the institutionalization of democracy in Latin America — mostly derived from the long-standing traditions of oligarchic liberalism and the heavy legacies of authoritarian rule. This is why Garretón (1994) coined the term 'authoritarian enclaves' to identify the persistent cultural and institutional blockages that hinder the consolidation of the democratic regimes in Latin America. And Guillermo O'Donnell, one of the most influential regime analysts, recognized:

> Our theories must come to terms with...the extent to which a poly-archical regime coexists with a properly democratic rule of law. For this purpose...even though it greatly expands the scope and complexity of the analysis, it is necessary to conclude that a solely regime-based focus is insufficient.
> *(O'Donnell, 1998: 21)*

The point here is that it is not enough to establish new rules to select the elites through competitive elections, to create checks and balances among the institutions of government, and a public accountability among the elites and the electorate, etc.—which the minimalist approach has specified as being some of the main procedural attributes of a polyarchy or political democracy. A behavioral compliance of the main political actors is also necessary, for these actors have to demonstrate through their individual actions that they abide by those rules, in order that such formal procedures may become effective.

Therefore, Munck proposes to 'disaggregate the political regime' into its two dimensions - the procedural dimension and the behavioral dimension. First, there is a procedural dimension that establishes the new 'rules of the game' for the transition to democracy. And second, there is a behavioral dimension - i.e., 'the strategic acceptance of these rules by all major political actors and the lack of normative rejection of these rules by any major political actor' (Munck,1966: 6) - which consolidates the new regime. This emphasis on the 'two-dimensional' character of the regime facilitates also its analytical disaggregation into a time-sequence, of 'de-consolidation/transition/ consolidation'. For when one distinguishes between the institutional procedures and the actors' compliance to them, one may grasp the political regime in its dependence on the strategic interactions among the relevant political actors, who have to initiate the transition and should also consolidate the new regime.

Certainly, several of the scholars reviewed by Munck (such as O'Donnell, Schmitter, Whitehead, Przeworski, etc.) emphasized as much as he did a time-sequence for the various stages of political democratization. But none of them made these stages so closely dependent on the individual compliance and independent behavior of the political actors, as did Munck:

> Regime analysis consists of three broad areas of inquiry which are characterized by distinct analytical issues: the creation of new rules by the actors, the central feature of the process of transition; the rules themselves, the central outcome of the process of transition; and the acceptance or rejection of the rules defined by actors during the transition phase, (which is) the core characteristic of the process of consolidation.
> *(Munck, 1996: 8)*

From this standpoint, Munck stands against alternative (collective and/or Marxist) conceptualizations of the political regime — such as that of Michael Mann (1993) where the regime is defined in terms of a 'dominant coalition': 'An alliance of dominant ideological, economic, and military power actors, coordinated by the rulers of the state' (Mann, 1993: 18-19). This is an interpretation that Munck considers 'reductionist', for it 'conceives of regimes solely in terms of actors or ... treats institutional rules as epiphenomenal' (Munck, 1996:20). And, 'because the importance of institutional rules in structuring politics is ignored, such a conceptualization tends to ignore the range of institutional diversity that can coexist with a similar set of actors". (Muck, 1996: 21) Munck also labels as reductionist social-democratic conceptualizations of the political regime, which analytically distinguish between 'regime of power' and political regime: 'The regime of power... always shapes and conditions the political regime' (Jaguaribe, 1973: 94-98).

The aim of all these critiques by Munck is very clear: collectivist or reductionist conceptions of the political regime "lead to a dramatic truncation of the research agenda (and) ignore the independent importance of institutions". (Munck,1996:21) The point is that the actors of the political regime, in order to be able to create those democratic institutions, must be individually free from other power actors and agencies. Moreover, we have seen above that according to Munck, the actor's compliance to the rules is not normatively defined, but instead is defined strategically. A normative component only appears in the actor's behavioral dimension *ex negationes* — as the 'lack of normative rejection of these rules by any major political actor'. Nevertheless, one may ask whether the actors' strategical compliance to democratic procedures does not need (or imply) a normative support to the democratic regime — and one that should be explicitly recognized.

In fact, this normative groundwork is all the more relevant to the behavioral dimension of the political regime, as some of the regime analysts have repeatedly pointed to the 'hybrid' character of the new democracies in Latin America. For instance, Guillermo O'Donnell (1996) has stressed the importance of 'another institutionalization' in Latin America and elsewhere, which is informal and even illegal — namely, that of clientelism, particularism and corruption. These widespread informal cultural and institutional practices are threatening the consolidation of the republican and liberal ideals of democracy and its very survival as a political regime in Latin America.

The 'two-dimensional' disaggregation of the political regime proposed by Munck helps to raise the question of **who** its political actors are. According to Munck (1996: 11) they are 'many...the leaders of multiple political parties'. But, considering the hybrid character of the new democracies, it is not enough to say that they are the political parties – however 'many and multiple'. In fact, parties and other political actors share the contingent nature of the political regime, i.e. they may enter into transition, consolidation, 'de-consolidation', etc. This happens as they either actualize through their behavior the rules and procedures of the regime, or else negotiate different rules for a new regime with other political actors. Thus, parties may even emerge and/or vanish suddenly from the political arena — as it happened, for instance, with the PRN of Fernando Collor de Mello in Brazil (there have been similar cases of outsider and antiparty-system candidates in other countries, such as Fujimori in Peru or Chavez in Venezuela).

In sum, relevant political actors emerge from society, and their commitment to the procedures of democracy can be tested even in regard to their behavior as plain citizens or subjects of a 'hybrid' society. This is a simple conclusion that regime analysts usually discard, and/or take for granted without integrating it properly into their empirical analyses. Certainly, due to their informal nature, such 'hybrid' behaviors and procedures usually lie outside the institutional focus and theoretical scope of the regime analysis approach. However, as they threatened to hinder the attempts at democratic institutionalization, regime analysts had to look for the basis of such anomalies in the actual behavior of political actors.

It is interesting to realize that this approach, which claims to hold a purely strategical point of view, often lapses into a 'quasi-moralistic' account of Weberian categories, when these are applicable to the informal traits of political behavior. Thus, a category like clientelism is often used more as an argument of authority, that dispenses its deployment as a heuristic category, for an analysis of specific empirical behavior (Zabludovski, 1989). (However, there are noteworthy exceptions, such as the study of clientelism in the Brazilian Congress, by Fabiano G. Santos, 1994). Accordingly, when regime analysts denounce candidates, incumbents and political parties for their particularism and hybrid practices, the electorate is often evaluated through overgeneralizations such as 'plebiscitarian vote', *caudillismo*, etc. — in spite of the apparent lack of interest by these scholars for the political culture and the value orientations of the elites, or in the population at large. (e.g. O'Donnell, 1994)

These critical evaluations are not intended here as an attempt to discard the contributions of the regime analysis approach. Munck's rigorous review of this literature highlights its many virtues and accomplishments, which certainly help to enhance the understanding of democratization in Latin America. However, all currents of interpretation have their shortcomings, and such limitations and unsolved problems do not diminish the importance of their results, but rather raise new challenges for future research. The great merits of the regime analysis approach (e.g., the economy of its model of the rational actor and his or her strategic actions) helped to raise it to its present salience in studies of democratization.

In fact, some of its limitations seem to arise from the approach's most appraised virtue — its rigorous and necessary focus on the institutional analysis of the political regime. These limitations also relate to the approach's internal limits, that stumbled on contradictory elements of the processes of democratization, lying beyond the formal institutions the approach was designed to study. But its present attempt at 'disaggregating the political regime' into its procedural and behavioral dimensions among the political elites had the great merit of unveiling the blockages that hinder, at this level of analysis, the processes of democratization.

THE CULTURAL STUDIES APPROACH

Cultural studies as a specific area developed originally in England, with Stuart Hall (1992) and his associates at the Birmingham Centre for Contemporary Cultural Studies, and its roots relate to British Marxian cultural historians, such as Raymond Williams under Gramscian influence. More recently, the area developed also a close dialogue with poststructuralist currents, under Foucauldian influence (Laclau and others, see Harris, 1992). The influence, in turn, of the cultural studies approach on Latin American research is very recent — though some of the latter research claims to share seminal mutual references with previous studies on social movements in Latin America, since the transitions from the authoritarian regimes in the 1980s. The book edited by Sonis Alvarez, Evelina Dagnino and Arturo Escobar (1998) - "The Cultures of Politics and the Politics of Culture: Revisioning Social Movements in Latin America" - seems to be the most representative of this line of studies in Latin America. This is the reason why this section focuses on some of the issues raised in the book in its controversy with the regime analysis approach.

In contrast with previous studies on Latin American social movements, the authors of this volume do not posite social movements as the bearers of structural resistance and emancipation from national and international domination. They prefer to look at the unfolding of a non-linear cultural process of social and political change, in which 'ambiguity' is a keyword (see the chapters by Yúdice, Schild and Alvarez.) The book portrays social actors as the responsible subjects and interpreters for the meanings and the political relevance of their actions, within their specific national contexts.

In fact, the analysis of social movements can only be properly done at the local and national levels (as the chapters by Yúdice, and Grueso et al. demonstrate clearly). One obvious reason for this is that there are not, as yet, comparative studies, that are capable of evaluating the relationship between social movements and democratization processes from a cross-cultural perspective — in spite of the growing importance of regional integration, and of worldwide communications (Ribeiro, 1998). Therefore, the authors of this book rightly emphasize the importance of national specifications in order to evaluate the relationship between social actors and the process of democratization (Jelin, 1998).

Of course, there is always an expectation that national differences and social diversity may be gauged through a comparative outlook, and Alvarez et al. select a 'cultural studies' approach as its focus of analysis (Introduction). We shall return to this point later on, because comparisons are of crucial importance to the study of democratization.

The contributions of this book are conceived as 'cultural studies', mainly to emphasize 'that the cultural politics of social movements enacts cultural contestation or pressupposes cultural difference' - write the authors of the Introduction. They add:

> We interpret cultural politics to be the process enacted when sets of social actors shaped by, and embodying, different cultural meanings and practices come into conflict with each other. This definition of cultural politics assumes that meanings and practices ... — all of them conceived in relation to a given dominant cultural order — can be the source of processes that must be accepted as political.... Culture is political because meanings are constitutive of processes that, implicitly or explicitly, seek to redefine social power. That is, when movements deploy alternative conceptions of woman, nature, race, economy, democracy or citizenship that unsettle dominant culturtal meanings, they enact a cultural politics. We speak of cultural formations in this sense: they are the result of discursive articulations originating in existing cultural practices — never pure, always hybrid but showing significant contrasts in relation to dominant cultures nevertheless — and in the context of particular historical conditions.
> *(Alavarez et al., 1998: 7-8).*

This is an innovative approach, that firmly questions the 'objectifying' trends of previous studies on 'political modernization' and 'political development', which imposed rigid 'Westernizing' categories to comparative research, such as the 'civic culture' of advanced Western democracies. Moreover, this cultural focus is firmly grounded methodologically through an openness to the meanings and ends social actors attribute to their actions. It thus takes a definite stance for the political emancipation of Latin American 'subaltern counterpublics' (Alvarez et al., 1998: Introduction). One may hope that this new focus on 'cultural studies' will be evaluated in the years to come in the same vein as its British counterparts (Hall and associates) who were assessed by an inner participant in a (not unsympathetic but often very rigorous) comprehensive overview:

> Gramscian work [in Cultural Studies] has opened a number of areas to critical inspection in a novel and interesting way. It has been responsible for the emergence of a critical sociology of culture and for the politicisation of culture, and these developments have generated very successful academic programmes of research and course construction. However... there are also a number of tendencies towards closure in Gramscianism too. Very briefly, for me it is far too ready to close off its investigations of social reality, to make its concepts prematurely identical with elements of that reality in various ways ... [They] are liable to premature closure by being too `strategic´for me, as well — by letting a politics priviledge analysis, both an explicit national politics, and a less explicit local academic politics. Such closures have benefits, but there are also considerable losses.
> *(Harris, 1992: 195).*

The new cultural approach to Latin American social movements certainly learned from previous cultural studies in Britain and elsewhere, in order to avoid the trends towards 'closure'. Perhaps this is the reason why Gramsci is seldom mentioned by the essays of this book, and 'hegemony (that 'fashionable floating signifier' in Harris'[1992:44] critique) is ruled out in the Introduction, because 'dominant political cultures in Latin America - with perhaps a few short-lived exceptions - cannot be seen as examples of hegemonic orderings of society'. And they add:

> In fact, all have been committed, in different forms and degrees, to the deeply-rooted social authoritarianism pervading the exclusionary organization of Latin American societies and cultures...This lack of differentiation between the public and the private — where not only the public is privately appropriated but also political relations are perceived as extensions of private relations — normalizes favoritism, personalism, clientelism and paternalism as regular practices of politics...Thus, emergent redefinitions of concepts such as democracy and citizenship point toward directions which confront authoritarian culture through a resignifying of notions as rights, public and private spaces, forms of sociability, ethics, equality and difference, and so on.
> *(Alvarez et al., 1998: 9-10).*

The emphasis of cultural studies on the actions and meanings emerging from the society ('never pure...always hybrid but...defying domination'), as the source for the expansion of a democratic regime thus provide an analytical focus to gauge the displacement and eventual replacement of that 'informal institutionalization' (clientelism, etc.) that pervades Latin American politics.

Certainly, this book's approach to 'cultural politics' introduces an understanding of the polity that is more open-ended and sophisticated than the interpretation of politics held by most previous studies on social movements in Latin America. Previous studies have usually relied on a rigid dichotomy between civil society and state (which was certainly relevant during the times of authoritarian/military rule). The studies of the book edited byAlvarez et al. introduce a more flexible and nuanced understanding of politics. The essays by Olivia Cunha, on the Brazilian Black Movement, by Veronica Schild on Chilean feminists, or by George Yúdice on Mexican Zapatistas, emphasize the ambiguities and non-linear development of the relations between social movements and the state in different historical contexts.

All the essays also take into account national institutional change, constitutional democratization and/or related transformations of the political structures. David Slater (1998) even introduces a useful distinction between politics and 'the political', in order to emphasize the specific political dimension of social movements. These contributions go far beyond the usual binary polarization between civil society and government, that was sustained by many previous studies of social movements in Latin America. The individual essays by Alvarez, Dagnino, Jelin, Baierle and the book's Introduction develop the concept of 'public sphere' as an extension or expansion of institutional politics outside the boundaries of government. These are important conceptual innovations, which improve the understanding of the political relevance of social actors and movements.

As might be expected, the Introduction by Alvarez et al. raises an acute critique of the regime analysis approach to democratization, which is considered to be supportive of the exclusionary elitism that prevails in current attempts at post-authoritarian institutionalization in Latin America:

> An alternative conception of democracy — one advanced by several of the movements discussed in this book — would view the very process of constructing democracy as encompassing a redefinition not only of the 'political system' but also of economic, social and cultural practices that might engender a democratic ordering for society as a whole. Such a conception calls our attention to a wide array of possible public spheres wherein citizenship might be exercised and societal interests not only represented but fundamentally re/shaped.
> *(Alvarez et al., 1998: 2).*

Alvarez et al. use the term 'subaltern counterpublics' coined by Nancy Fraser (1993: 14), where it is defined as 'parallel discursive arenas where members of subordinated social groups invent and circulate counterdiscourses, so as to formulate oppositional interpretations of their identities, interests and needs'. Fraser advances this definition as a critique of Habermas's conception of the liberal public sphere, characterized by her as 'informed by an underlying evaluative assumption, namely, that the institutional confinement of public life to a single, overarching public sphere is a positive and desirable state of affairs, whereas the proliferation of a multiplicity of publics represents a departure from, rather than an advance toward, democracy' (Fraser, 1993: 13). Alvarez et al. derive from this argument their emphasis on the 'expansion of the public sphere beyond the frontiers of the state'. At the end of this section we return to this topic.

It seems to me that the next step in this revalorization of politics for the study of social movements will be the recognition that an interpretation of both social and political democratization entails the adoption of a comparative scale to gauge 'political development' (again, this contentious word !). I surely realize that 'cultural studies' have a certain (and perhaps justified) resistance to words that imply quantifying, objectifying, and/or the making of linear comparisons which take the advanced Western countries as the benchmark. But I do not mean that one should return to the 'modernization' illusions of the 1950s/1960s. What I have in mind is Kohlberg and Habermas' 'cognitive/moral development', and its correspondence in socio-political democratization (Habermas, 1984-7; Kohlberg, 1981-4), which I have proposed elsewhere as a viable approach to the study of social movements during Latin American democratization (see especially Chapters 3, 5 and 7 of this book).

The point here is that the establishment of formal democratic rights in post-authoritarian regimes has allowed an expansion of the public sphere whereby social actors and movements are acquiring (and developing) new strategies, identities and a 'civic culture' — albeit incipient and limited by its historical conditions. In short, there is a process of social learning of democratic rights that may be assessed cross-culturally in specific political contexts, through the famous stages of 'cognitive-moral development' (See Chilton [1991] for a methodological approach akin to this proposal). It should be noted that Habermas's approach to 'cognitive-moral development' is multi-dimensional, including a cognitive dimension (the development of worldviews), alongside a normative dimension (moral and legal development) and a subjective dimension (the development of identities and personality structures). (Habermas, 1990)

Of course, institutional changes cannot be naively made parallel with subjective changes, and the various dimensions of social life have to be assessed through specific empirical studies. But 'cognitive-moral development' is only one example of proposals that may enhance the effectiveness of 'cultural politics' in tackling personal, social and political democratization from an overall perspective that may be amenable to comparative analysis. And it has also the merit of facing another methodological problem seldom considered by previous studies on social movements in Latin America: the issue of the unit of analysis. This issue has been especially debated outside Latin America, under the rubric of 'methodological individualism'(see Levine et al., 1987; Birnbaum and Leca, 1990), and studies in North America on 'resource mobilization' have raised it since the influential work of Olson (1965) on the 'logic of collective action'.

Some of the essays in Alvarez et al. have indirectly faced the issue in the terms of 'a new concept of social citizenship' (e.g., Paoli and Telles; Dagnino). Paoli conceives it as a notion of 'citizenship different from the liberal [conception]... and conceived as an active collective participation in dialogue and negotiation... related to the whole of society and its inequities". Dagnino defines this collective citizenship as the constitution of 'active social subjects (political agents)'. All the book's authors seem to endorse collective conceptions of citizenship, in some cases side by side with the more conventional interpretation of citizenship as the individual exercise of basic civil, political and social rights.

This definition of social participation as a form of collective citizenship is certainly relevant and accompanies the reappraisal and expansion of the political sphere already noted above. Nevertheless, it runs the risk of simply renaming an old bias of previous Latin American studies of social movements, namely their inability to integrate the personal and the individual into their focus of analysis. This refusal has often been justified elsewhere as an opposition to ego-centered interests, which are supposed to be the focus of 'rational choice' and 'methodological individualism' (though Elster [1987], Birnbaum and Leca [1990], Levine et al. [1987] and others have, from different points of view, rejected this criticism). Whatever the merits of this debate, it would be ironic if a line of cultural studies, that intends to underlay (among other cultural aspects of politics) the subjective dimension of social and political democratization, forgot the individual interests and personal motivations that drive people to social and political participation.

In fact, it is necessary to come to terms with the fact that social actors and movements are composed of individuals. And most previous studies of social movements in Latin America have tended, in the opposite direction, to attribute to social actors the characteristics of personalities and individuals - thus 'reifying' or 'essentializing' their actions and orientations. This lapse may be similar to previous Marxian conceptualizations on social classes (see Kowarick, 1995).

The poststructuralist focus of the book we are reviewing was capable of identifying many peculialities and diversities within social groups and movements, according to gender, age or race. For example: Kay Warren argues against the 'unified Marxian anti-capitalistic paradigm' in its approach to indigenous groups in Central America, and

Olivia Cunha argues similarly about Black movements in Brazil. A footnote in the Introduction also mentions some related positive advancements of the studies on 'resource mobilization'in the U.S. But something else should be done to account for individual and personal differences within Latin American social groups and movements. A research approach on cognitive-moral development, and its correspondence in the sociopolitical and normative spheres, could thus provide such a comparative standpoint on overall democratization.

Finally, I would like to mention another relevant contribution of these new cultural studies on social movements in Latin America. In their respective essays Ribeiro, Yúdice and Cunha stress the importance of the imaginary, myth and utopia to the cultural life of social movements. But should we not recognize that there is also 'ambiguity' in the sphere of the imaginary? In this sense, Paoli and Telles make a valuable sggestion: to look at present social conflicts and negotiations in Brazil as part of a 'social contract' that is being worked out through the expansion of the public sphere.

This kind of concrete utopia has the advantage of being amenable to empirical analysis through an evaluation of its outcome. Contract relations may be considered as an operative myth or utopia that offers or produces specific results that may partly actualize the hope of equity implied by the ideal of contract. (See the debates on Rawlsian neocontractarian analysis). Both James Bohman (1990) and Seyla Benhabib (1987) have shown, in different ways, that the 'generalized other' of the contractarian utopia's equity has to take into account the inequalities and diversities of every 'concrete other' - thus correcting Rawls and Kohlberg from a Habermasian perspective on 'communicative action'.

James Bohman (1990) has suggested that Habermas's definition of 'democracy as an institutionalization of discourses' implies that 'discourses are institutionalized to the extent that a social setting is created that permits collective, post-conventional agreements which, in turn, create whatever shared structures actors may have'. (Habermas, 1979: 73; see also Habermas, 1997). This is a sharp contrast with the poststructuralist emphasis on the role of discourses in 'articulatory practices', that 'diffuses and dilutes "politics" to mean almost any antagonism... [for] the issue is whether the connections between the elements in a articulatory practice are merely contingent or somehow necessary'. (Harris,1992: 34).

The focus on contract relations may thus enhance our understanding of Latin American democratization, in the context of the 'informal institutionalization' (O'Donnell, 1996) of 'non-liberal or hierarchical societies' (Rawls, 1993). For it provides one of the 'ideoscapes' (Yúdice, 1998), or 'material processes through which imagined communities interact' — i.e. it provides the means to evaluate the building up of the ideals and practices of democracy in the midst of the inequalities, prejudices and 'hybrid' experiences that have shaped the history of Latin American societies (thus correcting, incidentally, the unfair assessment by Nancy Fraser of Habermas's concept of the public sphere).

CONCLUSION

The two approaches to the study of Latin America democratization whose general lines we reviewed previously reveal a parallelism that is apparently insoluble, because they sustain different and competitive theories about democracy. It suffices to list some of their central themes to highlight this parallelism. Thus, regime analysts hold a minimalist concept of the public sphere, whereas cultural studies argue for an expansion of politics beyond the frontiers of government. Regime analysts focus, accordingly, on the individual actions of the political elites, whereas cultural studies center their attention on 'collective citizens' as their units of study. Regime analyses look at government and party officials as their relevant political actors, whereas cultural studies choose the 'subaltern counterpublics' as the source of democratization. The time reference of the first approach is the cycle of institutionalization-transition-institutionalization, whereas the second approach looks for on open-ended participatory expansion. The political regime of the regime analysis approach is the set of governmental procedures and behaviors, whereas for cultural studies the regime includes a confrontation between cultural politics and the ruling institutions, and so on.

Some of the conceptual and methodological problems of the two approaches are indicated earlier in the chapter and - though we cannot demonstrate this assumption here- they seem to relate to the internal limitations of each theory. If this assumption be plausible, one may suggest that such limits hinder each approach from including in its analysis exactly those aspects of democratization that are the focus of the other approach. This being the case, it is possible to say that each approach brings to light complementary aspects of the democratization processes. However, this is not to say that one should discard as irrelevant the basic theoretical disagreements that underlie both approaches. In fact, as their mutual critiques emphatically contend, what is at stake are different and competitive projects of democracy whose eventual reconciliation cannot be foreseen.

Nevertheless, in this analysis it is possible to note some thematic interfaces, and at least three of them are innovative when inter-related, for they may be of special importance for future studies on democratization:

1. The 'two-dimensional' disaggregation of the political regime into a procedural and a behavioral dimension by regime analysts (recently emphasizing the second dimension) resembles, to a certain extent, the central contrast of cultural studies betweeen the ruling institutions, on the one hand. and 'cultural politics' on the other (emphasizing, in the latter, the oppositional behavior of the 'subaltern counterpublics').

Cultural studies maintain, however, that cultural politics are also exercised by the ruling actors and institutions - which, in fact, is the *raison d'être* for the oppositional behavior of the subordinate sectors.

2. Therefore, the recent emphasis of regime analysis on the 'informal institutionalization' of clientelism, particularism, etc. - as the main obstacle to an

eventual institutionalization of democracy in Latin America - receives a fundamental analytical support from cultural studies. These studies help to specify historically the informal particularist traits in the conflicts for meaning and participation that help to change society, and 'expand the public sphere' starting at its roots in daily life.

3. Finally, the emphasis by the regime analysis approach on the individual behavior and strategic choices and interactions of political actors lacks an explicit recognition of the normative orientations of such actors in support of democracy. These normative orientations are present in the collective actors studied by cultural studies - in spite of the fact that these studies lack an interpretation of individual behavior capable of integrating their analysis of democratization from a comparative standpoint. Therefore, both approaches lack an explicit normative theory of democracy (like those of Rawls or Habermas) that is able to explain the political, social and personal changes effected by the processes of democratization from an overall perspective.

Most certainly, a return to a philosophy of history or of consciousness is not claimed here, or that democratization can only be understood through a metaphysical concept of humankind and its destiny. But democratization is a historical process of learning new values, attitudes and sociopolitical behavior, that capacitate groups and individuals to create and sustain a new way of life, and new institutions to organize this lifeworld. Regime analysis and cultural studies shed light on many aspects of this learning process, both at the institutional and at the cultural levels of Latin American societies. It is up to social cientists to accumulate fresh data and new insights about the learning of democracy in Latin America, in order to show that this historical process can be understood from an overall perspective which is both comparative and universalist.

REFERENCES

Alvarez, S. E. 1998. "Latin American Feminisms 'Go Global'. Trends of the 90s and Challenges for the New Millenium", in Alvarez, S.; E. Dagnino and A. Escobar (Eds.), 1998. **The Cultures of Politics and the Politics of Culture. Revisioning Social Movements in Latin America**, Boulder: Westview.

Baierle, S. 1998. "The Explosion of Experience: The Emergence of a New Ethical-Political Principle in Popular Movements in Porto Alegre, Brazil", in Alvarez/Dagnino/Escobar, O.Cit.

Benhabib, S. and Cornell, D. (Eds.) 1987. **Feminism as Critique**. New York: Basil Blackwell.

Birnbaum, P. and Leca, J. 1990. (Eds.) **Individualism, Theories and Methods**. Oxford: Clarendon Press.

Bohman, J. 1990. "Communication, Ideology, and Democratic Theory", **American Political Science Review**, 84:93-109.

Chilton, S. 1991. **Grounding Political Development**, Boulder: Lynne Rienner Pubs.

Cunha, O. 1998. "Black Movements and the 'Politics of Identity' in Brazil", in Alvarez/Dagnino/Escobar, O.Cit.

Dagnino, E. 1998. "Culture, Citizenship, and Democracy: Changing Discourses and Practices of the Latin American left", in Alvarez/Dagnino/Escobar, O.Cit.

Dahl, R. 1971. **Polyarchy: Participation and Opposition,** New York: Yale University Press.

Elster, J. 1987. **Making sense of Marx**. Cambridge: Cambridge University Press.

Fraser, N. 1993. "Rethinking the Public Sphere: A Contribution to the Critique of Actually Existing Democracy", in Robbins, B. (Ed.). **The Phantom Public Sphere**, Minneapolis: University of Minnesota Press.

Garretón, M. A. 1994. **La Faz Sumergida del Iceberg. Estudios sobre la Transformación Cultural**, CESOC/LOM.

Grueso, L.; C.Romero and A.Escobar, 1998. "The Process of Black Commmunity Organizing in the Southern Pacific Coast of Colombia", in Alvarez/Dagnino/Escobar, O.Cit.

Habermas, J. 1979. **Communication and the Evolution of Society**, Boston: Beacon Press.

_____. 1984/7. **The Theory of Communicative Action**. Boston: Beacon Press, 2 Vols.

_____. 1990. **Moral Consciousness and Communicative Action.** Cambridge, Mass: MIT Press.

_____. 1997. Between Facts and Norms: Constributions to a Discourse Theory of Law and Democracy, MA: MIT Press.

Hall, S. 1992. "Cultural Studies and its Theoretical Legacies", in Grossberg, L. et al. (Eds.). **Cultural Studies**, London: Routledge.

Harris, D. 1992. **From Class Struggle to the Politics of Pleasure. The Effects of Gramscianism in Cultural Studies**. London: Routledge.

Jaguaribe, H. 1973. **Political Development: A General Theory and a Latin American Case.** New York: Harper & Row.

Jelin, E. 1998. "Towards a Culture of Participation and Citizenship: Challenges for a More Equitable World", in Alvarez/Dagnino/Escobar, O.Cit.

Kohlberg, L. 1981-4. **Essays on Moral Development**, San Francisco, Harper & Row, 2 vols.

Kowarick, L. 1995. "Investigação Urbana e Sociedade". In: Reis, E., M. H. Tavares and Peter Fry (Eds.). **Pluralismo, espaço social e pesquisa**. São Paulo: Hucitec/ANPOCS.

Levine, A.; E. Sober and E. O. Wright. 1987. "Marxism and Methodological Individualism", **New Left Review**. n.162:67-84.

Mann, M. 1993. **The Sources of Social Power**, 2 vols., Cambridge: Cambridge University Press.

Munck, G. 1996. "Disaggregating Political regime: Conceptual Issues in the Study of Democratization", **Kellogg Institute Working Paper**, n.228.

_____, 1998. **Authoritarianism and Democracy. Soldiers and Workers in Argentina, 1976-1983,** University Park, PA: Pennsylvania State University Press.

O'Donnell, G., 1994. "Delegative Democracy?" **Journal of Democracy,** 5(1): 56-69

_____, 1996. "Another Institutionalization: Latin America and Elsewhere", **Kellogg Institute Working Paper** 222.

_____, 1998. "Polyarchies and the (Un)rule of Law in Latin America", **Kellogg Institute Working Paper** 254.

Olson, M. 1965. **The Logic of Collective Action. (Public Goods and the Theory of Groups),** Cambridge, Mass.: Harvard University Press.

Paoli, M.C. and V.S. Telles, 1998. "Social Rights: Conflicts and Negotiations in Contemporary Brazil", in Alvarez/Dagnino/Escobar, O.Cit.

Przeworski, A. et al. (Eds.), 1995. **Sustainable Development,** New York: Cambridge University Press.

Rawls, J. 1993. "The Law of Peoples", in S.Shute & S.Hurley (eds.). **On Human Rights.** New York: Basic Books.

Ribeiro, G. L. 1998. "Cybercultural Politics: Political Activism at a Distance in a Transnational World", in Alvarez/Dagnino/Escobar, O.Cit.

Santos, F.G. 1994. **Teoria das Decisões Legislativas: Microfundamentos do Clientelismo Político no Brasil,** Ph.D. Dissertation, Rio de Janeiro: IUPERJ.

Schild, V. 1998. "New Subjects of Rights? Women's Movements and the Construction of Citizenship in the 'New Democracies'", in Alvarez/Dagnino/Escobar, O.Cit.

Schumpeter, J. 1942. **Capitalism, Socialism, and Democracy,** New York: Harper & Row.

Slater, D. 1998. "Rethinking the Spatialities of Social Movements: Questions of (B)orders, Culture, and Politics in Global Times",in Alvarez/ Dagnino/ Escobar, O.Cit.

Warren, K. B. 1998. "Indigenous Movements as a Challenge to the Unified Social Movement Paradigm for Guatemala", in Alvarez/Dagnino/Escobar, O.Cit.

Yúdice, G. 1998. "The Globalization of Culture and the New Civil Society", in Alvarez/Dagnino/Escobar, O.Cit.

Zabludovski, G. 1989. "The Reception and Utility of Max Weber's Concept of Patrimonialism in Latin America", **International Sociology,** 4(1):5-66.

Chapter 2

CONTRIBUTIONS OF GRASSROOTS PARTICIPATION[*]

Daniel Drache, a Canadian expert in international economic relations, stated recently that 'the new message of the nineties from international oirganizations such as the World Bank is that public authority needs a more realistic view of governance, one that is not premised on simplistic ideas about the power of the markets'. (Drache, 1999: 2) And he added

> (T)he critical issue for our times is not statelessness – defined in its most extreme form as the end of the nation-state and the irreversible diminishment of national authority – but 'state-ness': finding the appropriate model, strategy, and resources for maintaining public authority in constrasting market economies.
> *(Drache, 1999: 7)*

Drache explains that his argument is based on Habermas's concept of the 'public sphere'. (Habermas, 1989):

> (T)he public sphere is not seen as a neutral meeting place. Its principal virtue is that public life is a series of collective engagements that are negotiated and change as the balance of social forces shifts from the elites to the democratic end of emporwement. The merit of Habermas's public sphere is its radical indeterminacy and openness.
> *(Drache, 1999: 27)*

This was written before the "Battle of Seattle", when 50,000 protestors were successful in preventing the World Trade Organization from meeting in November 1999. However, a commentator stressed that

> '[T]heir shut-down success also provided police and security forces with a worst case scenario from which to learn and devise more effective countermeasures against similar protests in the future. The result can be seen clearly in the cases of attempts to close the

[*] This report was based on research supported by the *Fundação de Amparo à Pesquisa do Estado de São Paulo (FAPESP)*. Judith Hellman helped with the editing of the English version. Thanks are due to José Reis, Eduardo Viola, Ilse Scherer-Warren, Ary Minella and Sergio Zermeño for their critical comments on an earlier draft of the text.

IMF and World Bank meetings in Washington D.C. in April 2000 and the OAS General Assembly in Windsor in June, which were successfully prevented. [After all]...there seems to be little sign of any cracks beyond the rethorical in the state-business consensus behind market reforms'.
(Leger, 2000: 10, 12, 13)

Nevertheless, the World Bank and other official agencies have been insisting on the issues of popular participation in, and the social impact of, the local projects they are supporting in Latin America. These policies have to do with the long transition in some countries (as is the case of Brazil) from authoritarian rule into more open and participatory political regimes. They also relate to the new forms of democratic life and grassroots organization that emerged in society in opposition to the previous authoritarian regimes. It had been predicted that the political transition would channel and integrate institutionally these forms of popular organization. However, it has been noticed that many local groups engaged in grassroots mobilization (such as some Catholic communities and agencies) tend to criticize participation in, and to continue opposing, official programs and policies.

This chapter will not explore the various definitions and controversies about 'grassrootism', or *'basismo'* as it is known in Latin America. The term is widely understood to mean the opposition of certain social movements to classic forms of institutional politics, political parties and permanent channels of political representation. However, it is necessary to go further and seek a more rigorous approach to the phenomenon and its effects in the political sphere.

The Mexican sociologist Sergio Zermeño wrote an evaluation of social movements in Mexico, with an analysis of the historical political dilemmas of these movements, under the title 'democracy as restricted identity'[1]. He says, for instance, that social movements tend to act at a 'restricted, grassroots level, inferior to the social classes and the grand historic actors' (political parties, government institutions), not only for self-defense against repression, but in order to create a 'structurally different style of democracy' — namely, participatory or direct democracy.

Zermeño's analysis is innovative and thought-provoking in more than one respect. Its innovativeness lies in the discussion of democratic identity, which has not so far been dealt with in depth in Latin America. His analysis is thought-provoking because one may assume that the usual problems of social movements (such as their discontinuity, limits and political restrictions) are not mere *weaknesses,* but are part of the specific contributions of these movements to processes of democratization. In other words, one may ask whether social movements, with their experience of democracy as 'restricted identity' may not be confronting the state with the challenges, stimuli and initiatives which belong precisely do their sphere of competence - particularly, but not exclusively, in 'late capitalist' societes[2]. It might thus be suggested that what is referred to (often pejoratively) as 'grassrootism', is in actual fact a permanent element of democratic order - an order we, in today's Brazil, are only beginning to experience and to study.

These arguments will be partly developed here, as a research note, starting with a look at Zermeño's analysis from the angle of its relevance to the discussion of social movements in Brazil, and then considering some research data on the question of whether the experience of 'democracy as restricted identity' has been a positive one for Brazilian social movements. It shall be indicated that this question can be answered through two types of data: 1) local changes in political culture which seem to result from participatory experiences of social movements; 2) the cumulative nature of these movements' experiences as a change in the conditions for political democratization (and as a broader definition of the frontiers of the polity).

THE MOVEMENTS' 'RESTRICTED IDENTITY'

Latin American social movements coexist with two opposing principles of political organization which, in a contradictory manner, preside over political processes and institutions: these, in Zermeño's words, are 'national-statist logic' and 'class-democratic logic'. The effects of the former are that

> In a country with a strong ancestral state, the political action of the elites, both in government and in opposition, tends to be organized around the position from which everything seems possible (the vertex) and in this shared fixation the socially, culturally and politically formed matrix is nourished and reproduced.
> *(Zermeño, 1987: 40).*

On the other hand, Zermeño says,

> Class-democratic logic is characterized as a bitter adversary of our pyramidal heritage insofar as from all directions at once the pillars of the strong state suffer constant erosion from the demands coming, with differing signs and - on other plane - antagonistically, from the working class, from capital and from the middle classes.
> *(Zermeño, 1987: 19).*

Zermeño also mentions the logic of 'modernization' and of civil society, which affects especially the new middle classes, the students and intellectuals. However, he does not find it important in Mexico (he writes before the *Zapatista* rebellion in Chiapas [1994] and the process of formal democratization which defeated the *PRI* in the national elections [2000]). But what matters here is to recall initially the effects of a political context of statist tradition on the constitution of 'democracy as restricted identity'. For Zermeño, two paradoxes can be observed in Mexico:

> First, social struggles, which are strongly oriented toward the state but find no intermediate bodies, spaces or channels through which to conduct their politics with a degree of permanece and continuity, create superpoliticization very early on.... In constrast with other matrices of practice in Latin America, it seems that in Mexico there is a high degree of social and political tranquility. But what there is in fact is a constant effervescence of movements that are swiftly split, coopted, truncated and isolated.
> *(Zermeño, 1987: 40).*

The second paradox:

> If the leadership thrown up by this contestatory action does not destroy itself by hurling itself against the state in direct action, it tends over time to insert itself into the anatomy of the power bloc, thereby seeking more influence for the attainment of its interests or those of the people it represents.
> *(Zermeño, 1987: 40).*

The conclusion: 'Thus, sooner or later the leadership itself is split, and there also occurs a split between the leadership and the grassroots, between social action and political action' (Zermeño, 1987: 42). Zermeño ends with a quotation from Alain Touraine saying that in Latin America 'social movements are not autonomous forces but rather positive or negative reactions to state intervention' (Zermeño, 1987: 42). This explains the social movements' experience of 'democracy as restricted identity', 'since experience has shown that other forms of social and political action lead to repression, co-optation and desintegration of the actor mobilized because his identity is transitory and deficient'. (Zermeño, 1987: 4).

In the case of Brazil, too, there have been studies which analyze the gap between social action and political action, as well as the differing dynamics which govern these two processes[3]. It is usual to emphasize the degree to which social movements depend on the state, and the peculiarities of *basismo* as a form of resistance to the statist tradition in Brazilian politics. But few have been so bold, as is Zermeño for the Mexican case, as to characterize the practices of Brazilian social movements in terms of 'democracy as restricted identity'[4]. Even though the terms of the debate in studies on Mexico and Brazil are not exactly the same, there are undoubtedly points of contact which are worth highlighting.

One such point that invites attention is that the experience of 'democracy as restricted identity' is certainly different from (though not necessarily, as Zermeño claims, 'inferior' to) the forms of political identity usually attributed to social classes, as well as those which may exist in the 'grand historical actors' (political parties, government, etc.). Here, however, it would not be amiss to ask, for example, to what extent there has been in any country (even in the advanced Western democracies) a case of fully realized 'class-democratic logic'[5]. Historical studies have shown that the institutional life of the liberal democracies of the West arose gradually from a long series of reforms creating public freedoms, in response to society's egalitarian demands — which in turn started from forms of direct or grassroots democracy practiced or envisaged by popular groups[6].

Thus, recognition of 'democracy as restricted identity' in social movements cannot overlook the influence and pressure such experiences might bring to bear toward reformulating and broadening the territory of politics. Even when the partial nature of these democratic experiences is recognized - i.e. their inability (or, as is often the case, their unwillingness) to reformulate or transform the entire political body.

The interpretation skillfully presented by Zermeño of social movements as an experience of 'democracy as restricted identity' is an innovative adaptation of the relational theory of the identity of social movements (Touraine, 1978) to the historical situation of Mexico and other Latin American countries - with their statist traditions and their chronic, seemingly interminable political transitions between authoritarian and liberal forms of political regime. But this interpretation tends to remain purely 'negative', in the sense that it emphasizes only what such a 'democracy as restricted identity' has *not yet become* (and may never be able to become). It is therefore necessary to raise some issues and questions regarding the 'positive' meaning such an interpretation could have for processes of partial democratization of the state, such as that of the present transition in Brazil.

LOCAL CHANGES IN THE POLITICAL CULTURE

The first set of points concerning the positive contribution of the experience of 'democracy as restricted identity' in Brazilian social movements has to do with the possible transformation of political culture produced thereby. Studies that have already been made of internal socio-cultural changes in the grassroots of some segments of the Catholic church in Brazil and the influence of the church on certain social movements indicate significant changes in patterns of orientation and behavior among these groups. This may, in turn, have broader effects on the formation of a pluralist political culture[7]. It is true that these studies show a vast diversity of situations in many different regions of the country. Yet, they do raise the issue of the role of grassroots resocialization in constituting new social actors - suggesting that these changes tend to negate or transform the authoritarian norms that prevail in the dominant political culture[8].

Thus a comparison in some parts of Brazil of the *CEBs-Comunidades Eclesiais de Base* ('grassroots church communities') shows that a dual process of identity construction goes on in these communities. (See Chapter 6 of this book for a more detailed account of these processes). On the one hand, they are carrying out a religious reformation inside the church, by instituting the participants as social actors with a renewed religious identity - an identity that is active rather than passive. Individuals assume responsibility for their own values and decisions and interact on equal terms with all other participants, thus challenging the differences between the clergy and the 'average person in the pew', as well as differences in the social division of labor within the community.

On the other hand, the *CEBs* also act as institutional mediators between church reform and social change. They arouse motivations and attitudes favoring social action and stimulate the participants to construct autonomous, participatory political identities. Through their reflection and action with other actors, the participants can focus on the problems of the 'world' around them and the ways and means to solve these problems. In other words, religious reformation or resocialization tends to lead to social action that is external to the church, usually has an egalitarian and participatory connotation, and is similar to, or an extension of, the process of reformation of the religious community.

Other studies of social movements at the grassroots level have also suggested the constitution of a 'dual pattern of interactions' which extend the process of identity building into the political system[9]. In the first place, militants from the same neighborhood take part in various groups and organizations (teachers and parents' associations, *CEBs*, neighborhood centers, mothers' clubs, youth groups, etc.) which have mutual relations reinforced by joint initiatives, thus constituting a 'territory for popular organization', unified through the personal action (or 'work') of these militants. Meanwhile, individuals inside these same movements also relate to institutions outside the neighborhood (such as parishes, trade unions, political parties, social and educational services run by the state) in which the predominant relationships are asymmetrical and authority-based. Some of these 'external' institutions have also 'branches', 'cells', agencies, services and leaders located in the neighborhood.

Therefore, 'pastoral agents', teachers, social workers, who work (and may even live) in the neighborhood are seen as authorities, as are the local leaders whose actions occur outside the neighborhood (in unions, parties, etc.). This 'dual pattern of interactions' introduces an ambivalence into the orientations and actions of the local movements, which is usually dealt with through strategies of cooperation, competition or even conflict. The most successful external agents are generally those who cooperate with local forms of grassroots democracy (this is the case with many Catholic pastoral agents, for example)[10].

There is no doubt that an exchange between the two levels of identity does indeed occur, so that even when popular 'democracy as restricted identity' is co-opted or repressed, or comes into conflict with broader cultural and political groupings, the latter are obliged to take it into account and to offer it some kind of response. It is possible that this says little about the democratization of the political system, or even of the national political culture taken as a whole. But it does state something regarding the emergence and influence of a participatory cultural standard at the grassroots of society, namely, that Brazilian society is no longer a homogeneous society entirely submissive to authoritarian traditions. Perhaps it is easier to verify in Brazil than in Mexico Zermeño's evaluation of the movements' 'restricted identity' as the emergence of a 'structurally different style of democracy'. In Brazil there are new sectors of the Catholic church, new social movements and new trade unions, which became permanently organized in the last decades, and which devoted themselves specifically to questioning the traditionally authoritarian political culture[11].

THE MOVEMENTS' 'PERMANENT NEGOTIATION'

A second block of questions or issues which have drawn the attention of researchers on the relations between social movements and politics has to do with the apparently discontinuous and fragmented nature of the identities assumed by social movements. Thus, these movements are usually recognized to be merely local and 'parochial' in their perspectives, discontinuous and ephemeral in their existence, engrossed in community experiences of direct democracy, and organized around specific demands addressed to the state for the concrete satisfaction of certain basic rights - a satisfaction which, paradoxically, would lead in most cases to the demobilization or extinction of the movements themselves[12].

It is relevant to ask, however, whether this discontinuity and fragmentedness is not more apparent than real, when the social movements' experience of 'democracy as restricted identity' is taken seriously in its *positive* contributions, both to the collective memory of society and to institutional reform. The fundamental question here is whether the experience of 'democracy as restricted identity' is not an experience of social equality which questions the state's monopoly on politics - and by doing so performs a process of resocialization of social groups in the specific fields to which they are related, in addition to stimulating institutional reforms in response to such a process.

But there are other striking features unveiled by the historians of Western social movements. These social struggles have mostly been mixed – 'mongrels' from the orthodox standpoint - because they combined immediate economic goals with projects for the future, visions and utopias, together with ideologies and concrete practices (which are apparently fragmentary and discontinuous)[13]. Yet, they are struggles that very often emphasized and pointed toward a search for an ideal future society. This is the ideal of a society politically emancipated and endowed with equality for all, regardless of the 'objective' group or individual interests (which clash mutually but become symbolically reconciled through the state). These struggles were not aimed (to use the language of Marxist orthodoxy) at replacing 'class dictatorship' with another dictatorship, but they questioned precisely the 'pyramidal' nature of politics (the state's monopoly over it) and hence aimed at eliminating the state through the absorption of political power by a self-governing society[14].

The point, therefore, is to find out whether it is not in the admittedly utopian nature of this egalitarianism of social movements that resides their ability to influence and bring pressure to bear on the state - which is responsible for the democratizing changes in politics in the advanced Western countries[15]. In this case, the apparent discontinuity and fragmentedness of 'democracy as restricted identity' would be the cause of substantial changes in politics and society that have taken place in these countries, but which can be understood only in the long term.

However, as the study by Zermeño emphatically contends, Latin American countries suffer from additional constraints which, far worse than in the advanced Western societies, deform and segregate politics from its base in society, in the contradictory clash of its mutually exclusive 'logics' of historical development. However, this does not necessarily mean that social movements are simply forms of manifestation dependent on the state, or that their 'democracy as restricted identity' has merely negative characteristics, those of evading, ignoring and being unable to influence the political sphere.

Numerous studies on social movements in Brazil during the period of political liberalization have been carried out and permit a more balanced assessment of the relations between the two phenomena in the recent past[16]. It is impossible to produce such a systematic survey within the limits of a research note. (See chapter 3 of this book for a broader discussion on this topic). Instead, I will focus on a sequence of studies on social movements in São Paulo, raising the questions pertaining to their apparent discontinuity[17].

One clear example, regarding the ephemeral and discontinuous nature of social movements, is that of the various movements which emerged - in different forms, sometimes simultaneous, and sometimes successively in time - during the last decades, in many outlying suburbs of metropolitan São Paulo, to demand solutions to the problem of low-cost housing. Some of these are movements of shanty-town dwellers (*'favelados'*), while others demand the legalization of 'clandestine'(illegal) housing estates which have sprung up without official planning permission. In some cases the movements organize the occupation of empty land owned by speculators, or in areas subject to litigation but originally registered as public property. The characteristics of these movements vary enormously, as regards not only their demands but also the conditions in which they arose, their organization, leadership and coordination, both internally and in their relations with other movements[18].

Nevertheless, several institutional changes have resulted from the action of these movements. For example, while Brazil was still under military rule, Congress introduced a change in urban zoning laws, to punish property speculators selling lots without official planning permission (the first time any such legal sanction was created in Brazil). And the last São Paulo mayor nominated by the military formally legalized all 'clandestine' estates in 1982. Moreover, under the first administration of the democratic opposition (1983-1985), the city government took steps to tackle the problem with more general measures, by offering subsidized loans to workers for home building along with other measures designed to alleviate the ill effects of property speculation.

However, these social movements and others like them, are still campaigning. While their demands and forms of organization have changed (and also vary with the area in dispute or with the forms of leadership), they tended to demand ever more drastic solutions to the problem of low-cost housing. For example, sit-ins have often been staged by several hundred people at the regional offices of the city government in the east of São Paulo, at the State Housing Department and at City Hall. These demonstrations demanded the fulfillment of previous promises made by the authorities. Underlying these protests was doubt as to the authorities' capacity to carry out their promises, giving real protection to owners of suburban lots against property speculators. Indeed, as soon as many of these groups had received promises of financing from City Hall, they were surrounded by would-be purchasers making offers no low-income family could easily refuse. Here we see a repetition, this time underwritten by City Hall and with direct financial support from the federal and state government, of the speculative drive which is typical of the real estate market in Brazil.

What examples of this type demonstrate is that changes in legislation and public policies concerning apparently limited problems entail more general reformulations of the state's public policy and an increase in the degree and forms of participation in decision-making by the popular groups involved. Moreover, it is clear that the reformulations of public policy regarding such demands result from initiatives undertaken by the interested parties, who thereby succeed (however partially and episodically) in influencing the political sphere (legislative, executive and judiciary), not just as passive recipients dependent on the state, but as active citizens struggling for their rights.

Finally, a medium-term view of processes such as these suggests that the discontinuity of social movements is only relative. There tends to be an accumulation of demands and experiences, with new movements seeking new demands emerging successively, in the same area of needs, once the previous demands have been won and the movements campaigning for them apparently have vanished. The words 'relative' and 'apparent' are used here, because studies have shown that the same leaders and participants in previous movements often crop up again in new movements, bringing forward new demands and communicating their previous experience, as the new strategies to be followed are polished.

For instance, in the example mentioned above, while the city administration agreed to legalize the 'clandestine' developments *en masse*, at first the situation changed only on paper rather than in practice. This led many groups from the previous movement to carry on the struggle and to demand enforcement of the legislation and the provision of public services required under the new zoning law. This led also to the emergence of new movements, such as groups of smallholders lobbying for negotiations on public financing to support owner-occupiers. Other movements, meanwhile, denounced the latter as a 'market solution' and demanded other forms of state intervention (eg. the São Miguel and other associations which discussed the access to a usufructuary provision by which the government could grant smallholders inalienable rights to their lots)[19].

These observations permit the conclusion that the needs which mobilize social movements are historical needs, that is, that they do not constitute a level of merely 'objective' wants which can be easily and straightforwardly quantified. The wants or needs in question undergo constant mutation but are anchored in the identity peculiar to the movements bearing them. The movements' identity itself is historically variable, and tends to be constantly re-elaborated as new responses and possibilities are offered by the state, their main interlocutor. These opportunities vary, in turn, in accordance with the central characteristics of the ruling regime, with regard to its acknowledgement of the needs experienced and expressed by social movements, or at least by the more dynamic and militant among them.

In the Brazilian case, such variances and advances of the political system - which became evident during the *'abertura'* (liberalization) process under the military regime, and have had institutional consequences under the liberal 'transition' - would be unthinkable without the emerging demands of the social movements. The continuity and cumulative effects of demands placed on the state by social movements can be described as a process of 'permanent negotiation'[20], but one which does not necessarily imply a linear evolutionary pattern. Just as defeats can occur (and have occurred) and ground may be lost, so an overall view of legislative changes and public policy in the field of low-cost housing shows that the action of social movements is not simply episodic and fragmentary, nor simply dependent on or reactive to the government[21].

In two specific cases discussed here (the *Sem Terras*, or 'landless', and the São Miguel association), the two movements had different aims, strategies and social bases (although both had a close link with the same sector of the Catholic leadership). Their results converged because both campaigned for the most favorable possible public policy changes on the issue of low-cost housing (both 'inside' and 'outside' the property market). This is, however, only one instance of the movements' 'permanent negotiation' - whose general results and consequences have to be appraised during the new stage of social negotiations surrounding the application of the advanced legislation on urban planning and participation, provided by the 1988 Brazilian Constitution.

CONCLUSIONS

In conclusion, it is possible to suggest, on the basis of research which ought to be extended to other parts of Brazil, that the experience of 'democracy as restricted identity' undergone by social movements has had a positive influence on the broader changes going on in the political and cultural system. It has been positive because it has led to an accumulation of demands and achievements centered on historical needs and on the fundamental rights of citizenship - precisely as these demands focus on specific issues or problems, of relevance to the communities in question. Moreover, the egalitarianism of grassroots democratic experiences has survived situations of interchange, negotiation and conflict with the governmental authorities.

By systematically reappearing whenever it becomes necessary and possible at the level of social movements, the experience of 'democracy as restricted identity' seems to be a conquest which tends to become a permanent channel for institutional and cultural expression by the subordinate groups in society. This persistence gives new meaning and comprehensiveness to the territory of politics and to the frontiers of the polity, in terms not only of a constant remodeling of institutions and policies, but specially of a politicization of every-day life which seeks to eliminate, or at least to reduce, the gap between society and politics.

The World Band (and other international) agencies are thus correct in insisting on local popular participation and on the control over the social impact of the development projects they are supporting in Latin America. For, in the present array of democratizing trends in the region, the people do tend to participate anyway - either in favour or against such projects. Furthermore, the studies are showing that social movements have become one of the main constructive channels for participation, through the influence they bring upon the democratization of political institutions and the political culture of Latin American societies.

REFERENCES

Cardoso, F.H. 1981. "Regime Político e Mudança Social." **Revista de Cultura e Política**. 3:7-26.

Cardoso, R.C.L. 1983. "Movimentos Sociais Urbanos: Balanço Crítico". In: Sorje, B. and Tavares, M.H. (Eds.), **Sociedade e Política no Brasil pós-64**. São Paulo: Brasiliense.

Drache, D. 1999. "The Return of the Public Domain after the Triumph of Markets", **Robarts Centre for Canadian Studies**, Toronto: York University.

Galtung, J. 1984. "Los Azules y los Rojos: los Verdes y los Pardos: Una Evaluación de los Movimientos Políticos Alternativos", mimeo. **Boletim de Ciências Sociais**, v.34, July.

Gohn, M.G.M. 1988. "Lutas Pela Moradia Popular em São Paulo". **Ciência e Cultura**, v. 40, n. 7, pp.637-645, July.

Habermas, J. 1984/7. **Theory of Communicative Action**. 2 vols. Boston: Beacon.

_____, 1989. **The Structural Transformation of the Public Sphere**, MA: MIT Press.

Heller, A. and Feher, F. 1985. **Anatomía de la Izquierda Occidental**. Barcelona: Península.

Kowarick, L. 1987. "Movimentos Urbanos no Brasil Contemporâneo". **Revista Brasileira de Ciências Sociais**, 3 (1): 38-50.

_____, 2000, **Estudos Urbanos**, São Paulo: Editora Trinta e Quatro.

Krischke, P. (Ed.). 1984. **Terra de Habitação vs. Terra de Espoliação**. São Paulo: Cortez.

Legler, T. 2000. "Transnational Coalition-Building in the Americas: The Case of the Hemispheric Social Alliance", **Centre for Latin American and Caribbean Studies**, Toronto: York University.

Maheu, L. 1983. "Les Mouvements de Base et la Lutte contre l'Appropriation Étatique du Tissu Social". **Sociologie et Sociétés**, 15 (1): 77-92.

Mainwaring, S. 1987. "Urban Popular Movements, Identity and Democratization in Brazil". **Comparative Political Studies**, 20 (2):131-158, July.

Mainwaring, S. and Viola, E. 1984. "New Social Movements, Political Culture and Democracy: Brazil and Argentina in the 80s". **Telos**, 61: 17-54, Fall.

Marshall, T.H. 1965. **Class, Citizenship and Social Development**. Garden City: Doubleday-Anchor.

Moore, B. 1987. **Injustiça, as Bases Sociais da Obediência e da Revolta**. São Paulo: Brasiliense.

Offe, C. 1985. "New Social Movements: Challenging the Boundaries of Institutional Politics". **Social Research**, 52 (4): 817-868.

Ollin Wright, E. 1985. "Que Hay de Nuevo en las Clases Medias?" **Zona Abierta**, 34/35: 105-150, January.

Portelli, H. 1981. "Democracia Representativa, Democracia de Base e Movimento Social". **Revista de Cultura e Política**, 3: 55-64, January.

Sader, E. 1988. **Quando Novos Personagens Entraram em Cena**. Rio de Janeiro: Paz e Terra.

Scherer-Warren, I. 1984. **Movimentos Sociais: Um Ensaio de Interpretação Sociológica**. Florianópolis: Editora da Universidade Federal de Santa Catarina.

_____, 1987. "O Carácter dos Novos Movimentos Sociais". In: Scherer-Warren, I. and Krischke, P. (Eds.) **Uma Revolução no Cotidiano? Os Novos Movimentos Sociais na América Latina**, São Paulo: Brasiliense.

Thompson, E.P. 1977. **La Formación Histórica de la Clase Obrera**. Barcelona: Laia.

Touraine, A. 1978. **La Voix et le Regard**. Paris: Seuil.

Vasconcellos, E. and Krischke, P. 1984. "Igreja, Motivações e Organização dos Moradores em Loteamentos Clandestinos". In: Krischke, P. (Ed.) **Terra de Habitação vs. Terra de Espoliação**. São Paulo: Cortez.

Zermeño, S. 1987. "Hacia una Democracia como Identidad Restringida: Sociedad y Política en México". **Revista Mexicana de Sociologia**, 49 (2): 57-88.

ENDNOTES

[1] Zermeño (1987). Quotations here are from the original typescript.

[2] This first approximation is inspired by the works of Offe (1985) and Heller and Feher (1985). On the characteristics of social movements in the central Western societies, see Habermas (1984-7). Careful research has yet to be done to point out similarities and differences between those movements and the Latin American movements. (See Chapter 3 of this book for a more general appraisal of social movements in Brazil).

[3] The classic example is an article by Cardoso (1981).

[4] Mainwaring and Viola (1984) defined the orientations of some of the new social movements (during the political liberalization processes in Brazil and Argentina) as 'radical democratic.'

[5] Different approaches to the classic Marxist argument with a view to possible application to the present can be found in Ollin Wright (1985); Scherer-Warren (1987); Thompson (1977). As to the Weberian opposition between bureaucratic and political trends in the Brazilian case, see Mainwaring (1987).

[6] See Marshall (1965). Similar results are shown from different perspectives by Moore (1987) and by Thompson (1977).

[7] On this topic, see various case studies edited by Krischke and Mainwaring (1986).

[8] What follows summarizes the argument and the conclusions presented by Krischke (1986).

[9] What follows expands an outline presented by Krischke (1987).

[10] These are some of the conclusions presented by Vasconcellos and Krischke (1984).

[11] Sader (1988) has shown how grassroots communities interacted with opposition leaders and new left cadres oriented toward democratic changes in the formation of new popular neighborhood movements in São Paulo.

[12] Krischke (1984: 70-88) discussed the 'paradoxical cycle' in social movements.

[13] Thompson (1977) is the best interpreter of this process for the English labor movement, but there are other interpretations, albeit from different perspectives and in different historical contexts: e.g. Maheu (1983).

[14] On this self-definition of social movements and the limitations of this definition, see for example Galtung (1984) and Portelli (1981).

[15] Habermas (1984-7) and Heller/Feher (1985) provide different contributions on this point.

[16] There are various surveys on the Brazilian social movements literature made from different perspectives. See e.g. Cardoso (1983) and Kowarick (1987).

[17] The data presented in what follows was collected by the author in São Paulo during 1985-1986 and later confirmed in a larger study by Gohn (1988).

[18] For a more detailed description and a comprehensive interpretation of all these movements, see Gohn (1988).

[19] The law has long provided for land usufruct under certain conditions and hence has been available to the ruling groups. Governments have indeed done so, for example, to attract business and to grant benefits to cultural and sporting associations. The fact that usufructuary land grants prohibit sale (usually for 90 years) would have made this an especially appropriate way to protect low-income families from the pressure of real estate speculators. The 1988 new Brazilian Constitution has also provided for urban '*usucapião*' (legal recognition) of property after ten years of undisputed occupation.

[20] The notion of 'permanent negotiation' dates back to 1982 when the *Movimento de Moradores em Loteamentos Clandestinos* took advantage of the new zoning law and the then imminent legalization of 'clandestine' housing developments to raise new demands for public services and facilities in over 100 neighborhoods. This strategy led to the creation of new and different movements in several of these areas. The use of the term here is designed less to stress its conscious strategic use by the movements than to underscore the cumulative nature of these struggles, which seem to be discontinuous, fragmented and lacking in a long-term strategy.

[21] We have seen above that this is the interpretation suggested by Touraine for Latin American movements in general. Overgeneralization may be misleading, for in São Paulo itself the situation changed drastically during the late 1980s, as the movements were repressed by the conservative Mayor Janio Quadros (1986-1988) but resurged with new impetus upon the election of the Workers' Party Mayor Luiza Erundina, in November 1988. Low cost housing continued to be a major problem in São Paulo throughout the 1990s. (See Kowarick, 2000). It is a priority of the government of the new *PT* Mayor Marta Suplicy elected in 2000.

Chapter 3

SOCIO-POLITICAL ACTORS AND
UNFINISHED DEMOCRATIZATION[*]

A process of democratization can be seen as the access of new actors to the public sphere: actors who learn to establish and support a stable and increasingly comprehensive democratic regime. This chapter will argue that Brazilian democratization is still unfinished. For instance, after more than a decade of formal recognition of civil and political rights by the 1988 Constitution, there is still a pattern of widespread violence against the urban and rural poor. (Méndez et al., 1998; Holston and Caldeira, 1998). Nevertheless, one must inquire about the positive contributions of the democratization process, even when its results are flawed and incomplete. People often learn from their experiences, and this learning may help them to devise new strategies and starting points to improve their future.

Several studies focusing on institutional development and elite replacement in Latin America have duly emphasized the obstacles and difficulties of democratization - when the process is compared, for instance, with advanced Western democracies (e.g., O'Donnell, 1988; Nun, 1988). In fact, other analysts (e.g. Morse, 1988; Wiarda, 1974; Hartz, 1958) have long sustained that Latin American societies are more likely to maintain similitudes with their traditional predecessors in Southern Europe, and their authoritarian counterparts in Central-Eastern Europe - though these European societies also began to democratize in the 1970s and 1980s, offering more grounds for comparative work.

Democratizing processes are always historically different, and many of them may eventually fail, deadlock or regress into oligarchic and dictatorial rule. Moreover, current theories of democracy were originally formulated on the basis of historical experiences in advanced Western democracies. Thus, these categories may seem insufficient on account of the complexity of existing contemporary societies - including the present societies of Latin America.

---

[*] This chapter is part of a report prepared for *FLACSO* and supported by *CNPq*. The author thanks the helpful comments – on earlier drafts of the text – made by Ilse Scherer-Warren, Eduardo Viola, Paulo Vieira, Benjamin Arditi and Maria Glória Gohn.

Many of the issues above have been considered by current studies and debates on democratization, in Latin America and elsewhere. For instance, several studies on 'new social movements' have questioned classical theoretical approaches, especially their capacity to explain the processes of democratization in Latin America (e.g. Evers, 1984; Laclau, 1986; Tourraine, 1986; Arditi, 1988). These studies concurred with similar research done in Europe (e.g. Offe, 1985; Heller/Feher, 1985; Habermas, 1984-7) which call for both a simultaneous revision of the classical approaches to democracy and modernization, and a historical 'radicalization' (or 'deepening') of representative and participatory democracy. Thus, all these approaches criticized the contemporary forms of socialism and liberalism - though from different standpoints and various degrees of conceptual 'radicalization'.

This chapter argues that the unfinished process of democratization in Latin America (taking as an example the Brazilian transition from authoritarian rule during the 1980s and 1990s) has been accompanied by two important elements. The first is the emergence of new social actors who have questioned both the legitimacy of the previous authoritarian regime (that was in full power in Brazil until 1985) and the conservative political culture[1] that continued to prevail in the country's political traditions and institutions. The second is the process of partial conflicts, negotiations and agreements that supported the expansion of the public sphere, and the growing institutionalization of an alternative democratic order - which is largely still in the making.

However, we should emphasize from the beginning that the two series of phenomena referred to above are not to be considered irreversible, in a linear or deterministic logic of institutionalization (repeating, as it were, what supposedly 'happened' in the advanced Western countries). In fact, historical studies (e.g. Thompson, 1977) have shown that such linear processes have not occurred in Europe either. On the contrary, what is suggested here is the ambiguous characteristics of the social actors who are emerging in the public sphere: an ambiguity that relates to the uncertainty surrounding current negotiations about the meanings and prospects of democracy.

Moreover, we are not suggesting that there is a discontinuity (let alone a contradiction) between social and institutional life — as if social and political democratization followed different paths, contrasting social actors to the institutional order (not even when this order was a full-fledged military-authoritarian regime, as that which ruled Brazil until 1985). In contrast, Brazilian research reveals a mutual influence, for instance between the rise of new social movements during the demise of the military regime, and the expansion of the public sphere that accompanied the transition to civilian rule. We will present some basic features of this interaction, as guidelines for this chapter.

If the rise of new social actors is said to relate historically and conceptually[2] to institutional democratization - in a new and alternative approach to democracy - it is necessary to recognize that the origins of the two phenomena are different, in spite of the fact that their results can often be complementary. Later in this chapter we will show that the aims and orientations which mobilize new and old social actors to satisfy their basic needs differ from - but relate to - the orientations and capabilities of political actors to promote and sustain democratic institutions. In short, historical analysis must use concepts that allow for a relational interpretation of the differences between social and institutional phenomena.

The interpretation offered below of some social and institutional changes that began in the 1980s in Brazil uses concepts of Agnes Heller's 'theory of needs', and Jürgen Habermas's 'communicative action' theory. The assumption is that these categories are compatible to each other, and applicable to this historical setting. This is not to say that these scholars share the same theoretical framework (though they may have common grounds in neo-Kantian philosophy), and no attempt is made to discuss the differences and similarities between their approaches. However, some indications will be made at the end, about the contributions of these concepts to the understanding of Brazilian unfinished democratization.

A final preliminary remark is in order. Both Heller and Habermas produced their theories in relation to a 'deepening' or radicalization of democracy in the central Western countries (and also in opposition to to the contemporary forms of liberalism and socialism). Latin American societies, however, are not fully established democracies - and are in fact at different stages of democratic transition and consolidation (at times, 're-consolidation', as in Chile and Uruguay). Therefore, the use made here of categories proposed by European scholars is intended to highlight the differences, rather than the similarities, between social and political actors in Latin America, and those that have been studied in the Northern hemisphere.

SOCIAL ACTORS: NEEDS AND UTOPIAS

Some critical overviews appeared in the late 1980s, in the vast and ever-increasing literature on social movements in Brazil (e.g., Kowarick, 1987; Cardoso, 1988). They reviewed an extensive bibliography - which offers different interpretations of the relationship between social action and the transition to democracy. Another general study, which focused on historical and conceptual restructuring, is the posthumous book of Eder Sader (1988). It added to previous works by Vera Telles (1986) and Tilman Evers (1982) which covered the same historical ground. Their focus was on the political reorientations of Catholic 'base communities', neighborhood associations and labor unions, among factory workers in São Paulo, from the mid-seventies. These studies complemented each other, as they emphasized different time periods, various forms of organization and mobilization, and diverse evaluations of these phenomena.

Evers's study looks at the 'Cost of Living Movement' (*Movimento do Custo de Vida - MCV*), that existed between 1973 and 1979, led by Church and union militants, neighborhood leaders and leftist cadres. The *MCV* prepared an open letter and a campaign of signatures, against the policy of 'wage freeze' and control ('*Congelamento salarial*') by the military regime. This letter was signed by one million two hundred and fifty thousand people from across the country. Of course, the military regime refused to receive the letter, alleging that it was 'subversive'. But the main aim of the movement was achieved, namely to publicly denounce the regime's wages policy, through a concerted action among those working to raise popular awareness and organization.

One of the results of the *MCV* was the election in 1978 of two of its leaders to the São Paulo state legislature through the only opposition party existing at the time. It is very likely that the *MCV* campaign influenced the orientations of industrial workers and the electorate at large, in their willingness to support labor strikes. These strikes were launched in São Paulo in 1978, and were the first labor outbreak since the late 1960s, and were led by the metalworkers' union of the '*ABC*'region (which includes Santo André, São Bernardo and São Caetano, the most industrialized cities of São Paulo's metropolitan area).

Vera Telles' research focused on the conditions that led to convergence and cooperation, from the early 1970s, among the various militants and organizers in the low income neighborhoods of São Paulo. This convergence among church sectors, union members and leftist cadres gave rise to the new movements of the mid and late seventies, thereby emphasizing the latter's originality vis-à-vis previous forms of mobilization. Vera Telles argued that this new experience of convergence and cooperation was important for three reasons. First, it overcame previous experiences of the workers' defeats and demobilization (1968/1972); second, it redefined the grassroots' (and their leadership's) actions and orientations toward alternative participatory forms of organization, in local churches, unions and other associations; and third, it adopted pluralist strategies, in tune with the living and working conditions of the new generation of more skilled industrial workers.

Sader's study subsequently identified the various cultural and institutional relations among the grassroots movements, in the neighborhoods, the unions and the workplace. He analyzed the different short and long term contributions of these cultural and institutional changes, to the 'opening' of the public sphere that took place under the official '*Abertura*'promoted by the military regime. Sader highlighted the specific contents of these changes in the processes of sociopolitical participation among the workers:

> The practices of the Church's 'mothers' club's' affirmed the values of sisterhood and of primary neighborly relations. In the local health committees an awareness of access to public resources was achieved. In union opposition ('*Oposição Sindical*') there was an appreciation of the grassroots struggles and forms of organization within the factory. In the labor movement there was a struggle to recover the union as the workers' public space, and the strikes and mass assemblies for political participation.
> *(Sader, 1988: 313)*

Sader analyzed the various 'discourse matrices' (of the new church, union and leftist sectors) that interacted in the formation of a participatory culture among the new generation of industrial workers. Such matrices originated from the crisis and restructuring of these groups and institutions - thus providing the central cultural features for the new institutions rising in the late 1970s. These new 'discourse matrices' expressed a cultural drive for self-reliance among the people, and their motivation to restructure their forms of representation. For instance, the 'new unionism' of '*ABC*' was soon able to found, in 1979, the national 'United Workers' Central Organization' *(Central Única dos Trabalhadores, CUT)*; new political parties were also founded, such as the 'Workers' Party' *(Partido dos Trabalhadores, PT)*, with the reform of the party system in 1979; and a national coordination of neighborhood movements was created in 1980 (*ANAMPOS*), by sectors linked to the 'grassroots church', *CUT* and neighborhood militants.

These new institutions began to negotiate with other social actors (allies and opponents), socialists, democrats, liberals and conservatives - in a growing expansion of the public sphere that would culminate in the 1984 street demonstrations for direct presidential elections (the *'Diretas Já'* Campaign), led by the opposition parties. Millions of people participated in these orderly street rallies in every major city of the country, waving colorful banners. At this moment it was possible to see in the streets the open and active presence of popular movements, with various political trends and constituents. Among them were the neighborhood movements linked to *ANAMPOS* and to *CONAN* (a more conservative neighborhood national coordination founded in 1982); the unions represented by *CUT* and *CGT* (this one representative of the more traditional unions); feminist, ecological, student and youth groups of various trends; as well as ethnic and other minorities.

Other studies also have focused on local convergences and differences within society, in the daily life of the ecological, feminist and church groups and other movements (e.g. Nogueira Porto, 1983; Mainwaring and Viola, 1984; Scherer-Warren, 1989). It seems that since the early 1980s a cross-fertilization began between popular movements and political parties, on the one hand, and other (mainly middle-class) democratic and minority sectors, on the other hand. This process had a considerable influence on public opinion and the urban electorate. The effects of this fertilization were clearly shown in the inclusion of participatory and minority demands (ecological, feminist, ethnic and cultural) in most parties' programs and many candidacies, since the time of the 1982 gubernatorial and parliamentary elections.

How should one interpret this convergence among wide urban and popular sectors, which finally manifested itself in the mass demonstrations of the *'Diretas'* campaign? In retrospect it is all too easy to focus on the failures of this campaign which was manipulated by the main opposition party - *Partido do Movimento Democrático Brasileiro, PMDB* - into a compromise with the military regime (an issue that will be considered below). Nevertheless, these campaigns effectively speeded-up the rather slow transition from authoritarian rule. In order to thoroughly assess their influence, it would be necessary to study the processes of popular mobilization in various parts of the country, similar to the research of Evers, Telles and Sader in São Paulo.

Such an evaluation would show, at the regional and national levels, how the ecological, feminist and other minority and middle class sectors interacted with the workers' movement, in response to the crisis and restructuring of Brazilian institutions, and how this interaction provided increasing support to a democratic transition[3]. But such studies could also simply indicate additional data about local changes, instead of explaining the generalization of democratic values and allegiances, expressed in the national convergence among these social actors (and also the influence of their messages and demands on the parties, the media and the electorate at large).

A comprehensive interpretation is thus required, in order to recognize the various contributions and differences that characterize social actors and movements: their cultural and material demands and orientations; their search for alternative life-forms; their capacity to engage in the electoral process; their often apparently spontaneous emergence; and their ability to negotiate in the public sphere. The theory of social movements proposed by Heller and Feher (1985) - on the basis of the 'system of needs' (a Hegelian concept greatly modified by Heller) - meets most of these conceptual requirements.

This approach relates 'radical' needs (e.g. for self-government)[4] to 'existential' (survival) needs. It also relates the autonomy of social actors to their capacity to generalize their claims among other social sectors. Thus, the movements are defined as (1) mobilized around issues raised by a lack of satisfaction of the 'system of needs'; (2) spontaneously contributing to the crisis or delegitimation of the political order; and (3) crossing over the frontiers of social classes and other particularist limits created by the social division of labor (Heller and Feher, 1985: 214).

This approach is very useful to historical analysis, for it avoids a lapse into teleology (which seeks to identify an end purpose for social action - for instance the utilitarianism of Olson's 'logic of collective action'). Instead, it captures the meanings produced by social actors themselves, the self-interpretation of their actions[5]. The studies mentioned earlier of São Paulo's popular movements showed the clear connection raised by those actors, among 'existential' (survival) needs, and their 'radical' needs for self-organization that challenged political legitimacy. This connection was indeed 'subversive' to authoritarian rule, as the military regime readily recognized.

The later convergence of the movements with middle-class sectors - ecological, feminist, youth and minority groups - expressed the growing diffusion or generalization of support for the radical needs within society. This is a capacity that Heller/Feher refer to as the 'rational utopia' of the new movements - in contrast with the 'irrational' or chiliastic utopias of self-centered movements that remain isolated, and look for a transcendental or non-historical destiny and outcome.

One may thus assume that a participatory 'rational utopia'[6] mobilized and exerted a mass democratic pressure, occupying the public space and re-signifying politics, during the street demonstrations of the 1984 *Diretas'* campaign. Even when this pressure was subsequently coopted by the official opposition and conservative parties, in their transitional pact among the elites in Congress. It would be hard to explain the civilian transitional government (1985/1989) without the generalized democratic pressures that justified this institutional change.

We also saw with Sader the complementarity of the heterogeneous trends that converged within the workers' movements, the unions, the workplace and the neighborhoods. Telles pointed out how this convergence responded effectively to the previous shrinking of the public sphere, under the military regime. These experiences of self-organization soon began to compete with alternative forms of organization, in the restructuring and expansion of the public sphere, beginning with the 1979 reform of the party system. For instance, *CUT* soon started to compete with the *CGT* for recognition as the dominant union coalition; *ANAMPOS* had to confront competition from *CONAN* among the neighborhoods groups. The pluralization of public space allowed the diversity of the social forces to emerge politically. As an example, the two state deputies elected by the *MCV* in 1978 went to different opposition parties with the reform of the party system in 1979 - and other examples of such pluralization were easily found.

This process of political and cultural pluralization reached one of its peaks in the unprecedented *'Diretas'* campaign in 1984. At this point the official opposition and the conservative forces took control of the transition that was negotiated with the military regime, and guaranteed that the new government would be commanded by the institutional elite. The first civilian administration was elected by Congress, with the agreement (and participation) of conservative politicians and the bureaucracy of the military regime. However, this is not to say that the conservative transition lacked popular and electoral support.

In fact, studies on specific social groups and movements indicate that their constituencies were not homogeneous and unified. These internal differences evolved toward a greater diversity and polarization during the process of institutional democratization, channeling opposing political orientations (and co-optation strategies) in regard to both 'existential' and 'radical' needs. These differences included conservative trends that became manifest both in the party system and in social organizations (e.g. Nogueira Porto, 1983; Viola, 1987; Gohn, 1988). Such diversity is not by itself a sign of weakness of the social movements because it may express the plurality of life-forms - that are created and channeled institutionally - through the relative influence of social actors on the various institutions and policies engendered to satisfy their needs (as will be demonstrated below).

However, these channels and processes of institutionalization were, in most cases, continuously and selectively controlled by the elites' transitional pact to maintain control of the federal administration. This control was exerted through a dual strategy - which on one hand, repressed the more radical and isolated social actors, and on the other hand, attempted to coopt or institutionally integrate the most organized and influential social movements. Moreover, the civilian government began numerous attempts at compensatory social policies (e.g. food distribution to the poor, low income housing projects, and even a project of agrarian reform). Most of these projects were never really implemented, but they were widely publicized, as means for political co-optation that used the media as the main instrument for persuasion and control. Finally, one of the government's most successful (but temporary) policies was its monetary adjustment policy, that created a new currency (the *'Cruzado'*). This maneuver simulated a policy of income redistribution, and succeeded in attracting electoral support for the 1986 gubernatorial and parliamentary elections.

It is possible to suggest, therefore, that the new social actors who rose in Brazil during the 1980s passed through different moments or stages in their relations with politics. First, they expressed the mobilization of urban workers and the middle-classes, in a challenge to the legitimacy of the military regime, and subsequently in popular pressure on the pacted civilian transition. This popular pressure resulted from the generalization of a rational democratic utopia that questioned the dominant conservative political culture and the country's political institutions. This utopian democratic ideal raised and organized a convergence of the 'existential' and 'radical' needs experienced by the various social actors at the grassroots.

However, this democratic utopia was in great part defeated throughout the mid and late 1980s: in the indirect Presidential election under the conservative pact of the '*Nova República*'; in the democratic rights approved by the 1988 Constitution, but to a large extent not regulated since then; and by electoral, party and media appropriation (or co-optation) of democratic demands from the ecological, feminist, union and other movements. For instance, since 1982 'token' representatives of black, native, union and gender minorities were elected to Congress, even by the conservative parties. But this 'window-dressing' representation had little effect on the social groups it was supposed to represent (with the important exception of the formal basic rights established by the 1988 Constitution, which will be considered below).

Such appropriation of central components (and protagonists) of the democratic utopia, under conservative rule, attempted (and succeeded to an extent) to neutralize the 'radical/existential' needs of the democratic forces, without providing the necessary institutional stability or consolidation for the democratic regime. It is important to recall, however, that political democratization does not mean only co-optation, but various forms of institutional and cultural channeling into the political order. This is why it is not enough to look only at the new social actors from the standpoint of the needs they express. We have seen that the contents of their needs explain to a large extent the origin and generalization of democratic demands. We also noted that these demands could be neutralized but not satisfied by the transitional government. Moreover: the grassroots could be divided, to benefit electoral support for conservative rule.

Therefore, in order to evaluate the contributions of social actors and movements to democratization, it is necessary to interpret both their limits and their innovations as **political** actors, vis-à-vis the dominant political culture and the processes of institutionalization. This is what we intend to do now, using concepts of Habermas's theory of 'communicative action'.

DEMOCRATIZATION AND JURIDIFICATION

Brazil's 1988 Constitution has been rightly appraised as a fragmented 'bricolage' of compromises between opposition and conservative interests, without a unifying democratic project. Certainly, civil and political rights have expanded since then, but the Constitutional text incoherently overlaps social and economic declarations of intent, and particularist interests that are often difficult, if not impossible, to reconcile. This fact was compounded by a stalemate in the Constitutional Congress, between presidentialist and parliamentarist currents – a stalemate that was only settled in support of Presidentialism by a referendum held in 1993. The 1988 Constitution maintained, however, heterogeneous legacies, which could have been corrected through parliamentarism. (See Limongi and Figueiredo, 1995; Power, 1998)

Progressive sectors of Brazilian society - such as the labor unions and some neighborhood organizations - attempted to counteract the conservative majority of the Constitutional Congress, presenting 'popular bills' to protect and expand citizenship rights in the 1988 Constitution. As a result, there were some advances in legislation - such as freedom for union organization, urban planning with social participation in major and mid-size cities. However, many such rights needed further legal regulation and approval at the state and municipal levels. Other basic points remained untouched - such as agrarian, fiscal and administrative reforms – because they were strongly opposed by various sectors of the political oligarchy in Congress.

In any case, the final revision of the constitutional reform was first scheduled for 1993, and then postponed indefinitely. It should ideally correct these shortcomings in the Constitution, and achieve a consolidation of the democratic regime. The expectation was that this reform at least could show the increased capabilities of the various political actors to establish policies of alliances, and provide a democratic focus for the necessary regulations and implementations of constitutional rights. To address the need for improvement in democratic governance and to provide a permanent solution to the fiscal crisis, four main sets of constitutional reform have been proposed by the current Cardoso government: social security reform, fiscal-tax reform, and political and institutional reforms. However, after strenuous and unsuccessful debates and negotiations in Congress, the reforms have not taken place and there are increasing doubts that they will be achieved in the near future. (Smith and Messari, 1998)

These facts suggest that a close evaluation has to be made of the capacity of political actors, since the start of the Brazilian transition from authoritarian rule in the mid-1980s. The setbacks and regressions, which became apparent in the Brazilian transition from the time of the failure of the *'Diretas'* campaign in 1984, indicate that the capabilities required of political actors during democratic institutionalization differ from the characteristics of social actors, that are related to their demands to satisfy their specific needs. Thus, social actors present their claims and demands to the political institutions; political actors, in turn, are expected to channel, represent, negotiate and respond to those social demands through the political institutions. This obvious difference requires, however, an explanation that avoids the classic dichotomy between society and politics that liberalism has always emphasized. Habermas's conceptualization is applicable to this aim, and therefore very useful to the study of processes of institutional democratization.

His view is that both social and political actors are (or should be) oriented toward mutual understanding, and thus aimed at a common ('intersubjective') comprehension of daily life[7] - which is usually distorted by the effects of political and economic domination. In order for actors to reach an understanding and overcome the distortions that are imposed on them, they must go through a gradual process of 'decentration'[8]. This process leads them beyond demands for self-centered particularist benefits, in the search for a common definition (by allies and opponents alike) of the possiblities for agreement that exist in every situation[9]. This is what Habermas calls 'communicative action' - in contrast to 'teleological' (strategic and instrumental) forms of action, that he sees prevail in 'systemic logic' and in particularist behavior[10]. Thus, 'communicative action' exists in the modern world only as a subordinate and alternative approach - since the 'lifeworld' is constantly 'colonized' by economic and political systems (the marketplace and government institutions)[11].

This approach may sound idealistic, but it is not conceived as such by Habermas. The cognitive and normative decentration of socio-political actors is considered by him as part of the ambiguous conquests of modernity - in a constant resistance to 'system colonization'. Thus, the plurality of ways that decentration opens for the search for truth (and for normative justice and veracity) among actors, leads them to a continuous revision of the traditions and values inherited from the past - thereby promoting a participatory reform of the institutions. In this way, the logic of communicative action only actualizes itself in confrontation with the logic of the systems - i.e., by subjecting instrumental and strategic ('teleological') actions inherent in the institutional order, to communicative aims geared to understanding.

Therefore, Habermas's 'communicative action' is by no means a denial of the importance of institutions, and rather proposes the contrary: it tries to reorient the main institutions to accomplish the 'unfinished tasks' of modernity. For instance, one of these unfinished tasks is present in the juridification of social relationships in Western societies. Though this juridification has obvious negative functions in the 'system colonization' of the 'lifeworld', it is also the point where that colonization can be faced and eventually reversed. (See also Habemas, 1997). This is considered a privileged point for communicative action, because Habermas thinks that law and morality are two of the main spheres for resistance to, and confrontation with, 'systemic logic' - ever since the establishment of the democratic state and the rule of law[12].

Therefore, the institutionalization of a public sphere, with the democratization of politics and the rule of law, provides a necessary precondition for the effective recognition and exercise of civil and political rights. Moreover, the consolidation of political democracy may be seen as a historically ambiguous process of juridification of social relationships - as a confrontation between the instrumental and strategic logic that is inherent in the institutional order, on the one hand, and the communicative logic defended by the universal orientations of certain social and political actors (such as new social movements and democratic parties) on the other hand. The normative and legislative establisment of democratic rights in the Constitution assures therefore the historical baseline and warranty for the exercise and implementation of such rights[13].

Moreover, in spite of the fact that juridification imposes rights and obligations that are not always obeyed, and implies an overload of the institutions through bureaucratic inertia, the so-called 'iron law' of political oligarchies, the manipulations of public opinion by 'media-regulated systems' in government and the marketplace, are seen as historical phenomena that result from the ambiguous confrontation between systemic and communicative actions, that may thus be corrected and overcome. Thus, the emphasis on juridification surpasses the classic dichotomy between the social and the institutional spheres by stating the historically relative character of the systemic blockades to the communicative actions of the social actors that emerge in the public sphere. However, these conceptual remarks are only a simplification that cannot encompass Habermas's sophisticated theory in its complexity. Nevertheless, they can be useful to the understanding of processes of political change and institutionalization in countries such as Brazil, in which democratization is not yet complete.

For instance, these concepts help us to understand the importance of what Sader called the 'discourse matrix' of new unionism in Brazil, that has converged with other cultural trends since the late 1970s — and also its crucial role for the generalization of democratic ideals in the institutional life of the country[14]. Sader compared the unions to the 'mothers' clubs' (linked to the grassroots church): the unions' leadership acted in institutions recognized in the political and legal system (controlled by the government until the late 1970s). Their importance derived from the fact that the unions were supposed to defend universal rights — that were recognized by law but denied in practice: the freedoms of collective bargainning, association, public representation, etc. Moreover, the normative decentration required from union organizers was much wider and pluralist than the orientations and values learned from religious and customary traditions (as was the case in neighborhood groups of the grassroots church).

These differences in juridification and morality do not indicate, however, that the restructuring of the unions and neighborhood groups of the working class were unrelated. The contrary is true: each of them contributed in their own way to the juridification of social relations during the transition from authoritarian rule. The mothers' clubs helped the workers' families to overcome their passivity and subjection under the military regime, as these families supported the 'wild-cat' strikes that started to change union conformity to government control. The strikes organized by the unions increased the awareness of the expansion of the public sphere, through the exercise of civil rights that were publicly recognized but until then hindered by government control.

It is thus not surprising that the military regime considered the industrial strikes of the late 1970s to be 'subversive' — not only because they freely acted for the strategic ('systemic') defense of salary and labor rights at the workplace, but also because they sought general democratic rights. The juridification of social relations already publicly recognized in the labor rights defended by the unions, provided the institutional groundwork for the implementation of those rights, and for their influence on the public sphere. Saders' study has shown that the existential and radical demands of the various popular movements converged, in this process of demise of authoritarian rule, to achieve basic rights of life and liberty — that were already implied in industrial relations and in labor legislation.

These facts help us to understand the generalization of public support for these demands from the most diverse groups, organized religions and ideologies, as well as the successes achieved by the strikers. The 'discourse matrix' of the new unions was thus a central example of communicative action — that subordinated a 'systemic' strategy to the end of achieving mutual understanding among those concerned with democracy in Brazil. For it stimulated the access of popular movements to the public sphere, with the communicative resignification of political action, the pluralization of political culture, the reform of the party system, etc. The example shows also that communicative action promotes a convergence among different sectors that hope for democracy.

Moreover, communicative action is not seen as a 'peaceful' form of action or compromise. The example surely illustrates the fact that the strikers and their supporters aimed to achieve the basic guarantees that democracy can provide. But the latter include the use of strategic and instrumental-legal resources for public negotiation, as a means of enforcing and expanding those rights in the public sphere. Consequently, communicative action not only summons support from those oriented toward democracy, but also strategically challenges and confronts actors who oppose the exercise of democratic rights.

One may also understand many other changes that took place in the 1980s from the point of view of juridification including: the reform of the party system, the conservative control after the '**Diretas**' campaign, and the subsequent civilian transitional government, with the new Constitution in 1988. During the 1980s there was a constitutionalization of the country, with the initial establishment of a formal democratic regime and the rule of law - that at least in principle began a juridification of social relations within Brazilian society. During these years the ambiguities of juridification were negotiated institutionally in the 'media-regulated systems'- the government and the marketplace. This transition to democracy included an attempt to exercise the rights formally recognized by the 1988 Constitution, gain increasing recognition for them - on moral grounds - from the population, and the latter's attempts to implement those rights in their daily life.

It is impossible to report in this space the numerous examples of how this juridification of social relations developed during the 1980s, and its effects after the 1988 Constitution. The effects of the Constitution on social relations were especially ambiguous, and an example is in order here, to illustrate this fact. During the first semester of 1989 the first civilian government launched a publicity campaign to demoralize publicly the industrial strikes that were spreading in various cities. The strikes were called 'anti-democratic', 'a threat of chaos', 'manipulated by agitators', etc.. The reason behind the apparent instability of the regime was that the government no longer could rely on police repression and labor corporatism to control the unions. In fact, the 1988 Constitution had instituted formal and universal right to organize, including the general freedom to strike - though this, like many basic rights, was left unregulated.

Nevertheless, a later evaluation of those 1989 strikes shows that they were highly positive for the union movement. The unions managed to start direct negotiations with companies and business associations, by-passing the previous government mediation. The unions appealed to judicial arbitration of those conflicts, and in many instances obtained legal support for their strikes. Moreover, the unions received wide support from their constituencies, due to their able and efficient leadership, and the orderly and prudent negotiations that they led. In spite of the fact that the economic results were meager (in a year of acute economic recession), the political consequences of these strikes for the union movement were noteworthy. In short, the unions assumed the strategic limitations existing in the open right to strike declared by the Constitution, and managed this ambiguity to improve their capacity for self-organization and negotiation in the public sphere.

The results of many studies of social movements in Brazil during the 1980s and early 1990s can also be interpreted using the categories of communicative action. For instance, Tavares (1989) presented an overview of rural movements (of peasants and salaried workers) showing that their various forms of struggle and organization had a common reference to the previous legislation on land tenure (the '*Estatuto da Terra*' issued by the military regime, that was considered more advanced than present Constitutional regulations). The other basic reference of rural workers was their national union confederation (*CONTAG - Confederação de Trabalhadores da Agricultura*) that was also established under the previous regime. The diversity of local movements did not hinder their convergence, in demands and processes of negotiation and juridification — i.e. their access to labor rights and land reform projects, that have been constantly demanded in various parts of the country. Of course, violence and patronage based or clientelistic relations are still widespread in the Brazilian countryside. But the convergence of agrarian workers around their access to democratic rights portrayed a process of juridification of social relations that was already in the making.

More specific and detailed studies have revealed differences in the capacity for decentration among agrarian workers, and thus their limited ability to influence political democratization - as was emphasized (see above), by Sader's study of São Paulo urban movements. For instance, a local study on the peasant 'Landless' movement in Santa Catarina (Lisboa, 1988) has shown its response to land reform policies promised by the government and its relations with other movements and institutions sponsored by the Catholic church (especially the '*Pastoral da Terra*', which supports 'landless' movements in various parts of the country). Perhaps due to church's influence, this movement seemed to be rather isolated from other democratic forces struggling for land reform and citizenship rights in the countryside (especially *CONTAG*). A later study of local experiences of land reform undertaken by the São Paulo government (D'Incao, 1993) presented similar results - though in this case the isolation of these experiences seemed to derive not only from church influence but also from radical sectors of the Workers' Party (*PT*). Nevertheless, these limited experiences can be understood as crucial attempts at self-organization under extreme conditions of economic hardship and political strife. They also influenced, albeit indirectly, the central juridification of social relations, promoted by *CONTAG* in the countryside.

The studies of rural movements in opposition to hydroelectric dams along the Uruguay River (Scherer-Warren, 1988; Scherer-Warren & Reis, 1988) also show convergences in processes of learning and normative differentiation among the grassroots, that effected interaction with the government, and resulted in juridification of social relations. The latter effects appeared in the recognition of citizenship and property rights among these sectors - reversing the violation of these basic rights under the previous regime. Significantly, these movements were also influenced by Catholic entities. Since their demands did not involve the contested issue of land reform, this fact may account for the easier access of these actors to the juridification of social relations. Certainly, the present 'Rural Landless Movement' (*Movimento dos Trabalhadores Rurais Sem Terras- MST*) that emerged nationally in the 1990s is the best example of institutional change through communicative action, but a general analysis of its evolution is still unavailable. Nevertheless, it is obvious that the *MST* was able to build on the above local developments. (See Pereira, 1998; Franco, 1998).

Finally, the studies on urban social movements during the 1980s (e.g. Jacobi, 1988; Nunes, 1988; Gohn, 1988) have evaluated processes of interaction with government; the selective biases of social policies; internal social and normative differentiations; the virtual convergence with other social actors and movements; and processes of institutionalization and juridification of social relations in which they participated — by supporting and/or opposing local governments and policies. Gohn's study is particularly enlightening, since it focused on numerous movements that emerged in São Paulo, around demands for low-income housing. These movements included groups in *'favelas'* (shanty towns), illegal settlements, government housing projects, and other situations. They were analyzed according to their different socioeconomic conditions, claims and demands; forms of organization and mobilization; diversity of orientation and ideology; rights previously acquired; alliances within the party system; and by their proposals for government intervention and urban reform, etc. This array of sociopolitical diversification became possible and achieved partial results, in the context of the new regime.

But the ambiguous juridification of social relations illustrated by these examples is not presented here as an apology for the new regime. To the contrary, these developments portray the severe limitations to democratic institutionalization under the civilian governments after the military regime. As the industrial strikes of the late 1980s clearly indicated, this conservative transition to civilian rule was much less capable than Brazilian social actors and movements of implementing the democratic consequences and regulations of the new constitution.

In spite of the limited capabilities of Brazilian popular movements - e.g., their obvious difficulty in achieving normative decentration, orderly negotiation of their demands, and open democratic allegiance to political parties and policies - they were often able to converge in processes of juridification of social relations and allocation of citizenship rights. This fact shows that many of these actors and movements acted as politically relevant social and political actors, capable of influencing the party system and negotiating with the government and the dominant sectors of Brazilian society. They assumed a democratic role in communicative action, opening up new spaces in the public sphere, and reversing the 'colonization' imposed on their daily life by the 'media-regulated systems' in government and the marketplace.

A specific example of the differences in democratic capacity between the elites and the popular actors already has been mentioned: the popular bills sent by many organized sectors of the electorate to the 1988 Constitution. Hundreds of thousands of signatures were collected by *ANAMPOS, CONAN, CUT, CGT, CONTAG*, and many professional and church organizations throughout the country[15]. These bills proposed urban and agrarian reform, urban planning, fiscal decentralization and many other related issues. They presented more than sectorial or particularistic demands: in many instances they created grounds for concerted negotiation, and specific proposals for practical implementation. Some of these items were (usually in softened and modified forms) included in the constitutional text. But most constitutional rights depended on additional legal regulation and/or constitutional changes to be implemented at the state and municipal levels. All of this received the anti-democratic opposition of local and provincial political oligarchies, who also have to a large extent (and until today) control of the national Congress. (Smith and Messari, 1998).

Several studies of social actors and movements in Brazil during the 1990s also have stressed their contributions to the expansion of a 'public sphere' beyond the frontiers of government (see Alvarez et al., 1998), through the 'identity politics' and the 'redistributive politics' (to use Fraser's [1997] categories) which they raise against the central state institutions. (See Avritzer, 1996; Costa, 1997; Silva 1999). This is often done in orderly fashion, but through strategies that include strikes, conflicts and mobilizations around the exercise of basic democratic and citizenship rights (Paoli and Telles, 1998). Much has been achieved in recent years, in terms of public awareness and the democratization of social and institutional life within civil society. But the reforms of political institutions, the party system, government elites and bureaucracy are lagging behind these developments.

The political impasse is clear. On the one hand, we saw the convergence among Brazilian social actors and movements, that promoted a plurality of alternative strategies of democratic institution-building in the public sphere. They thus contributed to the expansion and institutionalization of political democracy, through coalition policies among political parties, practical suggestions and ideas for party programs, government policies and the strengthening of the public sphere. On the other hand, we have the traditional political oligarchies that were, for the most part, bred or formed under the authoritarian military regime. These oligarchies are accostumed to a political environment composed of regional 'clicks', groups and families, who occupy the political institutions in order to defend their private interests and particularistic privileges.

Certainly, many individuals of these oligarchies eventually broke with the authoritarian regime, and helped to constitute the conservative transition government of the 1980s, as well as the Collor and Cardoso governments of the 1990s. Nevertheless, even when many traditional politicians formally adopted democratic aims and methods of government, they had to come to terms with the traditional clientelism and patronage inherited from the past, among their own constituencies. They were thus reluctant to engage in reforms that may have threatened these particularistic interests. A recent assessment of the conservative forces in Brazil considered that

> A more pragmatic breed of conservatism is emerging alongside the more traditional clientelistic variant...The conservative parties are more accepting of democracy than in the past. If these changes are consolidated, they would bolster the future of conservative parties in Brazil...The three presidential elections held under democracy have been won by candidates who promoted the conservatives' economic agenda, and the centrist parties have migrated rapidly toward conservative economic positions over the last decade. Thus, even if conservatives do not revitalize their electoral standing, they have temporarily won the battle to define much of Brazil's future.
> *(Mainwaring, Meneguello and Power, 1999).*

The strengthening of the process of juridification in wide areas of encounter, between social demands and public policies, will thus continue to depend mainly on the capacity of new social actors to become political actors (and on their increasing support by the electorate). This will happen as they engage in communicative action, through a process of decentration that will support the consolidation of democratic institutions, the rule of law, and the representativity of the party system[16]. Therefore, this is an ambiguous process, open to the decision-making of social actors and movements - and the population at large - in their choices to improve their capabilities as mature political actors. From this standpoint political regressions and deadlocks may also emerge, through the re-appearance of populist charismatic leaders, linked to the political oligarchies, who want to continue ruling through patronage and clientelism - supported by the culture of authoritarian legitimacy that still prevails among a large sector of the population. This is what happenned with the successful candidacy of Pres. Fernando Collor de Mello in 1989 - though this regression was partly reversed through Collor's impeachment in 1992.

In short, while we still do not have a systematic analysis of the contributions of the new social actors to the consolidation of democracy in Brazil, it is certain that the empirical data and the necessary conceptualization are available for this analysis - in the framework of communicative action. This analysis of the 'unfinished tasks of modernity' would provide a general survey of social and political forces, similar to that made by Offe (1985) of German society - which included the alternatives of alliances and oppositions among 'new' and 'old' social and political actors, as well as the possible scenarios and outcomes for further institutional development[17].

Therefore, we are not suggesting here a linear or evolutionary logic of 'modernization', that relates social action to its direct contributions to democratic consolidation. Rather, one of the important points of concepts such as decentration and juridification (as well as of the whole theory of communicative action) is that they are able to interpret the 'evolutionary *dynamics*'[18] in the processes of democratization — dynamics that are characterized by ambiguity. This ambiguity is constitutive of historical processes, open to conflicting trends that attempt to agree on an ever-expanding institutional framework of democratic legitimacy. The dilemmas of Brazilian politics do not derive only from the confrontation of particularistic strategic interests, or from the stubborn resistance of conservative elites and politicians. They relate also, and specifically, to the high democratic standards of participative democracy.

For when we understand social movements as Habermas (1979) does, as 'processes of learning through which the already latent structures of rationality may be translated into social practice, in a way to find finally an institutional embodiment, the next task then arises, of identifying the potential for rationalization of the traditions'. This is a task that cannot be blocked by any prejudice against society's potential for democracy, that is to be verified by social actors themselves.[19]

PROVISIONAL CONCLUSIONS

The research data reviewed above is rather limited, and does not permit a general evaluation of the contributions of social actors to the process of political transition and insitutionalization of democracy in Brazil. However, they indicate the existence of two inter-related phenomena. First, there was a questioning of authoritarian conservative cultural traditions by social actors and movements, due to orientations and demands originating from the 'system of needs'. These radical orientations and existential demands were generalized through a rational democratic utopia, which continued to expand - in spite of the many defeats, impediments and limitations it confronted at the institutional level. Second, during the 1980s and 1990s there was a pluralization of the public sphere and the institution of a formal democratic regime and the rule of law. These changes in the political institutions were able to channel, partly and conflictively, the changes that were occurring in society. These limits relate to the insufficient decentration of the main political actors, to the incipient juridification of social relations, the absence of a clearly representative party system, and other shortcomings of the new institutional order.

The latter institutional deficiencies can (and should) be solved through legal and institutional reforms, in order to improve, for instance, the legislation concerning parties, elections and government: in short, through the reform that the final Constitutional revision should achieve. However, the concepts of Heller/Feher and Habermas have helped us to see that the major problems of Brazilian democratic institutionalization lie elsewhere. Such concepts enable us to interpret the characteristics of Brazilian democratization as historical features of a delayed and unfinished transition to modernity, within the relations between society and the polity.

These characteristics show striking contrasts (but also some similitudes) with processes of 'democratic radicalization' studied by the above mentioned authors in the Northern hemisphere. The similitudes have to do with the rise of new social actors oriented by rational democratic utopias - whose capacity for generalization will be decisive in changing the conditions for liberal democracy, in Latin America and elsewhere in the Western world.

The differences have mainly to do with the conservative legacy that blocks political reform, and eventually undermines the attempts at democratic institutionalization in Latin America. We saw this legacy in the impediments to the institutionalization and expansion of the public sphere, during the Brazilian transition from authoritarian rule. This means that both the processes of decentration of political actors, and of juridification of social relations, only started to achieve a relative efficacy and possibility of institutionalization in the Brazilian case. (Other countries, like Chile and Uruguay, faced more favorable conditions, as they went through processes of democratic restructuring, or re-consolidation).

These provisional conclusions indicate that Brazil, as a Latin American country, faces two simultaneous and immeasurable tasks: on the one hand it must build up a representative democratic regime, and on the other it has to expand (radicalize) the regime through participatory democracy. History may show in due time whether either of these is possible. Nevertheless, these tasks remain urgent and indeed unavoidable - considering the present trends to globalization of internal relations, and the likely responses to this challenge by both 'new' and 'old' social and political actors. Since these tasks are overwhelming, we have then greater motivation than Heller and Habermas did to continue and further develop the critiques of the classic approaches (the liberal and Marxist orthodoxies) to social action and democracy. These classic approaches have been unable to recognize among us the plurality of life-forms, and the ambiguity of the methods, strategies and possible alternatives of generalization and consolidation, of a democratic utopia - that exists and expands within Brazilian society.

REFERENCES

Almond, G. 1957, "Comparative political systems", *Journal of Politics*, 18:391-409.

Alvarez, S.; Dagnino, E.; and Escobar, A. (Eds.), 1998, **The Culture of Politics and the Politics of Culture. Re-visioning Social Movements in Latin America**, Boulder: Westview Press.

Arditi, B. 1988, "Uma gramática pós-moderna para pensar o social", *Lua Nova*, 4 (3):105-123.

Avritzer, L. 1996, **A Moralidade da Democracia,** São Paulo: Perspectiva.

Cardoso, R. C.L. 1988, "Os Movimentos Populares no Contexto da Consolidação da Democracia", in Reis, Fabio Wanderley y O'Donnell, Guillermo (Eds.), **A Democracia no Brasil: Dilemas e Perspectivas**, São Paulo: Vértice.

Costa, S. 1997, "Contextos de Construção do Espaço Público no Brasil", **Estudos CEBRAP**, 47.

Evers, T. 1982, "Os Movimentos Sociais Urbanos: o Caso do Movimento do Custo de Vida", In: Moisés, J.A. et al., **Alternativas Populares da Democracia**, Rio de Janeiro: CEDEC/Vozes.

_____, 1984, "Identidade: A Face Oculta dos Novos Movimentos Sociais", *Novos Estudos*, Cebrap, 2(4):11 ff.

Franco, L.F. 1997, "El Movimiento de los Trabajadores Rurales sin Tierra y la Reforma Agraria en Brasil", *América Latina Hoy*, 17: 63-76.

Fraser, N. 1997, **Justice Interruptus: Critical Reflections on the "Postsocialist"Condition**, London: Routledge.

Gohn, M. G. M. 1988, "Lutas pela Moradia Popular em São Paulo", *Ciência e Cultura*, 40 (7):637-645.

Habermas, J. 1976, "Was Heisst Universalpragmatik?, in Apel, Karl O. (Ed.), **Sprachpragmatik und Philosophie**, Frankfurt a.m.: Suhrkamp Verlag.

_____. 1979, **Communication and the Evolution of Society**, Boston: Reacon Press.

_____. 1984/7, **Theory of Communicative Action**, 2 vols. Boston: Reacon Press.

_____. 1997, **Between Facts and Norms: Contributions to a Discouse Theory of Law and Democracy**, MA: MIT Press.

Heller, A. 1978, **Teoría de las Necesidades en Marx**, Barcelona: Península.

———. 1977, **Sociología de la Vida Cotidiana**, Barcelona: Península.

———. 1983, **A Filosofía Radical**, São Paulo: Brasiliense.

——— and Feher, F. 1985, **Anatomía de la Izquierda Occidental**, Barcelona: Península.

Holston, J. and Caldeira, T. 1998, "Democracy, Law, and Violence: Disjunctions of Brasilian Citizenship", in Agüero, F. and Stark, J., (Eds.), **Fault Lines of Democracy in Post-Transition Latin America**, Coral Gables, Fla: North-South Center.

ISER/MMMA. 1998. **O Que o Brasileiro Pensa do Meio Ambiente, do Desenvolvimento e da Sustentabilidade.** Crespo, S. (Ed.).

Jacobi, P. R. 1988, **Movimentos Sociais e Políticas Públicas**, São Paulo: Cortez.

Krischke, P. J. 1989, "Necesidades y Sujetos Sociales" *Revista Mexicana de Sociología*, 51(3):75-98.

Kowarick, L. 1987, "Movimentos Urbanos no Brasil Contemporâneo", *Revista Brasileira de Ciências Sociais*, 3(1):38-50.

Laclau, E. 1986, "Os Novos Movimentos Sociais e a Pluralidade do Social", *Revista Brasileira de Ciências Sociais*, 1(2),:41-47.

Limongi, F. and Figueiredo, A.C. 1995, "Mudança Constitucional, Desempenho do Legislativo e Consolidação Institucional", *Revista Brasileira de Ciências Sociais*, 29: 175-200.

Lisboa, T. K. 1988, **A Luta dos Sem-terra no Oeste Catarinense**, Florianópolis: EDUFSC.

Mainwaring, S.; Meneguello, R.; and Power, T.J. 1999, "Conservative Parties, Democracy, and Economic Reform in Brazil", **Kellogg Institute Working Paper**, 264.

Méndez, J.; O'Donnell, G.; and Pinheiro, P.S. (Eds.), 1998, **The (Un)Rule of Law and the Underpriviledged in Latin America**, Notre Dame, IN: Notre Dame University Press.

Movimento Popular, 1, April, 1989, São Paulo: POLIS/CPV

Morse, R. 1988. **O Espelho de Próspero,** São Paulo: Cia. das Letras.

Nogueira Porto, D. 1982, "A Militante Feminista e a Militante Feminina da Periferia: Estudo Psicossocial das Diferenças entre as visões de Participação Política da Mulher", M.A. Thesis, PUC/SP (mimeo).

Nun, J. 1988, "La Legitimidad Democrática y los Parecidos de Familia: Notas Preliminares", *Zona Abierta*, 46-47, Jan.-Jun.:189-222.

Nunes, E. 1988, "Carências Urbanas e Política", M.A. Thesis, FFLCH, USP.

O'Donnell, G. 1988, "Hiatos, Continuidades e Alguns Paradoxos", in Reis, F. Wanderley e O'Donnell, G. (Eds.), Op.Cit.

Offe, C. 1985, "New Social Movements: Challenging the Boundaries of Intitutional Politics", *Social Research*, New York, 52(4):817-868.

Paoli, M.C. and Telles, V.S. 1998, "Social Rights: Conflicts and Negotiations in Contemporary Brazil", in Alvarez et al., O.Cit.

Pereira, A. W. 1998, "An Ugly Democracy? State Violence and the Rule of Law in Post-Authoritarian Brazil", in Kingstone, P.R., and Power, T.J. (Eds.) **Democratic Brazil: Actors, Institutions and Processes**, Pittsburgh: University of Pittsburgh Press.

Power, T.J. 1998, "The Pen is Mightier than the Congress: Presidential Decree Power in Brazil", in Carey, J. and Shugart, M. (Eds.), **Executive Decree Authority**, New York: Cambridge University Press.

Sader, E. 1988, **Quando Novos Personagens Entraram em Cena**, Paz e Terra, Rio de Janeiro.

Scherer-Warren, I. 1989, "Redescobrindo nossa Dignidade: Avaliação da Utopía da Libertação na América Latina". *Religião e Sociedade*, ISER, Rio de Janeiro.

_____ and Reis, M. J. 1988, "O Movimento dos Atingidos pelas Barragens do Uruguai: Unidade e Diversidade". *Boletim de Ciências Sociais*, UFSC, Florianópolis,48:57ff.

Silva, C.P. 1999, **Participação Popular e Cultura Política**, Florianópolis: EDUFSC.

Smith, W.C. and MESSARI, N. 1998, "Democracy and Reform in Cardoso's Brazil: Caught Between Clientelism and Global Markets?", **The North-South Center Paper**, 33.

Telles, V.S. 1986, "Anos 70: Experiências e Práticas Cotidianas" in Krischke, P. y Mainwaring, S. (Eds.). **A Igreja nas Bases em Tempo de Transição**, Porto Alegre: LP&M.

Tavares Dos Santos, J. V. 1989, "Lutas Agrárias e Cidadania", in Krischke, P.; Scherer-Warren, I.; Viola, E. (Eds.), **Crise Política, Movimentos Sociais e Cidadania**, Florianópolis: EDUFSC.

Thompson, E. 1977, **A Formação da Classe Operária Inglesa**, (3 vols.), Paz e Terra: Rio de Janeiro.

Touraine, A. 1986, "Sobre as Possibilidades de Democracia na América Latina", *Revista Brasileira de Ciências Sociais*, 1(1): 5-15.

Mainwaring, S. and Viola, E. 1984, "New Social Movements, Political Culture and Democracy: Brazil and Argentina", **Telos**. (O.Cit.)

Viola, E. 1987, "O Movimento Ecológico no Brasl (1974-1986): do Ambientalismo à Ecopolítica", *Revista Brasileira de Ciências Sociais*, 1(3):5-26.

_____, 1988, "A Degradação Ambiental e a Emergência dos Movimentos Ecológicos na América Latina", *Boletim de Ciências Sociais*, UFSC, Florianópolis,48:1-31.

Wiarda, H. (Ed.) 1973. **Politics and Social Change in Latin America**. Boulder: Westview.

ENDNOTES

[1] Mainwaring and Viola (1984) offered an update and application of the concept of political culture for Latin American democratization. We propose here that the change of values and behavior of social actors arises from their social needs, as these are gradually assumed and generalized in society, during the communicative transformation of the political institutions.

[2] This paradigm change leads to the use of 'unifying concepts' (Thompson, 1977) that are relevant within 'paradigms (that) have in the social sciences an **internal** connection with the social context where they arise and operate. They express the self-understanding of social actors about their world, thus serving and mediating the interpretation of social interests, and the horizons of social wishes and expectations' (Habermas, 1984-7, I). (See also Offe, 1985: 829).

[3] Mainwaring and Viola (1984) proposed a sharp contrast between 'old' and 'new' movements, on the basis of the mainly instrumental orientations of the former. However, the eventual convergence of most movements around rational democratic utopias seems to indicate that their differences relate more to the **content** of the needs they express - which may be more "radical" or "existential" according to the situation. Thus, the more fundamental differences would arise in movements where purely quantitative basic needs tend to predominate (see e.g. the data provided by Gohn, 1988).

[4] Heller presents elsewhere (e.g. 1983:144) a more extensive list of radical needs: 'The need that humans may be in a position to influence social development, during a rational debate about its contents, directions and values, is a radical need. The generalization of freely chosen communities is a radical need. The need for equality among humans in their personal relations is also radical, and the abolishment of social domination and control. There is a radical need to overcome in the entire society, the contrast between the coersion of socially necessary work, and the emptiness of leisure time. The elimination of war and armaments is also a radical need. Today an increasing number of people also ask for a complete elimination of hunger and misery, and that action be taken against ecological catastrophy. The need to diminish the gap between high culture and mass culture is also a radical need. None of the above listed needs can be satisfied in a society founded in relations of subordination and domination'. Such radical needs are compared to 'existential needs', among them 'the need to be fed, sexual needs, the need for personal contact and cooperation, the need to be active' (Heller, 1987:171). It is also emphasized that the distinction between radical and existential needs 'is relative': 'In certain cases the former may coincide and absorb the latter'. Radical needs are sharply opposed, in turn, to 'alienated needs, that are quantitative (...for) the accumulation induced by quantitative-alienated needs can only be stopped through the development of qualitative needs' (Heller, 1983: 172).

[5] In the foreword to the Spanish edition of **Sociology of Daily Life** (1977:5-8) Heller discards any link to a philosophy of history, and proposes a focus to her topic that is mainly phenomenological. This approach may be very useful for historical studies of daily life in different countries.

[6] It is certain that the cultural orientations of religious grassroots groups are not usually similar to the rational democratic utopias conceptualized by Heller/Feher (1985). Nevertheless, it is possible to maintain (as Sader did) that new religious values and motivations have converged, and mutually influenced, new political identities that arose among the working class, and expanded through the unions into the public sphere. (See Sader, 1988: 222-3).

[7] 'I can introduce here the concept of the *lebenswelt* or lifeworld to begin with as the correlate of processes of reaching understanding. Subjects acting communicatively always come to an understanding on the horizon of a lifeworld. Their lifeworld is formed by more or less diffuse, always unproblematic, background convictions. This lifeworld background serves as a source of situation definitions that are presupposed by participants as unproblematic. In their interpretive accomplishments the members of a communication community demarcate the one objective world and their intersubjectively shared social world from the subjective worlds of individuals and (other) collectives... The lifeworld also stores the interpretive work of preceding generations. It is the conservative counterweight to the risk of disagreement that arises with every actual process of reaching understanding; for communicative actors can achieve an understanding only by way of taking yes/no positions on criticizable validity claims. *The relation between these weights changes with the decentration of worldviews*. The more the worldview that furnishes the cultural stock of knowledge is decentered, the less the need for understanding is covered *in advance* by an interpreted lifeworld immune from critique, and the more this need has to be met by the interpretive accomplishments of the participants themselves, that is, by way of risky (because rationally motivated) agreement, the more frequently we can expect rational action orientations... The more cultural traditions predecide which validity claims, when, where, for what, from whom, and to whom must be accepted, the less the participants themselves have the possibility of making explicit and examining the potential grounds on which their yes/no positions are based'. (Habermas, 1984-7, I:70-1. Emphasis in the original).

[8] '...Cognitive development signifies in general *the decentration of an egocentric understanding of the world*. Only to the extent that the formal reference system of the three worlds is differentiated can we form a reflective concept of "world" and open up access to the world through the medium of common interpretative efforts, in the sense of a cooperative negotiation of situation definitions. The concept of a subjective world permits us to contrast not only our own internal world, but also the subjective worlds of others, with the external world. Ego can consider how certain facts (what he regards as existing states of affairs in the objective world) or certain normative expectations (what he regards as legitimate elements of the common social world) look from the perspective of another, that is, as elements of alter's subjective world. He can further consider that alter is for his part considering how what he regards as existing states of affairs and valid norms look from ego's perspective, that is, as a component of ego's subjective world. The subjective worlds of the participants could serve as mirror surfaces in which the objective, the normative, and the subjective-for-another are reflected any number of times'. (Habermas, 1984-7, I: 69. Emphasis in the original).

Decentration is thus conceived by Habermas as a learning process, through which communicative action operates with the ambiguity of the lifeworld, by making reflexive the cultural traditions: The differentiation of the lifeworld involves the foundation of normative learning in two senses, one documented by cognitive development psychology (Habermas, 1979: 77-80) and the other by the possibility of transposing its results into a theory of social evoution. (Habermas, 1979: 118).

[9] '... It belongs to the communicative intent of the speaker (a) that he perform a speech act that *is right* in respect to the given normative context, so that between him and the hearer an intersubjective relation will come about which is recognized as legitimate; (b) that he make a *true* statement (or *correct* existential presuppositions), so that the hearer will accept and share the knowledge of the speaker; and (c) that he express *truthfully* his beliefs, intentions, feelings, desires, and the like, so that the hearer will give credence to what is said. The fact that the intersubjective commonality of a communicatively achieved agreement exists at the levels of normative accord, shared propositional knowledge, and mutual trust in subjective sincerity can be explained in turn through the functions of achieving understanding in language'. (Habermas, 1984-7, I: 307-8. Emphasis in the original).

[10] Habermas thus states this paradigm shift when discussing Weber's typology of rational action:

'... We call an action oriented to success *instrumental* when we consider it under the aspect of following technical rules of action and assess the efficiency of an intervention into a complex of circumstances and events. We call an action oriented to success *strategic* when we consider it under the aspect of following rules of rational choice and assess the efficacy of influencing the decisions of a rational opponent... By contrast, I shall speak of *communicative* action whenever the actions of the agents involved are coordinated not through egocentric calculations of success but through acts of reaching understanding. In communicative action participants are not primarily oriented to their own individual successes; they pursue their individual goals under the condition that they can harmonize their plans of action on the basis of common situation definitions. In this respect the negotiation of definitions of the situation is an essential element of the interpretive accomplishments required for communicative action'.
(Habermas, 1984-7, I: 285-6).

[11] Habermas insists on the distinction between instrumental (or functional) and communicative rationality, and also on the dichotomy between 'system' and 'lifeworld'. Long range social development involves the internal diversification of lifeworld components, and also the growing segregation of symbolic-communicative patterns from reproductive endeavors governed by standards of technical efficiency - a process which he describes as the 'uncoupling' of system and lifeworld. According to Habermas the main social domains dedicated to the enhancement of 'steering capacity' are the economy and the state. The 'steering mechanisms of money and power' are no longer coordinated with communicative patterns but begin to invade and subdue the latter. Thus the uncoupling of system and lifeworld is converted into a 'colonization of the lifeworld', that is, its subjugation to alien standards of technical control.

[12] Habermas shows that, in spite of originating from communicative action, juridification includes a strategic component, of compromise among particular interests, as well as

the institutionalization of positive freedoms and individual rights. In the second volume of his 'Theory of Communicative Action' he analyzes the development of the modern western state using this category. (Habermas, 1984-7, II, chapter VIII, [3], 2.)

[13] The practical consequences of the concepts of decentration and juridification are demonstrated by Habermas (1984-7, II: 558) in his distinction between 'offensive' and 'defensive' social actors and movements. The former are the feminist and ethnic movements for civil rights - before the latter resulted in 'the particularist affirmation of black sub-cultures'. They are seen as a continuity of the 'tradition of bourgeois and socialist liberation movements', for they claim 'to implement promises largely anchored in the universal foundations recognized by public law and morality'. The defensive movements are those of 'self-defense by possessive traditional social strata', and others that develop from 'an already rationalized life-world, through new forms of experience and cooperation'. Only 'offensive' movements are considered decentered and based on universal foundations. See also a critique of this distinction by Heller/Feher (1985:221), who nevertheless agree that 'new' social movements can only arise in an already established public sphere - however restricted it may be.

[14] The studies cited on the pages below adopted approaches that are specific and differ from those of Heller/Feher and Habermas. But they present data on normative decentration and juridification of social relations that question the assumptions of classic theories. The study by Gohn is a case in point (1988). It was based on studies by Castells and Lojkine on 'urban contradictions' (Marxist sociology), but its findings surpassed the limitations of this framework. The study provides a detailed description of the forms of organization, the aims and contents of these social actions - all of which point to various levels of decentration and juridification of social relations, in interaction with government agencies, the party system, etc.

[15] Cf. *Movimento Popular*. Polis/CPV, São Paulo, 1989.

[16] E.g.: Besides the *'Partido Verde'* (Green Party), which has a small constituency, there are environmental leaders and militants in various political parties. The ecological ideological spectrum penetrates almost all the party system, from the liberal center to the far left extra-parliamentary sectors. Even conservative and business sectors of the media are increasingly vocal about the benefits of environment preservation (See Viola, 1988; ISER/MMA, 1998). The feminist movement seems also to have increased its influence in the party system, and even an initial convergence has been found with ecological movements and grassroots Church groups. (See Scherer-Warren, 1989).

[17] Thus, it is very likely that one may see often again in Brazil the diffusion of that convergence, achieved in São Paulo since the late 1970s among various sectors of society — those who demonstrated in the streets in the national *'Diretas'* campaign in 1984. This in fact occurred with Lula's candidacy during the Presidential elections in 1989, 1994 and 1998, and also in the mass demonstrations for President Collor's impeachment in 1992.

[18] Cf. Habermas' (1979:118 ff) concept of social evolution, in which evolutionary dynamics is conceived as a process of learning that is neither linear, straightforward nor irreversible but the acquisition of ever-renewed skills for problem-solving.

[19] Cf. Habermas (1976:178). Verification (*Einlösung*) means intersubjective recognition of validity claims.

Chapter 4

NEIGHBORHOOD ORGANIZATIONS: CHANGES AND CONTINUITY[*]

During the initial transition from the authoritarian regime research on Brazilian social actors and movements mainly focused on the processes of social and political integration promoted by the government of the "New Republic" (e.g., Boschi, 1987; Cardoso, 1988; Jacobi, 1989). This focus was understandable, considering that this was the first civilian government after 21 years of military rule, analysts and practitioners alike were interested in the new opportunities for interaction and exchange under the new regime.

On the other hand, studies of the political-institutional transition from authoritarian rule emphasized the obstacles to institutional and cultural change, that occurred at the national level of political life (e.g. O'Donnell, 1987; Reis, 1989; Mainwaring, 1990). In particular, these studies pointed out fundamental conservative features of the Brazilian political tradition that re-emerged from the past populist (pre-military) regime, and from the legacies of the authoritarian regime (1964/1984) that are still found in the present party system and government. In a basic sense, the former approach (that looked at the " micro" level of social action) and the latter which stressed "macro" institutional traditions, converged in the appraisal that the democratization processes initiated by the *'Nova República'* were rather limited and not enough to establish a real democratic regime.

Cultural change, however, has not been sufficiently studied in Brazil, either at the 'micro' or 'macro' levels of political life. This is quite unfortunate, because cultural change could provide a useful focus for considering the problems highlighted by the studies of the Brazilian transition from authoritarian rule. Political culture can be seen as a pattern of relationships among social actors, the party system and government institutions (Garretón, 1992). This relationship may change significantly over time, decisively effecting the processes of democratization. In other words, cultural changes (even 'molecular' ones, that provide a base or groundwork for the political regime, cf.

---

[*] This study was supported by research grants of *FINEP* and *CNPq*. The author is grateful for the comments of Conceição D'Incao, Ilse Scherer-Warren, Juan Carlos Gorlier and Mario Toer.

Lechner, 1987) may influence both social action and the institutional life of the country - providing a privileged vantage point from which to approach a country's democratization.

This chapter proposes that a revised analysis should be conducted of the interactions between social actors and movements, on the one hand, and the processes of cultural and institutional change on the other hand. The chapter focuses on a specific historical analysis of neighborhood actors and movements that emerged in Florianópolis (the state capital of Santa Catarina) during the first transition government[1]. Neighborhood associations have a long history in traditional Brazilian politics - both in the populist (1945-1963) and the later authoritarian military regimes. These local entities thus provide useful indications that can be used to evaluate 'micro' changes affecting political culture, and the latter's influence on the institutionalization of democracy.

The first part of the chapter presents a general description of the emergence of neighborhood movements in Florianópolis during this period. The second part analyzes the historical changes observed in the cultural life of these groups throughout the period. The main conclusion is that studies of political transitions must consider what social actors have to say about their actions and expectations. This study shows that local neighborhood groups had a lot to say on their own openness to a future of democracy (even when, as it will be seen, conservatism still had a large influence within political culture).

THE HISTORY OF NEIGHBORHOOD
MOVEMENTS IN FLORIANÓPOLIS

Neighborhood movements began emerging in Florianópolis during the 1980s as a reaction to the social integration policies of the military regime - that were implemented as part of a national 'community development' project in the mid-1970s[2]. During its long period of '*Abertura*' ('opening') the authoritarian military regime, in its Second National Development Plan (1975) called for the creation of 'community centers' within low-income neighborhoods all over the country. These centers were regulated at the state or provincial level by specific decrees. In Santa Catarina state the decree regulating this matter (# 2840, of June 16, 1977) provided a series of very strict regulations concerning the organization of 'community councils'. For instance, their board of directors would be nominated by government officials, who also monitored the council's political and financial activities. The councils were thus designed to provide a tightly controlled channel for popular demands, as well as a local administration for the government's social policies (daycare, schools, food distribution and health programs, etc.).

A later decree (# 8558, issued in 1979) introduced several changes, aimed at integrating in government policies all of the existing neighborhood actors and movements, under government policies that established regulations that became gradually more comprehensive and less strictly controlling. A specialized agency was then created by the state government (*FUCADESC - Fundação Catarinense de Desenvolvimento*

Comunitário) to manage the relations between government and neighborhood groups, and to allocate the social services provided by the state.

During the late 1970s the main - and the only legal - opposition party (*MDB* – which after 1979 became *PMDB - Partido do Movimento Democrático Brasileiro*) the Brazilian Democratic Movement Party, supported in principle the formation of (voluntary) 'neighborhoods' associations'. These associations were organized to locally counteract the government strategy to form 'community councils' directly sponsored by the authoritarian regime. With the inauguration of the civilian transitional government in March 1985, the 'community councils' started to lose their source of federal resources, as well as their role in any national project for popular integration and control.

The national government was then headed by a party coalition between the *PMDB* and the *PFL* (*Partido da Frente Liberal*), The Liberal Front Party, a faction that splintered off from the conservative *PDS* (*Partido Democrático Social*), the Social Democratic Party, successor of *ARENA* (*Aliança Renovadora Nacional*) National Alliance for Renovation, which was the official party of the military regime.

The *PFL* was quite strong in Santa Catarina - where in the state government it supported the still ruling *PDS*. Thus, the community councils of Santa Catarina continued to be supported mainly by local and state officials and businesses - but also by the continued support from the *PFL* at the national level. This continued support was justified by the successful electoral results that *PDS-PFL* had received from this strategy of popular integration, since the 1982 elections for state government.

In November 1985 the first election was held for Mayor of Florianópolis (previously, mayors of state capitals were nominated by the military regime). The *PMDB* candidate won the election, but the conservative *PDS-PFL* held a majority in the City Council. The neighborhood associations linked to the *PMDB* (and other opposition parties) were called on during the electoral campaign (and then during the new administration) to debate a new policy to guide relations between the neighborhoods and City Hall, including issues such as the city budget, and the formation of a new citywide federation of neighborhood entities. A series of meetings was held with the neighborhood associations at which debate centered around the need for a new policy of relations between City Hall and the neighborhood movements. As an outcome of this debate, a sector of the *PT* (*Partido dos Trabalhadores*, the Workers' Party) that supported the *PMDB* candidacy, was appointed Secretary of Community Affairs in City Hall. They were in charge of the mayor's periodic meetings with the neighborhood associations, and of other municipal policies of popular mobilization.

Simultaneously, the political parties began negotiations to launch candidacies for the 1986 state gubernatorial elections. Opposition political leaders and leaders of neighbourhood associations in various Santa Catarina cities devised a strategy to form a statewide federation of neighbourhood groups (later on named *FAMESC - Federação de Associações de Moradores do Estado de Santa Catarina*). This federation was supposed to work out a statewide community policy, in order to replace that of the previous government agency (*FUCADESC*), inherited from the military regime. The neighbourhood associations of Florianópolis were then pressured to form their own citywide organization, to participate in the new state federation.

These facts led to a formal division between the currents that were attempting to form the Florianópolis neighbourhood coordination. Representatives of all local associations agreed upon the need for a new communitarian policy, in order to guarantee the independence and autonomy of the neighborhood associations vis-à-vis government agencies and policies. However, the associations linked to the *CEBs* (*Comunidades Eclesiais de Base*, the Catholic Church Base Communities) considered that a 'really autonomous' organization should be built 'from the bottom up'('*a partir das bases*'), and independent of 'electoral pressures'[3].

Nevertheless, a coordination of neighbourhood associations was formed in late 1986 (*UFECO - União Florianopolitana de Entidades Comunitárias*). It was founded by 32 local associations, including 10 of the previous 'community councils' formed under the previous regime. The first *UFECO* board was elected with the intention of representing all political currents, and included neighbourhood leaders linked to the *PMDB, PFL, PDS, PC do B* (the Maoist *Partido Comunista do Brasil*), *PT* and *PC* (the pro-soviet Communist Party). The chairperson of the board was a militant of the latter Communist Party[4].

A separate coalition was organized by twelve neighbourhood groups linked to the work of the Church (*CEBs*). These groups refused to join *UFECO*, although they had participated in the planning meetings between the neighborhood groups and the *PMDB* Mayor. This new coalition began to act as an alternative federation, with its own aims and strategies - though it resisted at this time assuming the status of a formal and structured organization. This group, which called itself 'Periphery' ('*Periferia*'), maintained informal contacts with *UFECO*'s leadership, but was generally opposed to the latter's support of *PMDB* policies at City Hall[5]. The group was initially very critical of any relationship with the government and all political parties. Nonetheless, it gradually began to interact pragmatically with government agencies, and eventually presented its own candidate for City Council through the *PT*, in 1988 – and to participate with other groups and movements, as will be seen below.

The *PMDB* was elected to the state government in the 1986 elections. As a consequence, *UFECO* received space in the state administration building formerly occupied by *FUCADESC* – which became the 'State Secretariat of Labor and Community Action'. *UFECO*'s statutes were approved in April 1987, opening participation to all neighborhood groups. The statutes affirmed the founder's aims at maintaining autonomy from government. However, no detailed regulations were established by the statutes to implement this general thrust (such as independent and autonomous funding from the associates, etc.). As a consequence of these flaws, and also due to lack of financial resources, *UFECO* became to heavily depend on government support for its survival.

Another point that later caused much trouble for *UFECO* was its indiscriminate policy toward new affiliations. The number of affiliated neighbourhood groups increased from the 32 original founders to 47 in early 1987. As a result, the weight of the community councils inherited from the previous regime increased considerably - surpassing the number of independent neighborhood associations that had originally founded the federation. By March 1989, almost all of the neighborhood groups in the city were affiliated to *UFECO*: 71 neighborhood groups (only the 12 *CEB* or Periphery neighborhoods still outside *UFECO*)[6]. One can thus see that during the *PMDB* administration, *UFECO* came to play the same role in the city as was previously performed by *FUCADESC* at the state level: namely, to channel an integrated negotiation between the neighbourhood groups and the government's community and social policies.

Financial support from the government and the affiliation of conservative groups began to reverse *UFECO*'s original intention of independence and autonomy vis-à-vis the government, according to most leaders from the first *UFECO*'s board. In fact, between 1987 and 1989, the members of the first board began to withdraw, and were replaced by conservative leaders, leaving the board in the hands of leaders linked to the *PDS, PFL* and the right wing of the *PMDB*. The chairperson of the Board, a member of the pro-Soviet Communist Party, was the last original founder to defect from the Board - in the context of a conflictive judicial process waged by the original founders of *UFECO* against its conservative leadership.

The left and center-oriented leadership that withdrew from the Board organized an opposition candidacy at *UFECO*'s internal election in 1989. This was done during the Brazilian Presidential campaign, when leftist and many center-oriented political currents of the country were against the candidacy of Fernando Collor de Mello (who finally won the Presidential election). This political context supported the coalition and educational strategy followed by founders of *UFECO*, to win back the leadership of this organization.

This changed context was already noticeable in the reorientation of the founder's understanding of politics. During the 1989 presidential campaign, the dissident leadership that had founded *UFECO* made a critical evaluation of the *PMDB* administration in Florianópolis (1986/1988). One of their principal conclusions was in partial agreement with the radical appraisal originally made by the neighbourhood groups linked to the *CEB*s ('Periphery'): that the policies of integrated representation implemented by *UFECO* had not helped to educate and organize the neighbourhoods 'from the bottom up' ('*a partir das bases*' – from the grassroots). Rather, these policies had stimulated individual disputes among the leaders, and the local associations as well, for special access to city resources, and for personal positions in government agencies.

Thus, the system of state clientelism or patronage inherited from the authoritarian regime was replaced by more modern forms of neo-clientelism. The former authoritarian structure established a direct dependency of the community councils on the government and its official party (PDS). The system of neo-clientelism that followed introduced competition among parties and politicians, on the one hand, and among the neighborhood groups and leaders on the other - around the exchange of public positions, services and policies, for votes and political support from the neighborhood groups[7].

This explained how *UFECO* had in fact replaced the old *FUCADESC* at the city level, and even inherited from the latter even its clientele. The dissident leadership which founded *UFECO* realized that a new community policy had to be adopted – one that was different from, and independent of, party politics (this was another conclusion they shared with the 'Periphery' group). This new policy should emphasize priorities for the city as a whole, instead of the piecemeal allocation of government resources according to the special demands of each neighbourhood (that had been stimulated by neo-clientelism). This new policy was in fact necessary for practical reasons, in view of the strategy of 'divide and conquer' implemented by the conservative *PDS-PFL* administration that won the elections to City Hall in 1988[8] and understandably discarded *UFECO*'s representativity.

This reorientation of the *UFECO* founders resulted in a well-devised program of institutional reform, that began with vocal opposition to *UFECO*'s conservative leadership in the assemblies preparing for the 1989 internal elections. This way, they managed to create a committee to revise the statutes, with the advice of the local Bar association (*OAB, Ordem dos Advogados do Brasil* – Florianópolis branch). The criteria for affiliation were revised according to *UFECO*'s original aims of independence and autonomy vis-à-vis the government and the party system and guidelines for decision-making and internal administration - respectful of the principles of representativity, majority rule, alternation in power were established. This reform of the statutes was voted by an assembly of the founding associations in May 1989, and the new internal elections were scheduled for November of that year. Before the elections there was a campaign to recruit new affiliations, according to the statutes and led by *UFECO*'s founders[9]. This campaign won over several conservative neighborhood groups to the new strategy of independence and representativity.

The program of institutional reform exposed the conservative leadership to open criticism from the grassroots of *UFECO*. The judicial process moved by the founders against the conservative leaders won popular support and local press coverage. Thus, the institutional reform succeeded in creating the legal and political conditions to replace the conservatives on *UFECO*'s board in late 1989. These conservative leaders tried various tactics to postpone internal elections and sought to sabotage *UFECO*'s reform in order to remain in power. But they finally decided to refrain from attempting re-election, since they anticipated defeat. Instead, they attempted to withdraw momentarily from public attention, and to await a victory of the conservative *PDS-PFL* coalition in the next Gubernatorial election - which in fact took place in 1990. The conservative leaders of *UFECO* expected that a restructuring of the traditional clientelist system would result from the return of the conservatives to state power. This expectation, however, proved to be unrealistic, due both to the shrinking of resources because of the state's economic adjustment policies, and (more importantly) to the greater competitiviness and visibility of neo- clientelist politics.

Thus, the second *UFECO* administration was elected in late 1989, with a Board of leftist and centrist leaders, mainly linked to the left of the *PMDB*, *PSDB* (*Partido da Social Democracia Brasileira*, a center-left splinter of the *PMDB*), *PC do B*, and a sector of the *PT*. The main thrust of this leadership, however, was that it no longer should attempt to reproduce the party system within *UFECO*'s leadership: they should strive for community policies which were independent of political party interests, focusing on priorities for the city as a whole - to be debated at City Hall and the City Council (regardless of the parties in power). Nevertheless, the new Board did not advocate a rupture with parties and government, but rather autonomy and an inter-dependent relationship, to negotiate politically its community policies.

One may notice several points of contact between *UFECO*'s new policies and the radical positions sustained by the 'Periphery' group from the time of its original separation. However, the 'Periphery' maintained its separate identity, and never considered affiliation with *UFECO*. In fact, the 'Periphery' had formed its own cadres and leadership, emphasizing different priorities through its solidarity with 'the poorest of the poor'. It supported, for instance, the 'Homeless' Movement (*'Sem Tetos'*), which worked with the problem of scarcity of urban land and low-income housing in the city through a radical strategy of occupation of vacant public and private land. The need for low-income housing had increased in Florianópolis during the 1980s, but had not affected the neighborhoods that founded *UFECO*. It was, however, very acute among the poorer neighborhoods of the 'Periphery'. Moreover, the links of the latter to the church led them to adopt the national Catholic policy of the 'preferential option for the poor' (*'opção preferencial pelos pobres'*)[10].

Thus, *UFECO* and the 'Periphery' constructed different parallel organizations, to intervene and participate in the city's public sphere. They were both created to counteract and replace the traditional forms of state integration and co-optation - i.e., the community councils formed under the authoritarian regime. Within the new competitive public sphere that opened up during democratization, the neighborhood groups worked out their basic differences of organization and leadership. These differences, in turn, influenced one another, and established points of contact and opportunities for cooperation[11].

Two examples of the history of both organizations help to illustrate these mutual influences: the priority given by the 'Periphery' to the issue of urban land, and the relationship between both groups and political parties. The issue of urban land relates especially to usufructuary rights - the Brazilian customary right of rural *'usucapião'* or undisputed land occupation - extended by the 1988 Brazilian Constitution to cases of use of urban land for low income housing. Some of the old community councils had demanded this right in Florianópolis since the late 1970s, and their demands were in part granted by the conservative administrations under the military regime. This was, incidentally, one of the reasons for the continued popularity of conservative politicians among these sectors.

Later on, with the increased pressure on housing supply caused by rural migration to the cities during the 1980s, this priority was adopted by the 'Homeless' movement, with support from the church and the 'Periphery'. The 'Homeless' movement grew considerably during the decade, attracting public attention to and press coverage of the issue of low income housing. Finally, the new conservative administration in City Hall created a committee in 1989 to deal with the issue, including representatives from the neighborhood sectors. The 'Homelessr' and 'Periphery' movements were obviously the most interested sectors, but they refused to participate in the municipal committee, alleging that 'it did not have representative parity' (i.e., the neighborhoods would have a minority vote). Thus, only *UFECO* represented the neighborhood groups in the committee, but it did so in consultation with 'Periphery' leaders, bringing them useful information and some influence in the committee's policies[12].

The relationship between neighborhood associations and the party system always was a hotly debated issue, from the time of the initial rejection of the community councils, by both **UFECO** and 'Periphery'. Both organizations criticized the subordination of community policies to party politics. However, the 'Periphery' was even more radical, rejecting ever since its ceation any connection whatsoever with the party system - as a matter of strategy in keeping with the influence of the church[13].

This radical position was later reformulated, when the 'Periphery' nominated one of its leaders as a candidate of the **PT** for City Council in the 1988 elections. This reformulation was further clarified, as a clear distinction (and positive appraisal) between the different (and complementary) roles of community policies and party politics. This reevaluation and gradual extension of the concept and the scope of politics opened further ground for cooperation and joint demonstrations among the 'Periphery' and other popular and left-center sectors. For instance, this convergence could be seen at a protest demonstration at City Council, when the city charter was voted in early 1990 (this will be considered below). In fact, the cooperation among most popular sectors (including the 'Periphery') and the left-center opposition was also noticeable throughout the national Presidential campaign in 1989, and especially in the second electoral round in December (when the center - left coalition was defeated).

CULTURAL DEMOCRATIZATION

We may now analyze the cultural changes and contributions to the process of democratization made by the neighborhood groups and movements in Florianópolis, the emergence of which was described above. A preliminary remark is in order here: at the end of the period (of the first civilian administration, 1985-1989) there were no longer any local neighborhood groups dependent on the state, in the terms previously imposed by the authoritarian regime. Therefore, the *'Nova República'* established an end to the institutional dependent relations that had characterized the community councils since the 1970s. It is necessary to stress this point, to highlight the specific differences introduced by neo-clientelism vis-à-vis the former authoritarian patronage relations.

In this new context, the differences among **UFECO**, 'Periphery' and other competitive neighborhood actors could be interpreted as alternative positions within the same public sphere - which was constituted in parallel to the government institutions and the party system - by the various neighborhood actors and organizations. This parallel public sphere was defined by these actors as an autonomous space for negotiations and representations, interacting with - but independent from - the institutional political order (the party system, government agencies, City Hall and others). Of course, this independent relationship was never complete, and included a variety of competitive and even conflicting interests. But the fact is that there was no longer formal *de jure* government coontrol of neighborhood groups (as there was with the previous community councils).

Nevertheless, even after the state clientelistic system ceased to exist in form and substance, the process of conservative modernization enforced by the authoritarian regime left a conservative legacy among the neighborhood organizations. This could be seen, for instance, in the continuity of a nucleus of conservative actors within the *UFECO* leadership (in its first Board). This group continued to exert great influence in support of the conservative *PDS-PFL* candidates in municipal and state elections - as well as in clear anti-democratic practices within the *UFECO* administration. In fact, the conservative legacy was not only present in the open militancy of the *PDS-PFL* '*cabos eleitorais*' (local political brokers) but also in some aspects of the other groups, which will be noted below.

Therefore, as one analyzes the composition of the parallel public sphere constituted by the neighborhood organizations, it is necessary to distinguish three different sectors which interacted in that sphere: *UFECO*, the 'Periphery', and the conservative sectors and trends inherited from the community councils. We will now analyze the main characteristics of their cultural changes and orientations, starting with the conservative sectors.

CONSERVATIVES: NEO-CLIENTELISM

This group of actors cannot be considered a social movement, for it is mainly constituted by the leaders and the grassroots membership of the former community councils created by the state (35 neighborhoods, in 1985). Many of them were outside *UFECO*, as a scattered and rather disparate network of neighborhoods, by the end of 1989[14]. A main feature of this group was its acceptance of dependent and subordinate (at times passive, other times negotiated) relations with the clientelist/patronage practices of conservative political parties and politicians. These practices were often (but not always) somewhat 'modernized', in the growing competitive context of neo-clientelism (in terms of a "conservative modernization". See Castro, 1988)[15].

These actors made little if any contribution to the democratization processes, as their community participation had its roots and continued to be supported by their passive role in the system of authoritarian legitimacy. Nevertheless, these sectors were gradually challenged to make new choices, in the face of the universal rights of citizenship increasingly recognized by public law and morality during the expansion of the public sphere in the political transition. Thus, some of the conservative sectors were able to re-orient their actions and allegiances, as was noticeable at the end of the first UFECO administration[16].

Conservative reorientation could even break with dependent relations (both from the traditional relations and from the more modern neo-clientelism). An early example of this rupture was the formation of the original leadership of the 'Periphery', which emerged in reaction to *PDS* electoral clientelistic practices in 1982 (see Chapter 6 of this book where these events are considered). At this time, members of the local *CEB* and the youth group of the community council (whose members later became leaders of the "Periphery") critically appraised the electoral manipulation of the local '*mutirões*' (voluntary work by the neighborhood groups, supported both by the church and by City Hall). Thus, they broke away from government control, and formed a new community organization, opposed to any political allegiance. But this was clearly an exceptional case of radical reorientation, stemming from specific circumstances (mostly, the political reorientation of the church, which in this city at that time was supportive of the authoritarian regime).

According to the Habermas and Kohlberg's (1990) theses on cultural and moral development, an examination of legitimacy principles (post-conventional morality) cannot be made by authoritarian/conservative sectors. For among these sectors, ethical issues are usually controlled by the routines of tradition, and thus excluded from public debate. However, the simple acceptance of legal obligations, in a context of growing democratic institutionalization, stimulates a conventional morality that is opposed to arbitrary practices (conventional legalism). A case in point was the attitude described above, of the conservative leaders at the end of the first *UFECO* administration: they recognized their defeat in the face of the reform of the statutes, and abstained from the elections for the new Board. Therefore, their contribution to this case of democratization was, at best, one of passive consent.

The basis of the conservative position thus rests on an opposition to both sociocultural and political democratization - e.g. we have seen that the conservative sectors did not distinguish between community action and party politics. Moreover, during their dominance in the first *UFECO* administration the conservative leaders omitted and distorted information that they passed to the constituency, manipulated *UFECO*'s resources for their personal interests, and tried to gain access to and positions in government institutions and agencies. They only gave up their anti-democratic practices after they were exposed through the media. They were then defeated by the campaign for institutional reform led by the original *UFECO* founders - i.e., the latter's 'appeal to the grassroots' at the assemblies, the judicial review of the statutes, and the public denouncement of the illegal practices of the conservatives, etc.

On the other hand, the conservative sectors displayed a thoroughly instrumental (or 'over-secularized', cf. Flisfisch, 1987, see Chapter 8 of this book) approach to politics, which they conceived of as a 'political market'. For they adapted clientelistic orientations to the new competitive context in the public sphere and institutional life, penetrating the party system and government agencies - regardless of the political programs and aims of the new patrons. This fact became clear starting with their strategy for participation in the first *UFECO* administration, where they managed to increase the affiliation of their traditional constituencies, established new links with the *PMDB* administration, and succeeded in isolating and finally excluding all other original members of the Board.

This is not to say that the conservatives were the only ones responsible for the restructuring of clientelism within *UFECO* (and in the latter's relations with government): the founders of *UFECO* recognized their own mistakes and their *naiveté* in abandoning their original effort to establish autonomy and independence from the government and the party system. But the fact remains that the conservatives were only displaced from their quickly acquired dominance of *UFECO* through the resistance and institutional reform promoted with great effort by the original founders of the organization.

Nevertheless, competitive neo-clientelism continued to prevail in the relations between the neighborhoods and the state agencies and government social policies. This allowed new opportunities for the pragmatic orientations of the conservatives. But an important difference between the new situation and traditional authoritarian patronage was that the competitive characteristics of representative institutions brought a new visibility to administrative procedures and negotiations - thus avoiding, or at least curtailing, the secrecy of relations based on special interests and patronage[17].

Finally, continuity within the conservative neighborhood sectors was largely dependent on the availability of public resources for social policies during the conservative state administration. These resources were likely to be scarce, in view of the current structural adjustment policies. Given the shortage of public funds that could be used to maintain patronage it is possible that the cooperation with other neighborhoods in search of federal resources (for instance) may have led the conservatives to a change of their practices and orientations. Or, at least, this may have happened with some sectors among the conservatives, as was already noticeable during the second *UFECO* administration.

Nevertheless, cooperation with the conservatives was extremely difficult, as the *UFECO* founders learned at great cost. Only a careful and continuous process of education and organization of the grassroots allowed the neighborhood movements to advance toward democratic representation. Conservative leaders continued to interact with the political oligarchy that inherited (and in fact, originally implemented) the conservative modernization policy devised by the authoritarian regime. This oligarchy continues to dominate to a large extent the political life of Santa Catarina, mainly (but not exclusively) through their 'brokers' (*cabos eleitorais*) in the neighborhoods.

UFECO: REPRESENTATIVE POLITICS

The actors who occupy the central position in the parallel public sphere formed by neighborhood groups in Florianópolis are the group of associations that originally founded *UFECO*. This central position expresses both their greater number, and their central influence among the neighborhood groups of the city. It also manifests their major (though disputed) influence on the local 'community policies' of the government. This group always emphasized the importance of maintaining a certain inter-dependence between the expansion of political representation in the party system, on the one hand, and the autonomous representation within *UFECO* of the different currents that existed in the neighborhood groups and movements, on the other. They have also emphasized the differences (and interactions) between community policies and party politics, social movements and representative institutions, civil society and the state, as complementary forms of social and institutional action.

The success of this approach became manifest during the democratic transition, by the group's ability to promote its ideals among the neighborhoods; through the foundation and later restructuring of *UFECO*; through the continuous campaign to educate and formally affiliate new members; and - last but not least - through their recognition of the virtues of struggle and conflict (though these were not always successful), in order to maintain and improve their original thrust of representativity and autonomy, vis-à-vis the government and other political institutions.

Nevertheless, the practices of this group have confronted many vicissitudes, as was noted in the crisis of the first *UFECO* Board. The group underwent continuous changes of political alliances and oppositions, passing through many defections and a high turn over in the Board's composition — related to frequent internal crises and external confrontations with other actors (political parties, public agencies, conservative groups, etc.). It is really a surprise to many observers that this leadership was able to maintain and improve their original cooperation and allegiance to *UFECO*, in spite of so many difficulties (and the opposition of the political oligarchy).

The contributions of this group to the democratization processes were particularly visible in the election campaign for the second *UFECO* Board (1989): the program of institutional reform that brought the organization back to its original aims; the careful reform of the statutes; and in the conquest of legal and popular support — even among sectors of the conservative groups. *UFECO*'s cultural democratization was revealed in this group's ability to raise the principles of legitimacy of the democratic regime in public law and morality (e.g., the procedures of representativity and alternating in power) — thus delegitimizing the basic authoritarian culture of oligarchic rule.

UFECO's founders consistently tried to maintain links of communication and cooperation with the 'Periphery' group, and worked out some common aims with the latter — e.g. the distinction between community policies and party politics. *UFECO*, however, always emphasized coalition strategies, both in community and political affairs. But this emphasis on coalition-building proved to be flawed on several occasions. Since divergent aims and motives among the partners were sometimes overlooked — this led to opportunism, co-optations and serious conflicts (such as those that took place during the period of the first *UFECO* board).

UFECO's emphasis on representativity could also easily lead to a lapse into unprincipled strategic compromises — both for the sake of maintaining a formal 'unity' and because of the desire to construct a general representation of the party system within the *UFECO* board. The contrasting emphasis of the 'Periphery' group on social participation, and on the importance of the final aims and values of social action, could (and did) influence *UFECO*'s orientations. One example of this influence was the participation of *UFECO* and 'Periphery' groups (together with leaders of the opposition parties) in the public demonstration against the approval of the city charter by the conservative majority of City Council, in early 1990.

UFECO's strategy around this issue was to attempt to influence the charter by providing consultation to progressive council members. The 'Periphery' in turn had collected signatures for the 'popular bills' it wanted to include in the charter. Both strategies produced meager results, as the solid conservative majority in the City Council refused to make concessions to the opposition. (However, Silva [1999] maintains that some positive legal provisions were achieved, albeit for the long-term). When this fact became apparent, most opposition forces participated in a mass demonstration in front of City Council chambers, to attract media coverage of a denouncement of the biased charter reform process. Thus, both *UFECO* and the "Periphery" learned from this process that they should converge — among themselves and other sectors — in order to have some participatory impact on the local institutions.

THE 'PERIPHERY': PARTICIPATORY POLITICS

The group alliance of neighborhood groups that became known as the 'Periphery' was characterized by its emphasis on maintaining a complete separation and autonomy vis-à-vis the state, the party-system and other political institutions. They thus opposed both the traditional clientelistic dependency of the community councils (and its 'modernized' versions in neo- clientelism) and the positions of *UFECO* that attempted to maintain an interdependent relationship between social movements and institutional representation in the party system. However, when the 'Periphery' presented its candidate for City Council through the *PT*, in 1988, this nomination was made through deliberation at the grassroots of its 12 neighborhood groups. In this manner, the movement took the initiative and control of the nomination process, overcoming the usual patterns of oligarchic nomination by the party system.

This policy also contrasts with the clientelistic practices of '*cabos eleitorais*' (local electoral brokers) chosen 'from the top down' by conservative parties and politicians. It contrasts as well with *UFECO*'s effort to establish interdependency with the party system, in which its Board and leadership were continuously tempted, by the various parties and agencies, to assume bureaucratic positions and/or electoral candidacies. Nevertheless, the capacity for generalization of the participatory line of the 'Periphery' is necessarily limited and partial — mainly due to its 'preferential option for the poor', and its linkages with grassroots Catholicism. The explanation of these limits is straightforward: not everyone in the population is a practicing Catholic; not every practicing Catholic is willing to assume the 'option for the poor'; and those who assume it may not identify this 'orientation to the poor' with the 'Homeless' Movement (sponsored by the 'Periphery').

However, these limitations do not imply that this choice of the 'Periphery' was naive or irrational; nor do they imply that it was purely religious or voluntaristic. In fact, it was an explicit ethical choice of high strategic rationality and considerable influence on the public sphere. It aimed at a 'reflexive equilibrium' (see Rawls, 1993) in the search for personal benefits and social solidarity: a balance between rational choice and a reasonable reciprocity, that is not dominant in Western democracies (let alone in Brazilian society, that is still in a process of transition to democracy). This approach defends civic and social rights of participation for the poor that may find support in public morality. An example of this possibility is the issue raised by the 'Homeless' movement on the 'right to housing' versus property rights — or even of the so-called 'social functions of property' traditionally voiced by Roman Catholic sectors (Cf. Tucker, 1980).

Perhaps this is one of the reasons why the 'Periphery' achieved a great deal of press coverage for its priorities, but often few practical results — though the latter problem also relates to its radicalism and reluctance to negotiate politically. For instance, we noted above that when City Hall established a special committee to handle the issue of urban land use for low income housing, the 'Periphery' refused to participate because the committee had not social parity (though UFECO served as the informal representative of the 'Periphery'). The point, however, is that it seemed more effective to the 'Periphery' to continue its policies of land occupation and public debate in the media than to engage in negotiations controlled by conservative and business sectors.

It is necessary to recognize that the 'Periphery' considerably expanded awareness in the public sphere of its priorities. This educational process took place within its own constituency, as well as among broader public opinion. Nevertheless, it seems that its religious overtones may have frightened more people than it attracted (support that it often tended to disregard). Its contributions to the generalization of rights recognized by public law and morality were very important, especially in the ethical sphere — due to the weight of religion in its orientations, and the support received from the local church hierarchy.

However, these groups did not seem to adopt an explicit aim of legitimizing the democratic regime (which established, for instance, the usufructuary access to urban housing, provided in principle by the 1988 Constitution). Instead, the 'Periphery' leaders apparently preferred to justify their actions and orientations in terms of a defense of 'natural' rights — probably seen as a transcendental, and thus a non-historical morality (see Flisfisch, 1987).

Therefore, the democratization of culture manifest in the actions and discourses of the 'Periphery' mainly occurred through an ethical education, contrary to the passive subordination that supported the traditional legitimacy of authoritarian and oligarchic rule. This dependency was overcome mainly through the organizational practices of its membership, in cooperatives, unions, and party activities, where these members may also have raised the the issue of the legitimacy of the regime in legal and political terms (thus reaching a post-conventional morality). The relations between these political practices and the group's communitarian ethics with religious overtones is a problematic issue that should be clarified through further research[18]. (See Chapter 6).

The 'Periphery' took an important step forward in its orientations when it clarified its relations with (and the differences between) sociocultural democratization and political democracy. This was done when it nominated its candidate for City Council through the *PT*. (Here, as elsewhere, the *PT* provided representation for new social movements in the Brazilian transition to democracy). From this step emerged, in the group's internal debates, the distinction between community policies and party politics (each as a legitimate engagement).

The recognition of these relationships - though still tentative and controversial within the group - has allowed an interaction at the political sphere with other groups, institutions and popular sectors that was less defensive and occasional. These experiences may have supported the gradual recognition by the group of the right to difference and the importance of pluralism among (and within) the various groups and currents of society. Tolerance and pluralism are cultural values and principles inherent to the concept of democracy as an aim and a value in itself, and not simply as a set of instrumental rules and institutions to be used for private purposes.

Nevertheless, until 1990 these actors mainly took an instrumental approach to the public sphere: 'We go there (City Hall) only to negotiate and achieve the most we can for ourselves, and not to reach any kind of compromise', one of the 'Periphery' leaders said. Eventually these leaders also acted in communicative (or intersubjective) terms, to reach understanding and consensus among their constituents - though here the relations between community and religious leaders should be better researched, to examine possible legacies of traditional dependency. Their instrumental actions, of land invasions, demonstrations and civil disobedience, were at times effective in reaching public opinion. But the group often tended to act in isolation from other popular groups and potential allies, discarding coalition alternatives and strategic considerations, which might eventually have produced better practical results and institutional solutions to their demands.

It is true, however, that the church's institutional support (especially foreign financial support) may, in part at least, have compensated for the lack of local coalition support. And it is also true that the group's predilection for the combative, expressive and participatory aspects of political life could be (and had already been) influential in the expansion of its support from public opinion. These practices cultivated and channeled the access of the rank-and-file (the 'man or woman in the street') to the media (at least when they did not attract excessive police repression). And they also educated members about participatory democracy, through regular contact with debates and decision-making within the neighborhoods. This way, not only was traditional passivity and subordination delegitimized, but individuals were personally enabled to assume the rights, values (and limitations) of participatory democracy.

CONCLUSIONS

In the above sections we have approached cultural changes within the neighborhoods, through categories from the Habermas/Kohlberg theory of cultural and moral development. These and other categories on cultural change are controversial, but they provide useful insights into the difficult issue of cultural democratization. In conclusion, this section presents a general outlook on the political culture of the three currents analyzed above, highlighting the main characteristics of each current of the neighborhood groups vis-à-vis the other two.

It is possible to say that the conservative sector of Florianópolis neighborhoods had a traditional political culture, whereas **UFECO** and the 'Periphery' emphasized complementary features of a democratic culture. Thus, the conservatives were to a large extent dependent on the authoritarian oligarchic legacy - though 'modernized' through neo-clientelism. This is because they were to a large degree dependent on political patronage, and saw the state institutions solely as providers of social policies, which addressed the demands of subordinate social actors (even when this was done through brokers such as political parties and politicians, and **not** through personal patrons as in traditional clientelism).

Political culture is considered to be democratic when it considers the characteristics of government institutions as part of a political **regime**. This is because democratic participation entails a debate on the principles that found and guide democratic governance (as in Habermas's postconventional morality). Thus, government is **not** simply considered as a source of material resources and as an addressee for economic demands. Garretón (1990) expands this argument, maintaining that the democratic regime must be considered from two different standpoints: (a) from the perspective of **how** it governs (the rules of its procedures and institutionalization); and (b) concerning the **relationship** between the state and the individual - where the actions of individuals, as citizens, may be guided by apathy, alienation, or participation.

Of course, these additional remarks on the democratization of political culture are not explicit in Habermas's categories. However, they are introduced here to help us interpret the dynamics of change among the neighborhood groups, within their parallel influence on the public sphere. For instance, the above analysis of the actions and orientations of **UFECO** leaders noted their emphasis on the establishment of procedural rules and institutionalization (related to **how** **UFECO**'s administration was to be carried out), and their legal conceptualization of democratic legitimacy, the issues of representativity, majority rule and alternating in power. In short, **UFECO** focused on the formal and instrumental resources to guarantee and institutionalize democratic government. They also emphasized an autonomous interaction with political parties and government agencies, centered on the pluralism of public interest representation. These emphases overcame (and denounced) the basic culture of subjection and patronage (be it traditional or in neo-clientelism).

The 'Periphery' was, in turn, the group that most stressed the relationship between the individual and politics. For it constantly called for active participation at all levels of political life - e.g. by the member of local cooperatives who organized his own economic survival in reciprocity with his neighbors; by the citizen who publicly demonstrated his rejection of traditional politics before City Hall, and so forth. The predilection of this group for the expressive, massive and egalitarian practices of participatory democracy reinforced its special strategy - which brought to public attention the priorities of the less fortunate and the destitute. The ethical, affective and religious features of its actions constituted a motivational foundation for awareness-building - a new approach to democratic life. This position attempted to overcome traditional (and 'conservative modernization') dependency, and also to solve the problems of apathy, demobilization and alienation - which **UFECO** leaders had difficulty solving among their grassroots.

Nevertheless, the 'Periphery' group hesitated to promote coalitions and often preferred to act in isolation in the public sphere —and at times received great publicity but few concrete results. Its strategies of occasional alliances were vulnerable to external deliberations and fortuitous circumstances, often defined by other institutional actors. Finally, at the end of the period studied, there was a *de facto* complementarity between *UFECO*'s emphasis on representation and the 'Periphery''s focus on participation (e.g., the city urban land committee; and the joint demonstration against the city charter).

But there are other legacies in Latin American political culture (as Morse, 1988, has sharply recalled): e.g., the medieval, hierarchical, sacral, stratified and authoritarian heritage derived from traditional religion and society. This legacy may be especially important in the provincial cities of Brazil, where the local elites managed to implement a successful process of 'conservative modernization' within the popular neighborhoods — sometimes with support from religious groups and institutions. Therefore, one has to adopt a sober appraisal of the democratization of Brazilian political culture, a process that had only begun during the transition of the first civilian government.

As a consequence of being a transitional and open-ended process, the democratization of political culture is bound to be unfinished and full of contradictions, in the actions and orientations of most social actors. For instance, the emergence of the 'Periphery' was notable not only for its radical innovations but also for its inheritances from the past: its often sectarian orientations; its reluctance to negotiate politically; its insistence on (transcendental/non-historical) natural rights; its instrumental perspective on politics; its reliance on religion and the influence of the clergy. All this is part of Brazilian popular culture, and has previously supported the traditional legitimation of authoritarian and oligarchic rule. These features continued to exist (however weakened and contradictorily) in the cultural traditions and motivations of the 'Periphery'.

Nevertheless, Habermas (1984-7) noted that concepts and categories should not be used as stereotypes but rather as 'real abstractions' open to the deliberation and ambiguity of social actors. If social actors are ambiguous, and they must decide on their future, one may ask which of the three faces of culture that we have identified will be more likely to prevail in the long run: the traditional, the representative or the participant? One may only observe, at this time, that the three currents or sectors of the neighborhood groups in Florianópolis were not so impervious or insulated as the above analysis might perhaps suggest. In fact, all three sectors jointly shared individuals, neighborhoods, practical aims, and the enormous problems of the city they lived in. This is why we were able to propose initially that they have converged in a parallel public sphere which they were building together (or, more often, in competitition or conflict with each other).

It would thus be hard to predict whether one of the neighborhood sectors would be able to win over, or to absorb, the other two. Probably this would not happen at all - at least not while these groups maintained their current positions. (This uncertainty seems to be a central feature of newborn democracies, in a transition that is an open-ended process toward eventual political institutionalization.) Nevertheless, one could see a process of democratic learning in all three neighbourhood currents - where, for instance, the different emphases on participation and representation (respectively sponsored by the 'Periphery' and *UFECO*) seemed to complement each other, and to jointly influence the conservative sectors, in a gradual dissolution of the cultural basis of traditional legitimation.

It is also certain that these progressive cultural trends toward building a democratic future only became visible in Florianópolis during the first civilian government. Before this, subjection and dependency prevailed everywhere, characterized by a false sense of security, and by the manipulation and secrecy of authoritarian oligarchic rule (with the exception of a few rebellious pioneers; Cf. Matos Machado, 1990). A more recent historical survey of civil associations in Florianópolis, part of a nationwide comparative research project on the subject (see Scherer-Warren et al, 1998) confirmed the findings of this chapter:

> The institutionalization of civil associations responded to constitutional democratic institutionalization...[The numbers of] new social movements and neighborhood associations increased [faster than other groups], showing a trend of civil associations to move toward social and political concerns and to the defense of new citizenship rights. *(Scherer-Warren, 1999: 125-7)*

Thus we can now recognize that the cultural changes we have analyzed above in the neighborhood groups really influenced the local processes of democratization. These changes have emerged as the effort to build a new and better world, and this struggle for democratic institutionalization has still a long way to go in Latin America.

REFERENCES

Almond, G., Verba, S. (Eds.) 1980. **The Civic Culture Revisited**. Boston: Little Brown & Co.

Archer, R. P. 1990. "The Transition from Traditional to Broker Clientelism in Colombia: Political Stability and Social Unrest", **Kellogg Institute Working Paper**, n.140, 36ps.

Boschi, R. 1987. **A Arte da Associação, Política de Base e Democracia no Brasil**. São Paulo: IUPERJ/Vértice.

Cardoso, R.C.L. 1988. "Os Movimentos Populares no Contexto da Consolidação da Democracia", in: REIS, Fábio W. e O'Donnell, Guilhermo (orgs.), **A Democracia no Brasil: Dilemas e Perspectivas**, São Paulo: Vértice.

Castro, M. H.G. 1988. "Governo Local, Processo Político e Equipamentos Sociais: um Balanço Bibliográfico", **Revista Brasileira de Informação Bibliográfica em Ciências Sociais - BIB**, 25:56-62.

Flisfish, Á. 1987. **La Política como compromiso democrático**. Santiago: FLACSO.

Garretón, M.A. 1990. "Las Condiciones sociopolíticas de la inauguración democrática en Chile", **Kellogg Institute Working Paper**, n.142, 20pp.

_____. 1992. **Transformación Cultural**. Chile: FLACSO.

Habermas, J. 1984/7. **Theory of Communicative Action**. 2 Vols., Boston: Beacon.

_____. 1990. **Moral Consciousness and Comunicative Action** Op.Cit.

_____. 1997. **Between Facts and Norms. Contributions to a Discourse Theory of Law and Democracy**, Cambridge, MA: MIT Press.

Heller, A. & Feher, F. 1985.. **Anatomia de la Izquierda Occidental**. Barcelona: Península.

Jacobi, P. 1989. **Movimentos Sociais e Políticas Públicas**. São Paulo: Cortez.

Jobert, B. 1983. "Clientelisme, Patronage et Participation Populaire". Genebra: UNRISD.

Lechner, N. 1988. **Los Patios interiores de la democracia. Subjetividad y política**. Santiago: FLACSO.

Lüchmann, L. 1990. **Cotidiano e Democracia na Organização da UFECO**. *M.A. Thesis*, Programa de Pós-Graduação em Sociologia Política, Universidade Federal de Santa Catarina.

Mainwaring, S. 1990. "Brazilian Party Underdevelopment in Comparative Perspective", **Kellogg Working Papers**, 134.

Matos Machado, S. 1989. **O Processo de Formalização Jurídico-Institucional dos Conselhos Comunitários em Florianópolis (1977-1983): Um Caso de Oposição Sistemática**. M.A. Thesis, Programa de Pós-Graduação em Sociologia Política, Universidade Federal de Santa Catarina.

Morse, R. 1988. **O Espelho de Próspero**. São Paulo: Cia. das Letras.

Nunes, E. 1990. "La Doble Dimension de la Democracia y el Gobierno de las Ciudades de Tamaño Médio en Brasil". São Paulo: CEDEC.

O'Donnell, G. 1987. "Hiatos, Impasses e Continuidade", in: Reis, Fábio W. e O'Donnell, Guillermo (Eds.), Op.Cit.

Pazmiño, G. W. 1990. "An Approach to Patron-Client Relationships from an Anthropological Point of View", **ISA Congress**, Madrid.

Rawls, J. 1993. **Political Liberalism**. New York: Columbia University Pres.

Reis, E. P. 1989. "Política e Políticas Públicas na Transição Democrática". **Revista Brasileira de Ciências Sociais**, 9 (3).

Scherer-Warren, I.; Avritzer, L.; Costa, S.; and Jacobi, P. 1999. "O Novo Associativismo Brasileiro", São Paulo:**ANPOCS**.

_____. 1999. "Associativismo Civil em Florianópolis: Evolução e Tendências", **Revista de Ciências Humanas**, 26: 115-134.

Silva, C.P. 1999. **Participação Popular e Cultura Política. As Emendas Populares na Assembléia Constituinte de 1989 em Santa Catarina**, Florianópolis: EDUFSC.

Tucker, D.F.B. 1980. **Marxism and Individualism**. Oxford: Basil Blakwell.

ENDNOTES

[1] Santa Catarina is one of Brazil's smallest states. It is located in the country's southern region. It is a convenient setting for the study of the political-cultural transition to democracy, because its political and economic characteristics lie between the modernity of Brazil's southeast region and the relative backwardness of the north-northeast.

[2] The fieldwork for this study was conducted in cooperation with students of the Graduate Program in Political Sociology of the **Universidade Federal de Santa Catarina**, Brazil. Simone Matos Machado, Kathia Muller, Ligia Luchmann and Francisco Canella wrote their M.A. theses on specific topics related to this project.

[3] Matos Machado (1990) covers this initial period.

[4] Interview with leader and founder of the 'Periphery', December 1988.

[5] Interview with the chairperson of the first **UFECO** Board, December 1988.

[6] Same as (5). See also Luchmann (1991).

[7] See Archer (1990) on 'broker clientelism'.

[8] Interview with the chairperson of the second **UFECO** Board, November, 1989.

[9] Interview with **UFECO** leader, March 1990.

[10] Interview with 'Periphery' leader, December 1989.

[11] See also Habermas (1997) for an expansion of his previous work on the public sphere.

[12] Same as (8).

[13] Same as (10).

[14] The interviews with conservative leaders were conducted in late 1988 and early 1989, when they controlled **UFECO's** Board.

[15] Traditional clientelism is also to some extent a negotiated relationship (see Pazmiño, 1990). However, it tends to be a onesided dependency, as a dyadic, personalized relationship. The case of 'broker clientelism' (Archer, 1990) is somewhat more visible and competitive. As such, it may be open to public questioning and accountability through party competition. See also Nunes (1990) on the effects of political transition on municipal administrations.

[16] For Habermas (1989), post-conventional morality discusses the principles or foundations of political legitimacy, and not only the political procedures, as in conventional morality.

[17] However, the centralized and unaccountable character of city administration, linked to a government party majority in the City Council, may favor the persistence of dyadic personalized negotiations outside public control (Nunes, 1990).

[18] Cf. Muller (1992).

Chapter 5

SOCIAL ACTORS AND THE LEARNING OF DEMOCRACY IN LATIN AMERICA[*]

The main argument of this chapter is very simple, almost commonplace: during the nineteen eighties and nineties Latin American countries experienced a dual process of crisis and democratization. On one hand, there was the crisis of the Latin American insertion into the world economy and the gradual economic rearticulation at the national and regional levels. On the other hand, there was a transition to and a permanence of political democracy in several countries. This dual process has not yet ended or been "consolidated" in many countries of the region. The chapter also presents the argument that social and political actors underwent strategic, identity and political-cultural changes during this period. These changes were different from location to location, but were always related to the processes of crisis and democratization that were taking place throughout the continent. It is impossible within this space to dwell on national characteristics — in spite of the fact that national peculiarities are most important — and this general survey indicates specific studies and research reports which support and develop the argument.

The first part of the chapter focuses on strategic changes, mainly among so-called "old" social actors. The second part considers the changes in identity, and their relationship with strategic changes, mainly among the "new" social actors. The third part introduces the issue of change in political culture among social actors. This cultural dimension of social action raised the main challenge faced by researchers and activists alike, during the attempts at democratic institutionalization in the 1990s.

A final preliminary remark is also in order: this overview lacks an explicit theoretical underpinning because it relies on the main arguments presented in the rest of the book. However, theoretical remarks are occasionally raised in the text, and some are more elaborated within the endnotes. This procedure is part of an intention to stimulate further

[*] This chapter was based on a report requested by the *Asociación Latinoamericana de Sociologia (ALAS)*. I thank the critical comments of Luis Gomez, Arturo Escobar, Elisa Reis, Ary Minella and Luzinete Simões.

historical research and debate around the topics and arguments of this survey — instead of focusing the debate on theoretical grounds.

STRATEGIC ACTION: CRISIS AND TRANSITION TO DEMOCRACY

The specific consequences of the neoliberal adjustment policies implemented by Latin American governments during the 1980s and 1990s have not yet been fully appraised. Nevertheless, it seems that these policies aggravated certain negative trends, inherited from what has been rightly named in Latin America as "the lost decade"[1]. The 1990 ECLA report, meaningfully titled "Productive Change with Equity", indicated, for instance, a remarkable increase in poverty. In 1980 there were 112 million people living below the poverty line or 35% of Caribbean and Latin American homes. In 1986, when the results of neoliberal policies started to be felt in large countries, such as Argentina, Mexico and Chile, there were already 164 million living in poverty throughout Latin America. In 1990, 183 million or 41% of Caribbean and Latin American households were poor. Other demographic and statistical data for the 1990s— e.g. on health, education, unemployment, mortality, etc. — also indicate the negative consequences of economic adjustment policies on the living conditions of the people. The data illustrate the aggravating effects of the curtailment of public services and policies as a result of the economic crisis and stagnation in most Latin American countries[2].

Crime and violence were some of the most acute symptoms of frustration, uncertainty and despair among the poor (e.g. Machado, 1991; Scheper-Hughes, 1992; Holston and Caldeira, 1998). Doris Cooper (1992) for instance documented the increase in criminality in Chile, in terms that could also apply to other Latin American countries:

> "The growth of the prison population(...)was closely related to the direct consequences of a relative economic growth with the highest social costs (...) Violence increased; and the number of armed assaults in Greater Santiago grew from 38% of all urban crimes in 1983 to 67% in 1991 (...) Unnecessary (excessive) violence, in assaults with murders and rapes, constitutes a new type of urban criminality (...) under the effects of drug abuse and a high content of frustration."
> *(Cooper, 1992:16-7)*

Other studies on violence also showed its connections with state adjustment policies in the period of transition from authoritarian rule - when there was a critical displacement of the security forces and judicial power to the context of civil government[3]. Moreover, one has to recognize the effects of the "drug war" launched by the U.S. government (as most recently highlighted by the so-called "Plan Colombia"), that places considerable pressure on the institutional life of various Latin American countries[4]. Finally, there is also a persistence of political violence in large areas of Colombia[5], and Mexico[6] - and which could eventually resurge in other countries of the region (the Zapatista rebellion for example has strong international connections, and disseminates new forms of "symbolic warfare" via the Internet).

One cannot pretend that all these diverse and acute symptoms of political and social crisis are solely the results (or are the only results) of the adoption of neoliberal policies by Caribbean and Latin American governments. But current research is showing that these economic and political changes have been accompanied by a crisis of social structures and orientations. These policies increased the visibility of previous ethnic cleavages and conflicts[7], and other problems of daily life, in the socio-cultural[8], socio-political[9], generational and family[10] spheres. Various studies even highlight the increase in some countries of racial and ethnic discrimination[11], as well as separatist, regionalist and national-chauvinist prejudices[12].

The facts above highlight a very "dark side" of the current policies of globalization in Latin America. In this light, the prevailing trends toward democracy and modernization were accompanied by new and unanticipated consequences - as well as by long-term problems left unsolved, and thus by very serious and visible threats of regression. However, it is also certain that current state and economic adjustment policies are related to some positive trends. For instance, various country specific studies[13], and studies of Latin America as a whole[14], underline the innovations and opportunities created by the new strategies for reinsertion in the world economy: e.g., programs of regional and subregional economic integration or cooperation[15]. The impacts and alternatives of economic international agreements have been frequently criticized[16]. But new challenges and opportunities have emerged in connection with these programs, (sometimes supported by the World Bank) even in rural areas of Latin America[17]. A case in point is the attempt to establish ecological projects and peasant cooperatives in some countries[18].

It is true that all policies of social and economic restructuring imply deep changes of mentality and strategic orientation, both among the elites and the popular segments of society; these changes will be considered below. They also imply the development and consolidation of public administration institutions - that various studies are emphasizing, at the national[19] and regional levels[20]. The majority of these studies point out the ambiguities and critical situations that have emerged in the political institutions. But they also show that the democratic transitions created options for new forms of state organization, and new experiments with the "logic of collective action" within society[21].

It is useful to recall that these joint impacts on social action by economic adjustment and the democratic transition had already been reported since (at least) the 1988 ALAS Congress in Montevideo[22]. Studies of this issue have multiplied during the 1990s, mainly (but not exclusively) in reference to changes of organization and orientation among socioeconomic actors. Research on the business elites, for instance, has increased and diversified, both at the national[23] and regional[24] levels. The same is true of studies on rural[25] and industrial[26] workers. Some studies of the working class have especially emphasized a growing convergence or complementarity of changes in collective action at the union and corporate level, on the one hand, and the constitution of new socio-political identities in the party system and the public sphere on the other hand[27].

Moreover, the emergence of what has been rightly named a "new left" in Latin America goes beyond the aims of class representation. This trend indicates a growing emphasis on the interclass character of (and the mass support for) the democratic institutions. It also implies an interdependency and relative autonomy between the experiences of social participation, and the new forms of institutional representation[28]. This linkage between participation and representation has spread mainly but not only among the so-called "popular sectors" — including the middle classes, urban workers and low income sectors. This also means that, alongside the "new left", a "new center" and a "new right" have also emerged in the political arena — though the two latter phenomena have been little studied in most countries. (See an exception for the case of Brazil in Mainwaring et al., 1999).

Nevertheless, the basic point, in all cases, is that a new form and content for politics has emerged in Latin America: the kind of politics which accepts the functioning of the democratic regime and a mass inter-class approach as its main characteristics - including the already noticed complementarity between social and political action[29].

The complementary relationship between social participation and political representation has strong effects on current processes of democratic institutionalization. This can be seen in studies about local politics, particularly of political administration at the municipal level. These studies usually criticize the persistent legacies of "*caziquismos*", patronage and clientelistic practices. But they also underline the opportunities opened to the participation of social actors — not only due to elections held at all levels of government (and by "checks and balances" introduced among state powers), but also due to decentralized practices created by local administrations[30]. Therefore, there is evidence of a coordination by the "logic of collective action" between social action and political representation — which helps to consolidate or at least to expand the democratic regime.

Nevertheless, these diverse approaches to the interaction between society and politics often highlight the emergence of new institutional and social problems and conflicts, seeming to threaten democratic stability instead of supporting its consolidation. It is thus necessary to recognize that the conditions prevailing in the "new democracies" of Latin America promote other dimensions of collective action — besides the capability for strategic interaction and public representation increasingly displayed by social actors since the transitions to democracy.

One may notice this fact when considering another large area of study of "old" social actors, namely that of "urban studies" on neighborhood movements and associations[31]. Lucio Kowarick (1995) evaluated the polarization among these studies in Latin America, criticizing both the Marxist structural emphasis on "urban contradictions" and the culturalist emphasis on a certain "spontaneity" among the grassroots of the "popular sectors" - considered, in both cases, as the sources of conflicts and negotiations with the government. He writes that

> "If history is not an impersonal process, the main thrust is not only to identify social actors that promote these changes, but also the types and fields of conflict that are essential to processes of social transformation. In other words: it is necessary to enquire where basic conflicts do occur, recognizing in advance that they do not relate only to the sphere of productive relations ... On the other hand, it is not enough to study our acute problems of poverty, and the socio-cultural and political inequities of our cities and societies. The reasons of social change do not derive from the magnitude of poverty, but rather from the complex production of historical experiences (that react) on it."
> *(Kowarick, 1995:13-4)*

In fact, when one considers these studies of neighborhood actors from a perspective that emphasizes a certain complementarity between strategies and identities, it is possible to suggest that, in spite of being different, these studies do not necessarily contradict each other. The literature on neighborhood actors and movements has often emphasized, during the transitions from authoritarian rule, the actors' instrumental and strategic orientations — in their struggle for access to goods and services of public and collective consumption[32]. In this sense, the "logic of collective action", with its individualist focus on "rational choice" (proposed by Olson, 1965) has been adopted at times, to interpret the struggles for access to the basic economic rights of citizenship.

On the other hand, approaches favoring spontaneity and "grassroots initiatives" ("*basismo*") revealed the importance of changes in values and orientations in order to allow construction of collective and personal identities - in spite of the fact that they often resulted in "restricted" identities (to overcome the apathy, atomization and subjection inherited from authoritarian regimes)[33]. Since the democratic transitions these emerging identities were often channeled through representative bodies for institutional negotiation - in institutions such as federations of neighborhood associations, party-related organizations and public agencies (such as municipal health, housing and education committees, etc.).

The above summary sounds very much like Weber's institutionalization of charisma. Nevertheless, even when the conflictive and radical character of these new identities was to some extent "normalized" during democratic transition, neighborhood and other consumption conflicts have often re-emerged in many places[34]. This results from the fact that there are always forms and degrees of participation which may be challenged in a democratic regime, with the continuous change of historical needs (and not only in reaction to the present restrictive policies). In fact, historical needs are not only material ones, and they may advance qualitatively, as people learn through participatory processes, and attempt to reshape their future.

Therefore, the studies of neighborhood actors also point to the importance of changes in the strategies of collective action, for the expansion of the public sphere (mainly, but not only at the local-municipal level). Moreover, these studies suggest as well that there is another important dimension that must be analyzed in collective action: the identities developed by these actors, to whom we now turn.

IDENTITIES, IDENTIFICATIONS AND SOCIAL INNOVATION

The already classic distinction between "new" and "old" social actors[35] has been gradually reformulated in recent studies, as a distinction between strategic actions and orientations, on the one hand (characteristic of more traditional and particularist trends, often prevailing among labor unions, neighborhood and party organizations, etc.); and, on the other hand, actions and orientations based on identities that are non-negotiable (because they are based on universalistic values that are characteristic of new trends and movements, such as the feminist, the ecologists, cultural and ethnical groups and minorities, etc.)[36]. Nevertheless, it would be useful to go forward in this reformulation, during the current attempts at democratic consolidation, and consider these "ideal types" as complementary dimensions of collective action - a complementation actualized in different forms and degrees by every social actor.

However, this is not to suggest that such complementarity can be worked out "automatically" in new institutions and forms of action. Neither could one pretend that this complementation may result "peacefully" from something like a "division of labor" among parties, unions and other social actors (as a casual observer could possibly attribute to the Brazilian Workers' Party — *Partido dos Trabalhadores* — and some unions and other social movements, such as the rural "Landless Movement", *MST*). In fact, such complementation (whenever it really occurs) between the identity and the strategic dimensions of collective action will probably never be "peaceful", "natural" or a necessary result of institutionalization processes - as Weber proposed [37].

Specific studies are showing that most social actors tend to combine strategic and identity actions and orientations, which may follow either particularist or universalist emphases. These actions and orientations have a high turnover, according to concrete developments and circumstances, considering the aims and sources of each action, as well as changes assumed by their interlocutors (both allies and opponents)[38]. However, the point here is **not** that "everything goes", in a voluntaristic way, but rather that actors do ponder and choose legitimate alternatives in most situations. Therefore, they may vary between identity actions and strategic actions, as they work out their search for social participation, and the expansion and development of the public sphere.

A historical example is in order here, to illustrate the importance of the combination (and displacement) between strategic and identity actions. In the late 1970s, when the transition from authoritarian rule started in Brazil, the metalworkers of São Paulo's *ABC* went on strike for better wages, and also demanded land reform in Brazil[39]. The military government pointed out that this was non-sensical, and indeed "subversive": land reform had nothing to do with the regular demands of industrial workers, and constituted only a challenge to the regime. Orthodox Marxists could certainly argue that land reform is part of the "long term" interests of the working class, for it may decrease the continuous pressure of the "reserve army of the proletariat" on wage levels. Nevertheless, the union's grassroots raised this demand in an attempt to publicize their new identity as autonomous workers, free from the restrictive labor legislation. Moreover, they wanted a new democratic regime (where workers of all kinds could be recognized as citizens, and thus represent their common interests and different identities). Therefore, the military regime seemed to be right about the strategic limitations of a union strike, and the "subversive" overtones of that event. Nevertheless, the metalworkers were then successful in their identity action for citizenship - although land reform is still being negotiated in Congress, 30 years later.

The more recent and successful example of combination between strategic and identity action is the trajectory of those social actors who were considered the "new" Latin American movements of the 1980s and 1990s: the feminist, ecological and ethnic-cultural minorities. For one thing, the vast and growing literature on gender movements shows that they have diversified[40] and gradually interacted with political parties and institutions[41]. Moreover, they have converged with other forms of identity, including ethnic, cultural and even religious[42], and have also merged with specialized structures and agencies to defend their needs and rights in the labor market, family life, trade unions, and other forms of social organization[43]. This means that Latin American feminists managed to work out flexible forms of identity and strategy - following the example of their sisters in the central Western countries. Thus, they were able to conquer public space and recognition in politics and the institutional sphere. Changes were made in the legislation and administration of their specific demands, and many other sectorial benefits were achieved that were previously unavailable to Latin American women.

Organized women thus formed one of the most active and successful sectors of the "new" movements, exactly because of their flexibility and diversity, in the use of strategic and identity actions. It is due to this capability for flexible intervention that gender movements have also achieved cultural influence and mutual exchange with other meaningful and prominent actors of Latin American culture and society. There are now so many deep changes in family life, in gender relations and in the cultural appraisal of the intellectual, scientific and artistic contributions of women, that it is almost impossible to disentangle them from the original (and continuing) feminist quest for gender equality. This was achieved in spite of the fact that the feminist movement never comprised large numbers (let alone most) of Latin American women.

Similar results have also been noticed among environmentalist actors[44], ethnic minorities[45], cultural and religious movements[46]. Appraisals are being made of their consequences, through a double evaluation of their strategic and identitary actions and orientations. This indicates that they have participated politically and have influenced the expansion of democratic institutions, on the one hand, and also culturally promoted and expanded within society their often universalistic values and aims, on the other hand[47].

However, the commemoration made above of the successes of gender movements, does not imply that the infamous Latin American "*machismo*" (male chauvinism) has been overcome. In fact, the struggles of Latin American women began long ago, and only recently have managed to achieve due public recognition. One must especially notice that these successes largely derived from the diversified character of gender movements, and the complementary flexible use of strategic and identity forms of action and orientation. Nevertheless, it is very likely that the women — as well as environmental, ethnic, ethical and cultural groups and minorities — will have to keep striving, simply in order to keep alive and progressive the affirmation of their identities and the conquest of their rights. The flexibility and diversification of their actions, both strategic and identity actions, and the convergence that the "new" actors may build among themselves, will surely help everyone of them to achieve and to maintain their successes.

These criteria will probably apply to both "new" and "old" social and political actors. What impedes, for example, a labor union from supporting gender struggles, even when the majority of its constituency is male? After all, current gender discrimination and inequality — in salaries, for instance — is a hideous employment practice that offends both the economic interests of the working class family and society's sense of justice. Similarly, one may ask: Why not build a majority in Congress that favors environmental policies, even when there are few "green" deputies, and most Congressmen are market-oriented conservatives? Such strategic advances could be possible, because they do not necessarily oppose the orientations of other social actors.

The real meaning of strategic advances such as these will mainly depend on the sustained autonomy and identity of the "new" actors - so that their universalistic values and aims do not become co-opted, neutralized or jeopardized, by conservative forces in political life, the media and the marketplace. And one should recall that these risks are always inherent in social participation and political representation, in any intervention in the public sphere.

Another useful example of changes among "new" social actors is the case of youth movements — especially in view of the scarce attention they have received, until recently, in Latin American research. Perhaps youth has been little studied as a consequence of the demise of the student movement, under the dictatorships of the 1970s. However, when one notices the important presence again of the students — for instance, in the mass demonstrations that led to the impeachment of President Collor in Brazil in 1992 — one realizes how unfortunate it is that the crucial interpretation of youth has been delayed in Latin America. With only a few exceptions, the meaning of student movements has not been systematically researched[48], neither with respect to the changes of youth culture under authoritarian regimes, nor with respect to changes since the transition to democracy[49].

An acute comparative evaluation of youth studies in Europe and Latin America was presented at the World Congress of Sociology in Madrid (Bendit, 1990). This survey emphasized some of the complex challenges faced by youth studies in Latin America - which are worth citing at length, because they are also relevant to the study of other social actors on the continent:

> "(International) **Integration**. Some of the central problems to be faced both by European and Latin American societies derive from regional and sub-regional integration — particularly those aspects related to professional training, the growth of competitive conditions in the labor market, as well as the development of new cultural identities.
> **Social disintegration**. One of the most important issues in Latin America is social disintegration and disorganization. This topic is especially acute in the big cities of Latin America, where it is mainly present within family life, in the marginalization of the young, and as a means of survival and construction of identity. Studies on this topic will surely tend to dwell on the links among these phenomena and the crises of the economy and of the populist-national state.
> **Regionalization**. There will be in the future inter-regional differentiations and national comparisons, as to the living conditions of the young within each nation.
> **Methodological pluralism**. Future studies will probably stress a combination among qualitative and quantitative research techniques, in research designs adapted to each region (...), and the development of longitudinal studies, to evaluate phenomena in their time sequence"
> *(Bendit, 1990: 15-7).*

This example of sociological evaluation of youth studies suggests the need for theoretical-methodological improvement of studies on social actors in general. This improvement should enhance our capacity to interpret phenomena within their historical setting, and the comparative use of research results at the national and regional levels. According to Bendit, there is

> A need to contextualize (theoretical and historically) concepts and approaches that are apparently similar - as a starting point for comparative work (...) on trends of development at the level of the general paradigms of social analysis, and of their impact on empirical and conceptual production, as well as on new developments in reference both to the 'object of study', and to the approaches to the theme, etc.
> *(Bendit, 1990: 17)*

The seriousness of these proposals for the study of youth is a warning about our inability to understand the renewal of society in the age groups, as well as in other areas of research on social action. But even when we update our studies in relation to youth studies in Europe, it may still be difficult to understand mass demonstrations such as those of the Brazilian students and other sectors of the urban population for the impeachment of Pres. Collor in 1992 (or similar events in Venezuela, later on). In this case, there was a convergence between strategic and identity actions where the "multichromatic" and "polyphonic" overtones of mass mobilization supported and stimulated the strategy of the opposition parties in Congress. But these critical moments of convergence between identities and strategies (moments that are often unpredictable and apparently spontaneous) also manifest a change of political culture — as another dimension of collective action, to which we now turn.

POLITICAL CULTURE, GLOBALIZATION AND DEMOCRATIC INSTITUTIONALIZATION

Comparative studies on processes of democratization in Latin America have emphasized a necessary correspondence between the possibility for democratic consolidation and the development of a civic culture[50]. This is an argument about the need and possibility for those nations to develop a political culture that is similar to that of advanced Western democracies. It is based on the understanding that the civic culture is oriented by the globalization and universalization of democratic values - through inter-subjective patterns and norms of communication, behavior and morality[51]. There would thus be a third dimension[52] of collective action: one that is coordinated in democratic regimes, with the strategic and identity dimensions of social actions and orientations.

Numerous studies have highlighted the enormous difficulties faced by the democratization of Latin American institutional and cultural life[53], though some progress has been noted in various countries since the early 1990s[54]. In any case, the central cultural problem of democratic consolidation and stability is now seen as a worldwide problem, relevant even to the deepening and expansion of democracy in the advanced Western countries[55]. This fact helps to overcome a certain self-depreciation among Latin Americans, who, following the classic functionalist studies on political culture begun in the early Cold War period, considered the countries south of the Rio Grande to be incapable of constructing and sustaining a civic culture.

The main importance of the civic culture for the study of collective action lies in its emphasis on social plurality and initiative, both within the life-world of social groups and organizations, and in their manifestations in the public sphere. For instance, in relation to the right of difference, as a norm to be preserved and cultivated: notice the civic initiatives of the citizens of central Western democracies, in actions of civil disobedience and others, for civil rights, gender equality, peace movements, and ecological demonstrations. Even when these actions also contain strategic and identity components, they manifest a sense of radical public tolerance among demonstrators and opponents alike, which renders possible the management of conflicts and the deepening of democratic institutional life. Social actors and movements that emerged in Latin America in the 1980s and 1990s have also contributed to the cultural transformation of the public domain.

Studies on the "new political culture" have shown the expansion of the civic culture among the youth of North America and Western Europe into new types of "post-materialist" actions and orientations[56]. These research projects are currently spreading to other continents, including Latin America. They interpret the relationship between changes in the political culture and "new" social movements, especially the youth and minority groups. According to Clark and Inglehart (1990) it seems that this "new political culture"

> "(1) redefines the classic Left-Right continuum in a way that (2) distinguishes fiscal from social issues, (3) stresses social issues, (4) emphasizes market and social individualism, (5) reassesses the welfare state, (6) focuses political debate on issues more than party loyalty, and (7) is supported by younger, more educated, affluent individuals and societies."
> *(Clark and Inglehart, 1990: 1)*

These findings need (and have received) further historical and theoretical questioning and explanation. The point, however, is that these changes seem to emerge among influential and growing sectors of the population (that are similar to those who have participated in the "new" social movements of the 1970s and 1980s). The electoral orientations and preferences of these sectors are already changing the party programs of municipal administrations in many cities of the United States and Western Europe, in the sense of "social liberalization" (support to minorities, the working women, the young, the elderly, etc.). They also support "fiscal liberalism" in a trend toward the decentralized and participatory administration of local social policies (Clark and Inglehart, 1990:15).

It is not yet possible to relate here these studies of the "new political culture" to the changes noted above in the new types of strategic and identity actions in Latin America. This issue still has not been systematically researched, and many studies should be made in the near future adopting this approach (especially on crucial actors, such as the "new" movements, youth, political leadership at the local level and others).

Nevertheless, general quantitative studies on political culture are being carried out in various countries, even in comparative terms at the regional level. Their results help in the appraisal of electoral trends, as well as in the evaluation of changes in values and orientations for social action[57]. It is not appropriate here to detail these results, but simply to stress their importance in the evaluation of current changes of political culture on the continent. In fact, these changes are now considered of central importance by many scholars, as a new dimension of social action in the processes of Latin American democratization[58].

For instance, Elisa Reis (1992) pointed out that

"In Latin America (...) the prevalence of state-led capitalism contributed to weakening social ties. Moreover, widespread poverty and persistent (even growing) inequality interact with a perverse culture that combines economic individualism with strongly hierarchical values. (This is) a peculiar political culture, fusing impotence and cynicism (...From this result) the high levels of private violence that openly challenge the state's monopoly, such as dramatically illustrated in Peru, Colombia or Brazil".
(Reis, 1992:15)

Various authors emphasize the importance of attaining a civic culture in processes of democratic institutionalization, but there are various evaluations about the main features of political cultures in Latin America. For instance, Garretón (1992) proposes a focus on changes in social action and political culture that differs from the above proposal (by Reis):

"The utopian principles emphasizing equality, liberty and national independence are now joined by another principle, that questions traditional forms of collective action. This is the principle of happiness and self-realization. This means that neither the suppression of exploitation or oppression, nor the desire for equality and liberty exhaust the imagination and the dreams of the people. They want to be happy, and do not believe that liberty and equality will grant happiness. This new demand is different from the former ones. It does not mean a triumph of individualism, or that the classic problems of inequality and oppression have been overcome. Rather, it is a new combination of struggles for individual self-realization and a togetherness that raises from the social groups as a whole. And it is not strange that this new principle and demand emerged within new social categories and movements - such as the gender and youth groups, and the sectors who have been most excluded from society, but were exposed to the universal images of a better world to be built."
(Garretón:1992: 8-9).

Differences in the appraisals of the current situation of Latin American political cultures result at times from the diversity of national conditions, as benchmarks for scholars to approach the continent as a whole. Chilean analysts, for instance, may be perhaps more optimistic than Brazilian scholars, as a result of deeper and longer democratic traditions in Chile. Nevertheless, their different opinions may also be related to diverse methodological approaches to the study of political culture. It is possible, for example, to criticize Garretón's emphasis on "happiness" — in the new types of movements and social action — from the standpoint of statistical mass studies of political culture. For the latter studies rely on aggregate national data that do not easily detect emerging qualitative changes. (We have seen above that this problem has been solved in European and North American studies, perhaps because in these regions "new" cultural trends have already achieved important electoral impacts.)

In any case, the convergence or coordination between qualitative and quantitative research methods might be very useful to clarify the scope and the meaning of changes in political culture. Such "methodological pluralism" could perhaps make it easier to discern why social actors engage in decision- making, elect priorities and assume identities, that are often very different and even contradictory, within diverse situations of their life. In other words: to articulate priorities in the strategic, identity and political-cultural dimensions of social action is something that remains for every actor to do. This in fact occurs in their daily life, and in electoral and social mobilizations. A methodological plurality of studies on political culture will be able to appraise the advances and setbacks of civic and cultural action — both in national aggregate data, and in qualitative studies of sectors and groups, the elites and the institutions of society.

Finally, one must recognize that the civic-cultural dimension of collective action, with an emphasis on the global insertion of Latin America, already has been discussed for some time, around the controversial topic of "post-modernity"[59]. This topic has been debated since the late 1980s, and it is not untimely — considering the problems of biased and incomplete modernization that have consistently plagued Latin America (especially now, with the current uncertainty on the alternatives for democratic consolidation). In fact, the issue of modernity has often been debated in Latin America in connection with cultural, esthetic and literary movements. This was the case of the Modernist movement in Brazil of the 1920s and 1930s, or the Latin American literary "boom" of the 1970s.

The rupture with the avant-gardes of political modernization (both the populist-developmentalist and the revolutionary one) was more delayed in Latin America than the diffusion of mass culture and the rupture with the esthetic avant-garde of modernism. There is now a new sensitivity or "climate" (called "postmodern" by the midia). It tends to promote within society the search for a "good" life, as an ideal of personal and collective realization —an ideal that far transcends and sometimes dismisses the usual forms of integration by the state and the marketplace. However, this is only a casual note, involving a research topic that has yet to be thoroughly revised, in the current array of political and cultural changes in Latin America. (See the book edited by Alvarez, Dagnino and Escobar, 1998).

In any case, the present context of Western globalization requires that effective social action be oriented by a civic culture that values the search for a "good life", both at the individual and the collective levels. That may be interpreted as the "politics of life" proposed by Giddens, or as the "cultural movements" of Tourraine, and yet as the "happy society" of others - though from diverse standpoints[60]. One could call it "happiness", "self-realization", "good life" or whatever... The point is, however, that it is neither simply "subjective" nor individualistic, but part of the democratic orientations and institutions of a fully developed civic culture — which is desired (and already being constructed) in Latin America and elsewhere.

In conclusion, one must recognize that the strategic, identity and civic-cultural changes of social action in Latin America have stimulated the studies in the field to a growing consensus (though many disagreements continue, and should also be stimulated) about the linkages among these diverse dimensions of social action, on the one hand, and the consolidation of new democratic regimes and political cultures, on the other. This also creates a need for an urgent revision and updating of theories and paradigms of action concerning democratic cultures and institutions — a review that has yet to be conducted. This dual conclusion also applies to studies of social action outside Latin America, and this finally indicates that we must face our tasks ahead in cooperation with social scientists from around the world, during these current times of globalization of science and society.

REFERENCES

Note - Texts cited as LASA, IIS and ISA were presented, respectively, in the Congresses of the **Latin American Studies Association,** the **International Institute of Sociology,** and the **International Sociological Association.** Texts cited as ALAS and ANPOCS were presented, respectively, in the congresses of the **Asociación Latinoamericana de Sociologia,** and the **Associação Nacional de Pósgraduação em Ciências Sociais** (Brazil).

Abrucio, F.L. and Couto, C.G. 1996. "A Redefinição do Papel do Estado no Âmbito Local", *São Paulo em Perspectiva*, 10(3), Jul./Sept.

Albornoz, O. 1992. **La Educación y la Crisis de la Democracia Social: del Populismo al Neoliberalismo.** Caracas:Tropykos.

Alvarez, S., Dagnino, E., and Escobar, A. 1998. **The Cultures of Politics and the Politics of Culture. Re-visioning Social Movements in Latin America.** Boulder, Westview Press.

Anchard, D. *et al.* 1994. **Las Élites Argentinas y Brasileñas Frente al MERCOSUR,** Buenos Aires: BID/INTAL.

Andrade, R.C. (Ed.) 1998. **Processo de Governo no Município e no Estado. Uma Análise a Partir de São Paulo,** São Paulo: EDUSP.

Arditi, B. 1992. "La Intervención Social ante las Transformaciones de la Política", Asturias: **Encuentros Internacionales de Juventud.**

Avritzer, L. 1995. **A Moralidade da Democracia,** São Paulo: Perspectiva.

Azevedo, S. y Prates, A.A. 1991. "Cidade: Planejamento, Pobreza Urbana e Participação Partidária", *Ciências Sociais Hoje*, ANPOCS/Vértice, São Paulo.

Baierle, S.G. 1998. "The Explosion of Experience: The Emergence of a New Ethical-Political Principle in Popular Movements in Porto Alegre", in Alvarez *et al.*, O.Cit.

Baño, R. and Faletto, E. 1992. "El Apoliticismo: El Factor Generacional", **Documentos de Trabajo,** 25, Santiago:FLACSO.

Bauman, Z. 1990. "Philosophical Affinities of Post-Modern Sociology". *The Sociological Rewiew*, 38(3):411-444.

Bebbington, A. and Thiele, G. 1993. **Non-Governmental Organizations and the State in Latin America: Rethinking Roles in Sustainable Agricultures**, London: Routledge.

Bendit, R. 1990. "Tendencias Convergentes de la Investigación sobre Juventud en América Latina, España y Otros Países Europeos". ISA (German Youth Institute.).

Bergquist, C.W.; Penaranda, R.; and Sánchez, G. 2001. **Violence in Colomboia, 1990-2000: Waging War and Negotiating Peace**, Wilmington, DE: Scholarly Resources Inc.

Bieber, J. 1997. "Race, Resistance, and Regionalism: Perspectives from Brazil and Spanish America", *Latin American Research Review*, 32(3): 152-168.

Birnbaum, P. and Leca, J. (Eds.) 1990. **Individualism. Theories and Methods**, Oxford: Clarendon Press.

Boschi, R. 1987. **A Arte da Associação: Política de Base e Democracia no Brasil**. Vértice, São Paulo.

Brown, P. 1998. "Cultural Resistance and Rebellion in Southern Mexico", *Latin American Research Review*, 33(3): 217-229.

Caldwell, K.L. 2000. "Racialized Boundaries: Women's Studies and the Question of 'Difference' in Brazil", **LASA** (California State University).

Calvert, S. and Calvert, P. 1990. **Argentina: Political Culture and Instability.**, Philadelphia, PA: University of Pittsburgh Press.

Cardoso, F.H. et al., 1991. **Eigth Essays on the crisis of Development in Latin América**. CEDLA, Amsterdam.

Casar, M.A. 1992. "Business and Government during times of Conciliation: New Actors, Alliances and Rules of the Game". **LASA** (CIDE, México).

Castillo, H.; Zermeño, S.; Ziccardi, A. 1988. **Juventud Popular y Bandas en la Ciudad de México.**, México:UNAM.

Carr, B. 1997. "'From the Mountains of the Southeast'. A Review of Recent Writings on the Zapatistas of Chiapas", *Journal of Iberian and Latin American Studies*, 3(2).

Catterberg, E. 1991. **Argentina Confronts Politics. Political Culture and Public Opinion in the Transition**, Boulder, CO: Lynne Rienner

Caudillo F., G.A. 1991. "Contenido Étnico de la Violencia Política en Peru". **ALAS** (CELA, UNAM, México).

Chalmers, D. *et al.* (Eds.) 1997. **The New Politics of Inequality in Latin America: Rethinking Participation and Representation**, New York: Oxford University Press.

Clark, T.N. y Inglehard, R. 1990. "The New Political Culture", **ISA** (Universities of Chicago and Michigan).

Cohen, J. 1985. "Strategy or Identity: New Theoretical Paradigms and Contemporary Social Movements", *Social Research*, 52(3):663-716.

Cohn, A. 1995. "NGOs, Social Movements, and the Privatization of Health Care: Experiences of São Paulo", in Reilly, C.A. (Ed.), **New Paths to Democratic Development in Latin America: The Rise of NGO-Municipal Collaboration**, Boulder, CO: Lynne Rienner Publishers.

Conroy, A. et al. 1992. "Political Culture and Democracy in Central América". **LASA** (University of Pittsburgh).

Cooper, D. 1992. "Delincuencia y Violencia", **Congreso Chileno de Sociología.** (Universidad de Chile).

Córdova, A.; Leal, G.; Martinez, C. 1990. **El Ingreso y el Daño. Políticas de la Salud en los Ochenta.** Ed. UAM-X. México.

D'Incao, C. 1992. "A Reforma Agrária no Cotidiano dos Trabalhadores", *Revista de Ciências Humanas*, 8 (12): 45-70.

Dale, P. and Marsall, J. 1991. **Cocaine Politics.** Berkeley, UCLA Press.

Davis, C. and Speer, J. 1991. "The Psychological Basis of Regime Support among Urban Workers in Venezuela and Mexico", *Comparative Political Studies*, 24(3): 319-343.

Deuseen, T. 1992. "Rebellion in the Guatemalan Highlands: a Comparative Look at Indian Resistance". **LASA** (Ann Arbor:University of Michigan).

Diaz, L.M. 1995. "Globalization and the Transnationalization Processes: New Migratory Trends Between Colombia and Venezuela", IIS (Bogotá).

Diniz, E. and Boschi, R. 1997."Estabilização e Reformas Econômicas no Brasil: Visão das Elites Empresariais e Sindicais", *Teoria e Sociedade*, 1, UFMG.

Drogus, C. 1992. "Religion and the Politics of Gender: a Comparative Perspective". **LASA** (Hamilton College).

Echegaray, F. 1994. "Working-Class Atittudes towards Democracy in Brazil", **LASA** (Universidade Federal de Santa Catarina, Brazil).

_____ and Elordi, C. 1994. "Democracy in Latin America: In Search of 'Regularisation'", *The Public Perspective*, March/April: 22-33.

Eckstein, S. (Ed.) 1989. **Power and Popular Protest. Latin American Social Movements.** Berkeley, UCLA Press.

Ellner, S. 1999. "Obstacles to the Consolidation of the Venezuelan Neighborhood Movement: National and Local Cleavages", *Journal of Latin American Studies*, 31(1): 75-97.

Escobar, A. y Alvarez, S. (Eds.) 1992. **The Making of Social Movements in Latin America. Identity, Strategy an Democracy.** Boulder, CO:Westview Press.

Feiteiro C., R.M. 1991. "Formas de Gestão Política no Movimento Estudantil Brasileiro". **ALAS** (UNESP, Brasil).

Feliz, R. 1992. "Price Controls: Credibility Issues". **LASA** (CIDE, México).

Frank, V. 1992. "Attitudes to Democracy among Chilean Labor Leaders". **LASA** (Univ. of Notre Dame, Indiana).

Fraser, N. 1998. "La Justícia Social en la Era de las 'Políticas de Identidad': Redistribución, Reconocimiento y Participación", *Apuntes de Investigación del CECYP*, 2(2/3): 17-36.

Friedman, J. 1989. "The Latin American **Barrio** Movement as a Social Movement: Contribution to the Debate". *International Journal of Urban and Regional Research*, 13(3):501-510.

Gaitan P. 1988. "Política y Elección Popular de Alcaldes en Colombia: los Desafios de la Democracia Local", **ALAS** (Bogotá).

Gallardo, M.E. 1992. "Institutions and Elites in Central American integration". **LASA** (FLACSO, Costa Rica).

Garcia D. 1988. "Democracia y Ajuste Estructural. El impacto de las Políticas de Estabilización sobre las Lógicas de la Acción Colectiva". **ALAS** (Univ. de la República, Uruguay).

Garretón, M.A. 1992. "Transformación Cultural". **Documento de Trabajo, 25,** FLACSO, Chile.

Gibbins, J.R. (Ed.) 1989. **Contemporary Political Culture. Politics in a Postmodern Age,** London: Sage.

Giddens, A. 1990. **Consequences of Modernity,** Stanford, CL: Stanford Univesity Press.

Glazier, S.D. 1995. "Latin American Perspectives on Religion and Politics", *Latin American Research Review,* 30(1): 247-255.

Gonzales G. M. 1992. "Redes invisibles en la ciudad de Montevideo: las comisiones vecinales"(CIESU, Uruguay).

González, L.E. 1992. **Political Structures and Democracy in Uruguay,** Notre Dame, IN: Notre Dame UniversityPress.

Gorlier, J.C. and Toer, M. 1993. "O Movimento Estudantil na Transição à Democracia: Estudo de uma Agrupação da Universidade de Buenos Aires*". Revista de Ciências Humanas,* 8 (13).

Grillo, O. 1988. "La Transición Democrática a Nivel Local: el Caso de la Ciudad de Buenos Aires". **ALAS** (UBA).

Habermas, J. 1984/7. **Theory of Communicative Action.** 2 Vols, Boston: Beacon Press.

Hargreaves, C. 1992. **Snowfields. The War on Cocaine in the Andes.** New York, Holmes & Meier.

Healy, K. 1992. "Comparisons of Anti Indigenous Political and Economic Elites in Bolivia and Ecuador". **LASA** (Inter-American Foundation)

Herculano S. 1990. "Do Desenvolvimento (In)Suportável à Sociedade Feliz", in Herculano, S. *et al.,* **Ecología, Ciência e Política,** Rio de Janeiro: Editora Revan.

Hewitt, E.W. 1990. **Base Christian Communities and Social Change in Brazil.** Nebraska: University of Nebraska Press.

Hindess, B. 1991. "Rationality and Modern Society", *Sociological Theory,* 9(2):216-227.

Hochstettler, K. 1992. "Think Nationally, Act Nationally: the Environmental Movement in Brazil and Venezuela". **LASA** (University of Minnesota).

Holston, J. and Caldeira, T. 1998. "Democracy, Law, and Violence: Disjunctions of Brazilian Citizenship", in Aguero, F. and Stark, J. (Eds.), **Fault Lines of Democracy in Post-Transition Latin America,** Coral Gables, Fla.: North/South Center.

Inglehart, R.; Nevite, N.; and Bazánez. 1994. **Convergéncia en Norteamérica: Comércio, Política y Cultura,** México: Siglo XXI.

_____, 1997. **Modernization and Postmodernization. Cultural, Economic and Political Change in 43 Societies,** New Jersey: Princeton University Press.

Jaquette, J.S. (Ed.) 1989. **The Women's Movement in Latin América.** Boston, Unwin Hyman.

Jauberth, C. et al. 1992. **The Difficult Triangle: Mexico, Central América and the United States.** Boulder, CO:Westview Press.

Jelin, E. 1990. "Citizenship and Identity", in Jelin, E. (Ed.), **Women and Social Change in Latin América**. New York, Verso.

Kearney, M. and Varese, S. 1995. "Latin America's Indigenous Peoples: Changing Identities and Forms of Resistance", in Halebsky, S. and Harris, R.L. (Eds.), **Capital, Power and Inequality in Latin America,** Boulder, CO: Westview Press.

Kelsey, S. and Levitsky, S. 1994. "Captivating Alliances: Unions, Labor-Backed Parties and the Politics of Economic Liberalization in Argentina and Mexico", LASA.

Kowarick, L. 2000. **Estudos Urbanos**, São Paulo: Editora Trinta e Quatro.

Krischke, P. and Gorlier, J.C. 1992. "Atores Sociais no Cone Sul: da Transição ao Neoliberalismo", **Revista de Ciências Humanas**, 8(11): 9-16.

_____ (Ed.) 2000. **Ecologia, Juventude, e Cultura Política**, Florianópolis: EDUFSC.

Lamounier, B. and Souza, A. 1991. "Democracia e Reforma Institucional: Uma Cultura Política em Mudança", **Dados.Revista de Ciências Sociais**, 34(3): 311-348.

Laurell, A.C. 2000. "Structural Adjustments and the Social Production of Representations and Identity by Indigenous People's Organizations of Latin America", **International Sociology,** 15 (2): 306-325.

Ledesma, M.L. 1992. **Los Empresarios y el Cambio Político**. UNAM, México.

Leite, M. 1992. "O Trabalhador e a Máquina na Indústria Metalmecânica". **Revista de Ciências Humanas**,8 (12): 7-44.

Long, N. 1990. "From Paradigm Lost to Paradigm Regained? The Case for an Actor-oriented Sociology of Development". **European Review of Latin American and Caribean Studies**, 49:3-24.

Lovell, P. 1992. "Race, Class an Gender in Brazil". **LASA** (University of Pittsburgh, Philadephia).

Lowy, M. 1990. "Modernité et Critique de la Modernité dans la Théologie de la Libération". **Archives des Sciences Sociales des Religions**, 71:7-223.

Machado, L.A. 1991. "Violência Urbana: Representação de Uma Ordem Social". ANPOCS, Caxambú.

Machin G., H.B. 1988. "Ideología y Subjetividad Social". **ALAS** (Univ. de la República, Uruguay).

Mainwaring, S. and Viola, E. 1984. "New Social Movements, Political Culture, and Democracy: Brazil and Argentina in the 1980s", **Telos**, 61, Fall: 17-52.

_____. 1992. "Interests, Ideas, and Choices of Political Institutions: Brazil in Comparative Perspective". LASA (Notre Dame).

_____ and Scully, T. 1995. **Building Democratic Institutions: Party Systems in Latin America**, Stanford, CA: Stanford University Press.

_____, Meneguello, R. and Power, T. 1999. "Conservative Parties, Democracy, and Económic Reform in Brazil", **Kellogg Institute Working Paper**, 264.

Maira, L. y Vicario, G. 1991. **Perspectivas de la Izquierda Latinoamericana**, Santiago: Fondo de Cultura Económica.

Mato, D. 1997. "On Global and Local Agendas and the Social Making of Transnational Identities and Related Agendas in Latin America", **Identities: Global Studies in Culture and Power**, 4(2): 167-212.

Mello, M.A. 1992. "State Retreat and the Restructuring of Patterns of Interest Intermediation: the Case of Brazilian Social Policy". **LASA** (MIT/UNICAMP).

Méndez, J., O'Donnell, G., and Pinheiro, P.S. (Eds.) 1998. **The (Un)Rule of Law and the Underpriviledged in Latin America**, Notre Dame, IN: Notre Dame University Press.

Merlinsky, M.G. 2000. "Desocupación y Crisis en las Imágenes de Género", **LASA** (Universidad de Buenos Aires).

Moisés, J.A. 1992. "Democratization and Mass Political Culture in Brazil". **LASA** (Universidade de São Paulo, Brasil).

_____. 1995. **Os Brasileiros e a Democracia. Bases Sociais da Legitimidade Democrática no Brasil**, São Paulo: Ática.

Moreno, J.A. 1992. "La Cultura Política de la Democracia: el Caso Dominicano". **LASA** (University of Pittsburgh).

Moreira, C. 2000. "La Izquierda en Uruguay y Brasil: Cultura Política y Desarrollo Político-Partidário", in Mallo, S. and Moreira, C., **La Larga Espera: Itinerarios de la Izquierda en Argentina, Brasil y Uruguay**, Montevideo: Editorial Banda Oriental.

Murillo, G. 1992. "Reforma del Estado en el Ámbito de la Democratización Política y de la Liberalización Económica en Colombia y Venezuela". **LASA** (Univ. de los Andes, Colombia).

Navarro, M. 1992. "The Gendered Politics of Populism". **LASA** (Dartmouth College).

Nelson, P. 1996. "Internationalizing Economic and Environment Policy: Transnational NGO Networks and the World Bank's Expanding Influence", **Millenium: Journal of International Studies**, 25(3): 605-633.

Nigh, R. 1992. "Organic Coffee Production Cooperatives: A Socially and Ecologically Appropriate Alternative for Central América". **LASA** (Centro de Ecología, México).

Offe, C. 1985. "New Social Movements: Challenging the Boundaries of Institutional Politics", **Social Research**, 52(4):817-868.

Olson, M. 1956. **The Logic of Collective Action**, Cambridge, MA: Harvard University Press.

Oviedo, J. 1992. "Postmodernism and Democracy in Central América". **LASA** (City Univ. of N. York).

Paiva A.R. 1992. "The Gendering of Technological Change". **LASA**, (IUPERJ, Brasil).

Palermo, V. 1999. "Interpretações sobre os Processos Políticos Latino-americanos. Brasil e Argentina em Perspectiva Comparada", **Revista de Ciências Humanas**, 26: 149-179.

Pateman, C. 1989. **The Disorder of Women**. Stanford,CA: Stanford University Press.

Paul, S. and Israel, A. (Eds.) 1991. **Nongovernmental Organizations and the World Bank: Cooperation for Development**, Washington, DC: World Bank.

Pearce, J. 1997. "Between Co-option and Irrelevance? Latin American NGOs in the 1990s", in Hulme, D. and Edwards, M. (Eds.), **NGOs, States and Donors: Too Close for Confort?**, New York: St. Martin's Press.

Pelupessy, W. (Ed.) 1990. **Perspectives on the Agro-Export Economy in Central América**. Pittsburgh, PA: University of Pittsburgh Press.

Pereira Da Silva, A.F. 2000. "Jovens em Busca de Emprego. Perfil do Jovem Desempregado de Baixa Renda e Efeitos Sociais do Desemprego", **LASA** (Universidade Federal do Rio Grande do Sul, Brasil).

Pierucci, A.F. and Prandi, R. 1996. **A Realidade Social das Religiões no Brasil: Religião, Sociedade e Política**, São Paulo: HUCITEC.

Phillips, L. (Ed.) 1998. **The Third Wave of Modernization in Latin America: Cultural Perspectives on Neoliberalism**, Wilmington, DE: Scholarly Resources Inc.

Place, S.E. 1998. "Society and Nature: Recent Trends in the Study of Latin American Environments", *Latin American Research Review*, 33(2): 221-236.

Postero, N.G. 2000. "Bolivia's Indigena Citizen: Multiculturalism in a Neoliberal Age", **LASA** (University of California at Berkeley).

Przeworski, A. 1992. "Democracy, Markets and Liberalization East an South". **LASA** (Univ. of Chicago).

Pucci, F. 1992. "¿Internacionalización de Intereses o Conflito Privado?". **LASA** (CIESU, Uruguay).

Rabkin, R. 1994. "The Lessons of Chile: Economic Expertise, Social Learning, and the Consolidation of Market Reforms", **LASA**.

Ramires, R. 1990. "Urbanization, Housing and the (Whithdrawing) State: the Production-Reproduction Nexus", in Datta, S. (Ed.). **Third World Urbanization, Reappraisals and New Perspectives**. Uppsala: Swedish Science Press.

Ranis, P. 1991. "View From Below: Working-Class Consciousness in Argentina", *Latin American Research Review*, 26(2): 133-156.

Ramires C., J. 1991. "La Religiosidad Popular en Cuba: sus Características y Significación Social y Política. Princípios Teóricos y Metodológicos para su Análisis". ALAS (Academia de Ciencias, Cuba).

Reilly, C.A. (Ed.) 1995. **New Paths to Democratic Development in Latin America: The Rise of NGO-Municipal Collaboration**, Boulder, CO: Westview Press.

Reis, E.P. 1992. "Transitions East and South: the Theoretical Challenge". (IUPERJ, Rio de Janeiro, Brasil).

Reyes, M. 1992. "Gender Issues and Social Diversity: A Latin American Perspective". **LASA** (University of Connecticut.).

Rosenau, P.V. 1992. **Post-Modernism and the Social Sciences, Insights, Inroads and Intrusions**. Princeton Univ. Press.

Rubin, J. 1992. "Ambiguity within Popular Movements: Hierarchy, Gender, Inequality, Images of Violence and Cultural (Mis)Representation". **LASA** (Amherst College).

Ruccio, D.F. 1992. "At the Margin: a Postmodern Perspective on Economic Development in Latin América". **LASA** (University of Notre Dame, Indiana).

Sam-Colop, E. 1992. "1992: The Discourse of Concealment". **LASA** (Centro de Documentación e Investigación Maya, Guatemala).

Sapsin F., K. 1992. "Social Violence and Human Rights during Transitions from Authoritarianism: Towards a Needs Based Theory". **LASA** (University of Massachussetts).

Shaper-Hughes, N. 1992. **Death without Weeping. The Violence of Everyday Life in Brazil**, Berkeley, CA: UCLA Press.

Scherer-Warren, I. 1999. **Cidadania Sem Fronteiras**, São Paulo: HUCITEC.
_____, and Krischke, P.(Eds.) 1987. **Uma Revolução no Cotidiano? Os Novos Movimentos Sociais na América Latina**. São Paulo: Brasiliense.
Schutte, O. 1992. "Women's Rights as Human Rights: Gender and Ethics in Latin América". **LASA** (University of Florida).
Selverston, M. 1992. "Politicized Ethnicity and the Nation State in Ecuador", **LASA** (Columbia University).
Sheanan, J. 1997. "Effects of Liberalization Programs on Poverty and Inequality: Chile, México and Peru", *Latin American Research Review*, 32(3): 7-38.
Sikkink, K. and Keck, M.E. 1992. "Transnational Issue Networks in the Environment and Human Rigths". **LASA** (Universities of Minesota and Yale.).
Slater, D. 1991. "New Social Movements and Old Political Questions", *International Journal of Political Economy*, 21(1):32-65.
Smith, G. 1990. **Livelihood and Resistance: Peasants and Politics of Land in Peru**. Berkeley,CA: UCLA Press.
Soares De Lima, M.R. and Cheibub, Z.B. 1996."Instituições e Valores: As Dimensões da Democracia na Visão da Elite Brasileira", *Revista Brasileira de Ciências Sociais*, 31: 83-116.
Stallings, B. and Kaufman, R. 1989. **Debt and Democracy in Latin América**. Boulder, CO: Westview Press.
Stevenson, L.S. 1999. "La Política de Género en el Proceso de Democratización en México: Eligiendo Mujeres y Legislando Delictos Sexuales y Acciones Afirmativas", *Estudios Sociológicos*, 17 (50): 519-558.
Sylva C., P. 1991. **La Organización Rural en el Ecuador, Autogestión, Desarrollo y Movimiento Social**. Quito: CEPP/Abya-Uaala.
Tavares, M.H. and Moya, M. 1997. "A Reforma Negociada: O Congresso e a Política de Privatização", *Revista Brasileira de Ciências Sociais,* 34: 119-132.
Tirelli, J. 1999. **Reinvenções da Utopia: A Militância Política de Jovens nos Anos 90**, São Paulo: FAPESP/HAECKER.
Touraine, A. 1992. "Beyond social movements?" *Theory, Culture and Society*, 9:125-145.
Turner, F.C. and Martz, J.D. 1997. " Institutional Confidence and Democratic Consolidation in Latin America", *Studies in Comparative International Development*, 32(3): 65-84.
Valadares, L. 1990. "Family and Child Work in the Favela". in Datta S. (Ed.) **Third World Urbanization. Reappraisals and New Perspectives**. O.cit.
Vazquez, M.G.L. 2000. "El Integracionismo en América Latina: Neobolivarianismo y Neopanamericanismo", **LASA** (Universidad de Guadalajara, México).
Viola, E. *et al.* 1995. **Meio Ambiente, Desenvolvimento e Cidadania: Desafios para as Ciências Sociais**, São Paulo: Cortez.
Vigevani, T. 1997. "Mercosul e Globalização: Os Atores Sociais", São Paulo: **CEDEC**.
Ward, K. (Ed.) 1990. **Women Workers and Global Restructuring**. Ithaca, ILR Press.
Weber, M. 1964.**Economía y Sociedad**, México: Fondo de Cultura Económica.

Weiskof, R. 1992. "Income Distribution and neo-liberal policies in Latin America: a survey". **LASA** (UCLA).

Winant, H. 1992. "The Fact of Blackness in Brazil". **LASA** (Temple University.).

Wolfe, A. 1989. **Whose Kepper? Social Science and Moral Obligation,** Berkeley CA: University of California Press.

Uzín, M.M. 2000. "Elecciones Legislativas de 1997: Nuevas Estratégias deIntegración Femenina en Política?", **LASA** (Universidad Nacional de Córdoba, Argentina).

Zaluar, A. 1998. " La Peur et les Nouveaux Conflicts des Mouvements Sociaux au Brésil", *Lien Social et Politiques*, 40(80): 149-157.

Zermeño, S. 1990. **Los Hijos del Libre Comercio**. México: UNAM..

ENDNOTES

[1] Luis Maira recalled that "the real prices of a package of 27 basic products exported by Latin America, including oil, deteriorated 35% between 1980 and 1989 (...) Since 1982 we have paid 230 billion dollars to the developed countries. Were these resources to stay in Latin America, they would have induced economic growth (...) Adjustment policies imposed by the IMF followed the logics of creating capacity to repay the Latin American foreign debt at any cost. This obliged governments to drastically curtail public expenditures, notwithstanding the fact that such reduction meant a collapse of health, education and housing programs." (Maira and Vicario, 1991:46-7). See also Cardoso et al., 1991; Stallings, 1989; Sheanan, 1997; Laurell, 2000.

[2] For example, Córdova, 1990; Cohn, 1995; Albornoz, 1992.

[3] Sapsin, 1992; Méndez et al.,1998; Holston and Caldeira, 1998.

[4] Dale, 1991; Hargreaves, 1992.

[5] Bergquist et al., 2001; Diaz, 1995.

[6] Carr, 1997; Brown, 1998.

[7] Deussen, 1992; Caudillo, 1991; Bieber, 1997.

[8] Smith, 1990; Mato, 2000.

[9] Kearney and Varese, 1995.

[10] Castillo et al., 1988; Valadares, 1990.

[11] Healy, 1992; Sam-Colop, 1992; Kearney and Varese,1995.

[12] Rubin, 1992; Selverston, 1992; Bieber, 1997.

[13] Mello, 1992; Reilly, 1995.

[14] Weiskof, 1992; Feliz, 1992; Laurell, 2000.

[15] Przeworski, 1992; Pelupessy, 1990; Inglehart et al., 1994.

[16] Jauberth et al., 1992; Phillips, 1998; Vázquez, 2000.

[17] Paul and Israel (Eds.), 1991. A growing literature has emerged about the relations between the World Bank, global and local NGOs, and Latin American governments. See Nelson (1996) and Pearce (1997) for different appraisals of such relations under neoliberal policies.

[18] Sylva, 1991; D'Incao, 1993; Bebbington et al. 1993.

[19] González, 1992; Tavares, 1997; Palermo, 1999.

[20] Murillo, 1992; Laurell, 2000; Mainwaring and Scully, 1995.

[21] García, D. 1988; Krischke and Gorlier, 1992; Davis and Speers, 1992; Rabkin, 1994; Kelsey and Levitsky, 1994.

[22] For example, Machin, 1988. See also Long, 1990; Scherer-Warren, 1999.

[23] Ledesma, 1992; Diniz and Boschi, 1997; Soares and Cheibub, 1996.

[24] Gallardo, 1992; Casar, 1992; Anchard et al, 1994.

[25] Nigh, 1992; D'Incao, 1992.

[26] Pucci, 1992; Ranis, 1991; Echegaray, 1994;Vigevani, 1997.

[27] Frank, 1992; Leite, 1993; Moreira, 2000.

[28] Mainwaring, 1992; Maira, 1991; Avritzer, 1995.

[29] This is argued by Maira (1991) and debated by many analysts (e.g. Jelin, 1990; Slater, 1991; Eckstein, 1989; Chalmers, 1997).

[30] Gaitán, 1988; Grillo, 1988; Baierle, 1998; Andrade, 1998; Abrucio and Couto, 1996; Reilly, 1995.

[31] Ramires, 1990; Friedman, 1989; Kowarick, 2000.

[32] E.g. Boschi, 1987; Azevedo and Prates, 1992.

[33] See the first part of Scherer-Warren and Krischke (Eds.) 1987; Alvarez, Dagnino and Escobar (Eds.), 1998.

[34] Zaluar, 1998; Ellner, 1999; Cohn, 1995; Sheanan, 1997.

[35] Mainwaring and Viola, 1984.

[36] Escobar and Alvarez, 1992.

[37] On this distinction/complementation see the contributions of Offe, 1985; Cohen, 1985; and Fraser, 1998.

[38] A corollary of this differentiation between the strategic and identitary dimensions of collective action is the recognition of the provisional and precarious character of social identity. This dimension should be rather considered in terms of "identification", to avoid a connotation of rigidity implied by the concept in social psychology and other disciplines.

[39] Agrarian reform was not part of the list of union labor negotiations, but a central issue of the political and civil liberties demanded by the strikers. Cf. **Sindicato dos Metalúrgicos de São Bernardo do Campo**, 1980. **Carta ao Povo Brasileiro - Por que continuamos em Greve**.

[40] Jaquette, 1989; Reyes, 1992; Pateman, 1989.

[41] Navarro, 1992; Stevenson, 1999; Uzín, 2000.

[42] Schutte, 1992; Drogus, 1992; Caldwell, 2000.

[43] Paiva, 1992; Stevenson, 1999; Ward, 1990; Merlinsky, 2000.

[44] Viola et al., 1995; Herculano, 1990; Hochstettler, 1992; Place, 1998.

[45] Winant, 1992; Bieber, 1997; Kearney and Varese, 1995; Postero, 2000.

[46] A previous and more militant approach to the study of religion during the transitions to democracy in Latin America has been now replaced by more sober appraisals, emphasizing the ambiguities of religious influence on cultural life during the institutionalization of democratic regimes. E.g. Lowy, 1990 ; Hewitt, 1990; Ramirez, C. 1991; Glazier, 1995; Pieruci and Prandi, 1996.

[47] The multiple identifications of social actors in various movements - as well as the cooperation among the latter at the national and international levels - have been

thematized by various scholars in terms of "networks". Cf. Lovell, 1992; Gonzales, G., 1992; Sikking, 1992, Mato, 2000.

[48] Feiteiro (1991) reviews the evolution of the Brazilian student movement up to the 1980s. Gorlier and Toer (1993) studied a sector of the Argentinan student movement during the transition to democracy. Tirelli (1999) studied some changes of orientation among Brazilian youth, and Krischke (Ed., 2000) discussed the "post-materialist" trends of the youth in the electorate of Southern Cone countries.

[49] There are a number of studies of Latin American youth cultures, their lifestyles, music, sports, etc. However, no effort has been made so far to relate these phenomena to political democratization. This is just one example, showing that it has been often difficult to recognize, let alone to solve, theoretical and practical problems in the study of Latin American democratization.

[50] E.g. Reis, 1992; Przeworski, 1992; Touraine, 1992; Inglehart, 1997.

[51] Moisés, 1995; Turner and Martz, 1997; Avritzer, 1995. Garretón (1992) proposed a broad operational definition for the study of political culture and social action, to be applied in processes of democratic institutionalization: "We call political culture the relationship among the state, the party system and social actors, in a specific time and society (...) The style and direction of politics, usually contradictory; the ways of doing politics in a society, and the role played by politics in the life of a collectivity" (Garretón, 1992:4). There is an array of actor-oriented definitions in the literature on political culture; however, Garretón's proposal has the merit of not subsuming social actions and orientations to any "ideal type" of civic culture (and also of ackowledging that they are "usually contradictory").

[52] This would be a fourth dimension of collective action, if one accepted the distinction proposed by Habermas (1984-7) among normative-evaluative actions, other actions that are symbolically expressive, and instrumental-strategic actions - besides "communicative action" itself, that coordinates the other three forms of action through the inter-subjective orientations of the social actors. However, civic-cultural actions may be interpreted as a dimension that encompasses both the normative-evaluative aspects of collective action, and the coordinative role of "communicative action". This loose appropriation of Habermasian categories certainly requires further theoretical and methodological specifications (e.g. on the broad parallelism suggested above between "identity" and symbolic-expressive - "dramaturgic", Habermas says - forms of action).

[53] Baño and Faletto, 1992; Calvert and Calvert, 1990; Catterberg, 1991.

[54] Moisés, 1992; Moreno, J. 1992; Conroy, A. 1992; Lamounier and Souza, 1991; Echegaray and Elordi, 1994; Garretón, 1992.

[55] See Touraine, 1992; Reis, 1992; Wolfe, 1989; Gibbins, 1989.

[56] Clark and Inglehart (1990). There is also a worldwide comparative study by Inglehart (1997). For a sub-regional comparative report on NAFTA see Inglehart, Nevitte and Bazánes (1994).

[57] See for instance the "Latinobarómetro" survey reports released every year since the mid-1990s.

[58] E.g. Garretón, 1992; Lechner, 1992; Inglehart et al., 1994.

[59] A CLACSO book of 1987 (**América Latina: La Modernidad en la Encrucijada Posmoderna**) presented several contributions on this topic. Other works were

presented in ALAS, 1988. Other approaches are showing the links between post-modern orientations in social movements and the institutional expansion of democracy (e.g. Arditi, 1992). Oviedo (1992) and Ruccio (1992) underlined the revelance of post-modern approaches for Latin American social sciences. There are also different critical appraisals (e.g. Bauman, 1991; Roseneau, 1992; Gibbins [Ed.], 1989; Inglehart, 1997) about the theoretical foundations, limits and influences of post-modern approaches.

[60] Tourraine (1992) deplores a dual external influence on current studies of social movements: on the one hand the influence of "rational choice" theory (that he calls "economic"), and on the other hand, from studies based on "political philosophy". One may understand the need to stress the autonomy of sociological studies on social movements. However, no progress could be made in any social science without interdisciplinary exchanges and debate. Moreover — and perhaps more important still — such progress will always depend on a permanent revision of the theoretical foundations of the social sciences. On the other hand, various authors have already indicated, from different standpoints, that rational choice should not be confused with the ego-centered utilitarianism of neoclassical economics. (e.g., Birnbaum & Leca, 1990; Hindess, 1991). The line of studies of Latin American democratization focusing "regime analysis" (see Chapter 1 of this book) demonstrates the importance of rational choice to study the institutionalization of the "new democracies".

Chapter 6

CHURCH BASE COMMUNITIES AND
SOCIO-POLITICAL CHANGE[*]

Throughout the 1980s, Brazilian society has experienced a process of political liberalization, culminating in December 1989 with the first direct presidential election in 29 years. Cultural institutions have contributed to this process, for example the political influence of the Roman Catholic church's internal reforms, which have been debated in Brazil since the mid-1970s (e.g., Bruneau, 1974; Camargo, 1971). The Brazilian bishops were considered to be among the most politically progressive in the worldwide Roman Catholic hierarchy (e.g., Della Cava, 1986; Mainwaring, 1986). In the 1970s and 1980s, they have encouraged the formation of some 80,000 local community reflection groups, especially among workers and peasants, known as *Comunidades Eclesiais de Base (CEBs)*, or church base communities.

These christian communities were said to mobilize more than 2 million people, for each of them brings together between 15 and 25 people to debate regularly (weekly or fortnightly) the problems of their daily lives in the light of the Bible. These grassroots groups of lay people were organized through the local initiative of 'pastoral agents', that is, bishops, priests, nuns, and trained lay leaders. The expectations were that the CEBs would make the laity aware of their ethical and practical problems, supporting their initiatives for social and political solutions. The church has de-emphasized this strategy during the 1990s, in part due to the fact that the present Pope has replaced some of the most progressive bishops with others who are considered more conservative. A recent survey of 'Religious diversity in Brazil'(Pierucci and Prandi, 2000) recognized that

[*] This report was based on research projects supported by the *Fundação de Apoio à Pesquisa do Estado de São Paulo (FAPESP)*, the *Conselho Nacional de Desenvolvimento Científico e Tecnológico (CNPq)*, the Ford Foundation and the Social Sciences Research Council. The first draft of the report was written when the author was a research-fellow at the Kellogg Institute for International Studies, University of Notre Dame. Thanks are due to Maria Victoria Benevides, José Reis, Tilman Evers, Eduardo Viola and Scott Mainwaring for their critical suggestions.

The CEBs [have been]... efficient 'producers of militants', people who have efficiently influenced the formation of community leaders and leftist partisans...Although [the movement] is currently in visible decline, it still has a following of 2 per cent of the total population,that is close to two million people.
(Pierucci and Prandi, 2000: 630)

These facts pose important classical questions about the relation between religious reform and sociopolitical change. More specifically, they raise the issue of whether church reform influences - and if so, how - the process of sociopolitical democratization which is now taking place in Brazil. This is one of the reasons why the debate on the political effects of the CEBs has continued to attract the attention of social scientists and to receive the coverage of the media. The number of studies on the CEBs (e.g., Azevedo, 1986; Banck & Koonings, 1988; Hewitt, 1986; Krischke & Mainwaring, 1986; Levine, 1986; Macedo, 1986) has grown steadily during the last decades, providing a variety of data and different interpretations about their political relevance. Other general studies on religious change in Latin America have also recognized the importance of the CEBs (e.g., Mariz, 1994; Bastian, 1997; Pierucci and Prandi, 1996).

Most studies recognized the innovations brought about by the CEBs, in terms of religious values and practices and sociocultural orientations. But they also underscore the CEBs' organizational limits, both within church structures and vis-à-vis the wider constraints of the polity (e.g., Banck, 1989; Doimo, 1986; Hewitt, 1986; Ireland, 1986). Of course, the institutional analysis of the organizational limits of the CEBs is very important. However, it would be hard to ascertain whether church or political authorities could unilaterally control the actions and orientations of CEB members (or the effects of the latter upon the polity).

For example, cases of alleged CEB involvement in politics have usually received wide press coverage during and after presidential elections (1989, 1994, 1998). Lula, the candidate of the Workers' Party (*Partido dos Trabalhadores, PT*) often received considerable electoral support in some areas of the country where the party is not strongly organized. His opponents - who have won the elections - accused the progressive church of providing official electoral and organizational support for the *PT*, but were unable to present concrete evidence to back the argument. In fact, several bishops prepare leaflets to provide ethical guidance for electoral choices by church members in various parts of the country, but these are general guidelines, which seldom discriminate in favor of specific candidacies. And even when such discrimination did occur, it has been difficult to establish its empirical connections with actual electoral trends.

It has been argued elsewhere (see Chapter 2) that all grassroots popular organizations may have a crucial importance in the process of democratization, when they relate, however indirectly, to local changes in the political culture, for these changes may lead to sociopolitical participation and to cumulative democratic changes in state institutions[1]. Here we want to argue that church grassroots organizations may support the process of democratization without being necessarily linked to a party's political line or to specific ideological commitments. In short, the argument put forth here is that church reform interacts with other processes of democratization, and that cultural and social democratization is influential in the democratization of the polity but is analytically different from the latter.

This chapter will indicate, more specifically, that local and regional research on the CEBs helps to clarify in more detail the question, posed above, on the interpretations of the CEBs' political relevance. The data shows that in Brazil the plurality of political institutions and popular movements is as great as the variety of local socioeconomic and political conditions, all of which interact decisively with the educational work of the CEBs. Therefore, the relation between the CEBs and politics is not only defined by church officials, but in the light of increasing differentiation and plurality in Brazilian society, the CEBs are an integral part of this ongoing process, participating in and contributing to it.

Second, although the CEBs play a part in the transformation of the religious and secular consciousness of their members, one cannot suppose a direct linkage between religious reform and political commitment. Our findings suggest that religious reform may have different form and content from place to place - and its political consequences may depend on local conditions that the CEBs cannot control. Therefore, some of the alternatives described by the literature - for example, between the 'CEBs as transformers' and the 'CEBs as channels to broader political involvement' (Krischke & Mainwaring, 1986) - can only be appraised at the local level.

Habermas's (1975) analytical distinction between the motivational and the legitimation orders of society seems to be especially relevant to the study of these changes in cultural institutions. It is necessary to understand the motivational effects of religious reform in political participation through a theory that distinguishes analytically between the religious/ethical dimension of social identity and the latter's political aspects. This framework could be further developed from Habermas's (1984-7) theory of 'communicative action'- for example, when he studies the development of Western democratic polities through the impact of modernization on traditional 'lifeworlds'. One could say that the CEBs modernize the church, for they motivate their membership to overcome traditional submissiveness in a search for new values of participation, initiative, and mutual respect.

Some of Habermas's categories are tentatively used in the present study of the CEBs. The hypothesis is that the CEBs' religious reform is part of a motivational crisis and reorientation which eroded the legitimacy of traditional political culture and institutions in Brazil during the past few decades (Krischke, 1985) - a reorientation that could now support the democratization of the political system. The diffusion of religious reform converges with, and is mutually reinforced by, the plurality of political currents and institutions building up a competitive political arena as an end and value in itself. Communicative action provides a useful focus to evaluate these changes, for it relates the increasing pluralism of the normative order to the consolidation of democratic institutions. However, the test of these theories requires further research on several crucial changes in Brazilian society and polity, and the analysis of the CEBs' relation to politics will need many empirical studies at the regional level to overcome the present state of overgeneralization which characterizes the literature[2].

Therefore, it will not be possible to demonstrate these arguments within the limits of this chapter, but only to present some insights drawn from comparative research data on the CEBs in Brazil. The data comes from several interviews with leaders of grassroots groups related to the progressive church: in the first part of the study, among popular movements influenced by the CEBs, in the second part, among CEB leaders. Nevertheless, the *avant garde* discourse of the progressive church has to be assessed as a minority position that is not representative of the practical positions and commitments of the church as a whole, in spite of the influence of that discourse on the CEBs' educational and religious work.

The first part of the study summarizes and compares some results of two research projects in two different cities, examining the influence of the CEBs on urban neighborhood associations of low income groups. Here it will be seen that the CEBs' educational work interacts with other forms of social and political identity through strategies that include cooperation, competition, and conflict - according to the alternatives of social organization available to the popular groups. In any case, the data point to significant local changes in political culture in which the CEBs participated.

The second part of the chapter presents the results of a comparative research project contrasting some CEBs in poor outlying districts of the city of São Paulo with others in two different areas of the Brazilian countryside. The focus here is on the CEBs' internal processes of resocialization, highlighting their motivational consequences for social and political change, which are different from place to place. It is hoped that this comparative approach will provide a better undertanding of the interactions between the religious reform conducted by the CEBs and overall social and political change in Brazil.

LOCAL CULTURAL CHANGE IN NEIGHBORHOOD ASSOCIATIONS: TWO EXAMPLES OF THE CEBs' INFLUENCE

The spread of the CEBs in Brazil took place in the mid-1970s, at the same time that other forms of grass-roots organizations emerged in popular neighborhoods (low income residential areas), labor unions, and peasants' associations, in several parts of the country. This fact had several practical and theoretical consequences. One of them was that the CEBs were often seen as just another 'new social movement' opposed to the military regime. Consequently, the religious reform promoted by the CEBs was considered by many as having immediate political and ideological consequences. Of course, the church hierarchy always drew careful guidelines in its official documents about the ecclesiastical character of the CEBs. But many within the rank and file, the popular activists, as well as the military regime, tended to see the CEBs as 'subversive' ideological organizations. And in the repressive context of the 1970s, this interpretation was not farfetched: it had been shown that the church tended to perform a surrogate political role (Della Cava, 1978), in the absence of legitimate political channels.

It was only by the late 1970s that a clear distinction was drawn in the literature between (religious) community and (political) society (C. Boff, 1979). Research has later been done on the interactions among the grassroots popular movements of the 1970s (e.g., Evers, 1982; Sader, 1988; Telles, 1986), showing the specific contributions of each movement within the popular neighborhoods of São Paulo[3]. The main conclusion of these studies was that the popular neighbourhoods became, during the 1970s, a meeting place for union militants, leftist cadres, and religious activists — who were themselves critical of their own previous strategies of political confrontation with the military regime. These sectors converged to form new forms of local organization, oriented by participatory strategies and attuned to the experiences of the new generations of more skilled industrial workers. These neighborhood organizations started then to influence their members' experiences, with the factory shop, labor unions, political parties, and the community services provided by the government.

Therefore, it became possible to distinguish in the action of the church among these popular groups two simultaneous and complementary processes: (a) the church's internal restructuring at the grassroots level; and (b) its participation in the constitution of new social and political actors, such as neighbourhood associations, labor unions, or political parties. The two processes worked out differently in terms of their aims, organizational strategies, leadership capabilities, and institutional resources — in spite of the fact that very often the same individual church members participated simultaneously in both processes.

The assumption underlying the distinction between these two processes is that the constitution of the religious and ethical aspects of social identity occurs at a motivational level that is different from its political dimension[4]. For instance, many mothers' clubs created by the church during the 1970s in São Paulo's popular neighbourhoods never had any direct linkage with politics, and they often oriented their self-help activities as a form of resistance to governmental 'assistentialism' (Sader, 1988). However, these clubs restored to these women a sense of collective belonging, dignity, and mutual trust, which they had lost in their daily lives. Hence, these women were able to understand, encourage, and support family members and neighbours when the latter decided to engage in the wildcat industrial strikes of 1978/1979, which started a new age of union liberty in the country.

Examples like these could be multiplied, to show that religious and ethical resocialization operates in the motivational order and is analytically distinct from the sociopolitical and ideological positions that are sustained in the public arena - and also, in turn, that these public positions interact with the motivational sphere of social identity which articulates values and norms (Habermas, 1975:76)[5]. On the whole, these 'molecular' changes in the motivational order may account for local changes in the political culture, when they are shown to relate - as Sader's study did - to sociopolitical participation and to cumulative changes in the public institutions.

We shall see later some examples of how religious restructuring is carried out by the CEBs. Now we shall look at the influence of religious reform on motivations for sociopolitical action, first through some data on a popular movement in São Paulo in the 1980s[6], and then by looking at another neighbourhood movement in Florianópolis (southern Brazil). In São Paulo, interviews were conducted with the leaders of a citywide committee that was organized by workers who were living on lots of land with irregular deeds, in that the properties did not comply with the legislation on urban development. This movement was founded in 1976, and by 1982 it included more than 100 **bairros** (local neighborhoods) throughout metropolitan São Paulo[7]. The 40 leaders interviewed were typical members of the regional boards of the movement in the different areas of the city where it was active[8]. The interviews contained various references to the church made by the interviewees on their own initiative, in answer to questions about their neighborhoods' most important organizations, what organizations they took part in, where they contacted people to call meetings of the movement, and so forth.

The interviews yielded an initial conclusion that the church was seen as a strategic channel through which the local meetings of the movement were called. This was considered by many leaders a good strategy to overcome the neighborhoods' social and cultural heterogeneity[9], because 'the church transcends the specific differences among residents, who often have contradictory interests', as one of them said. Second, the church provided an 'entrance point' to and institutional support for the movement. It was seen not only as a physical space where meetings of the movement could be held, but as an institution with a network of organizations throughout the neighborhood. This network included the **Pastoral Operaria** (the church's specific pastoral groups for the labor movement), CEBs, youth groups, mothers' clubs, and so forth. Many of the interviewees participated in these church groups, and most saw these organizations as the most important in their neighbourhoods. All this seems to point to the church as the main source of support for the movement.

Yet, when asked how they entered the movement or how the movement started to work in their neighborhood, most interviewees stressed that they had entered it 'on their own initiative', and that the movement had started 'spontaneously'. Thus, from the leaders' standpoint, the church did not exert an overt organizational influence, although it did provide institutional support for the residents' initiative. A third conclusion drawn from the interviews was that the church's network was seen by the movement leaders as part of a 'social arena' occupied by popular organizations, which went beyond the limits of their neighborhood. This social arena was seen as unified by actions of the people in the various spheres of their lives. Individuals who were active in the movement, or in parents' and teachers' associations, CEBs, unions, health neighborhood committees, and so forth, were not seen in a fragmentary way, but as agents building and organizing their own social space, as the 'subjects of rights and obligations' in the various spheres of their activity[10].

A dual pattern of interactions was recognized in these activities. On one level, there were relations of reciprocity among the local bodies in which the residents took part. On another level, there was an asymmetry of authority, as in the case of institutions that went beyond the limits of the neighborhood — the church, the school, other social services, unions, and parties. The latter institutions were seen as 'two-way streets' through which the local popular arena was able to relate to the political and cultural system as a whole — by means of interactions that could involve cooperation, competition, and conflict[11]. Thus, for example, a leader of one group living or working in the neighborhood could either cooperate with the movement and other local institutions, or come into conflict with them. Similarly, such a leader's activity outside the neighborhood could reach the point of representing the 'popular arena' in its interactions with the other institutions belonging to the political and cultural system.

A fourth finding of the research was a convergence between church influence and the use of participatory methods of local organization. Many of the leaders mentioned an organizational strategy that 'strengthened the movement internally, in a joint search for the best solution to problems', through dialogue, voting, consensus, and so forth. This was considered to be a central aspect of the organization of the 'popular arena', because it implied overcoming the divisive effects of sociocultural heterogeneity in the neighborhood — and also the 'dominant external influences, which deal with the residents' problems in a fragmentary manner', one leader said[12]. The fact that these interviewees also referred positively to the work of the church in their neighborhoods could mean that the local church often took up methods of democratic resocialization to support the residents' struggles 'to construct their rights as citizens, both inside and outside the *bairro*, as one of them said. The idea is that the religious reform promoted by the CEBs was able to sustain a pluralistic motivation, to help construct the democratic strategy of the 'popular arena'[13].

In brief, this research led to the perception that the resocialization process promoted by the CEBs and other church groups in the poor districts of São Paulo sustained motivations that promoted democratic actions and awareness among neighborhood leaders. The data showed a convergence between references to the church and the leaders' self-confidence regarding their initiative in achieving the movement's aims, the use of participatory methods to solve problems, a strategy oriented to overcome the barriers of sociocultural heterogeneity, the creation of a social arena of popular organization, obtaining support from the various bodies in which the interviewees took part, and so forth.

Moreover, there was a noticeable change in local political culture, expressed in the dual pattern of interactions, which reversed what interviewees called the previous pattern of 'passivity and submissiveness' to authoritarian rule. This new pattern was in fact responsible for the many public demonstrations staged by this movement during the early 1980s, which brought hundreds of families to City Hall and other public arenas of São Paulo. Church leaders were often present in these demonstrations, but the main spokespersons for the movement were the average rank and file of the popular neighborhoods: men and women of the working class who had learned to speak for themselves. It is hardly surprising, then, that they soon learned to participate politically with other sectors, parties and movements, electing their representative to the City Council, and finally to City Hall.

Another example of a popular movement influenced by the CEBs is in order to examine more closely how this influence worked in an urban setting different from the industrial context of São Paulo and in a more recent period of the national political transition. Florianopolis has a population of nearly 300,000, and is the capital city of the southern state of Santa Catarina. Here the military regime was able to implement successfully, from the mid-1970s onward, a strategy of 'conservative modernization' of the popular neighborhoods, establishing community councils mainly oriented by electoral clientelistic practices[14]. The councils attracted basic facilities and improvements to their neighbourhoods, and local community centers were built with government funds, providing day-care facilities, youth clubs, and public social services. Some of these improvements were made by the voluntary work of the residents on weekends, under the technical supervision of the government, which also provided the construction materials.

One of these *bairros* is a hillside *favela* (shantytown) near the center of the city. As it was situated within the parochial jurisdiction of the cathedral, priests and nuns ran social and educational services there and supported the voluntary work of the residents during the military regime. However, as the first free elections for state government were scheduled for the end of 1982, the clientelistic-electoral connections of the conservative modernization program came to the fore. One of the priests decided to live in the *favela* and to start a CEB. Simultaneously, the son of one of the community leaders became the leader of the local youth club. Both CEB and youth club members began internal evaluations of the voluntary work carried out by the community council. Their conclusions were:

1. The government raised taxes from all citizens in order to provide basic services and facilities. The residents of the *favela*, however, had to do voluntary work in order to have access to these facilities; thus 'the residents paid twice for the same right'. Moreover, the government presented these improvements as a 'favor to be exchanged for votes', in clear violation of the residents' freedom of choice.
2. As the residents had worked so well for the government, they could also instead 'work for themselves, organizing the community on a cooperative basis' — so that the many unemployed and underemployed could make a living.[15]

The new youth leader was elected chairman of the *favela*'s community council. The strict government-enforced regulations of the community council, which limited the right to vote to regular, dues-paying associates, were overruled by the majority of the assembly, which extended universal suffrage to adult residents in the neighborhood. Special committees were then set up by the new board, in order to plan, implement, and direct cooperative projects among the residents. By 1984 five such cooperatives were working regularly. One of them produced soap for local consumption and sale outside the neighborhood. Another cooperative bought some sewing machines and started producing clothes for the neighbors and also met the requests of some downtown shops. A consumers' cooperative started a weekly marketplace, with products brought directly by fishermen and small farmers from villages near the city, thus avoiding the intermediation of retailers. A housing cooperative was established to build houses for the poorer families of the community and for newly arrived migrants. An educational committee was created to integrate the various educational activities within the neighborhood, including the local elementary school, two day-care facilities run by the state, and the youth club.

Some of the practical results of this experience by the late 1980s showed that 'there was a sharp decline in infant mortality due to malnutrition' in the *bairro*. There was also 'a decline in the drop-out rate at the local school, an absence of juvenile delinquency, and continuous participation of the neighbors in the cooperatives'. Forty-two neighbors were then responsible for the committees that ran the cooperatives, and the community council regulations was entirely reshaped to allow for the representation of these committees in the board's decisions.

Another important outcome of this experience was its influence beyond the community. In 1983 the CEBs of the city started to meet on a regular basis to exchange their experiences and to plan their strategies. Since then, they have organized the urban 'Landless' (*Sem Terras*) and 'Homeless' (*Sem Tetos*) movements, striving to support the work in the *favelas* and land occupations by new migrants. The local experience with cooperatives in the *favela* downtown was extended to other neighborhoods, and the latter managed to form a federation of 12 *bairros* to press jointly for government improvements in their communities. Simultaneously, these communities started negotiations with other opposition groups in different *bairros*, aiming at the formation of a citywide confederation of popular neighborhoods. This latter attempt faced great difficulties because other opposition groups and neighborhoods were accustomed to clientelistic-electoral practices inherited from the authoritarian regime. (See Chapter 4).

In 1986 a citywide confederation of bairros was formed by the opposition groups. It was sponsored by the new mayor, a member of the *Partido do Movimento Democrático Brasileiro* (*PMDB*), the leading party of the 'New Republic', the center-right coalition that replaced the military regime in 1985. By 1988 this confederation included most of the community councils created by the military regime, counting more than 70 neighbourhoods, including some middle-class *bairros*. The 12 neighborhoods linked to the CEBs refused to participate in this confederation. They continued, however, to negotiate access to government funds and services and to debate with the citywide confederation their priorities on city planning and budget[16].

In 1988 the 12 CEB neighbourhoods decided to participate in the municipal elections to the City Council, and they appointed the same youth leader who had chaired the first cooperative experiences as a candidate through the *PT*. He was not elected, but he assessed the action positively: 'We made a contribution to the discourse of the *PT*, which was then mainly a group of academics and union leaders. Now we are speaking the language of the people and can be understood by all'. Moreover, the experience also benefited the local communities, for 'now we learned to appraise (positively) the different contributions of community policies and party politics'. Before, 'we were afraid of the state. Now we go into politics to struggle for our rights, to talk over priorities about the city with other groups and social classes'. However, 'we have to be cautious to preserve our community's unity beyond party politics; here people vote for different parties, but we have local common problems which have to be solved'.

This example shows a change in local political culture that is similar to the one in São Paulo. Neighborhood leaders achieved a sense of initiative and pluralism which had to do with their exposure to a change in orientation of the religious community. The reactive nature of this ethical-religious change vis-à-vis the changes in the political process is clear. As the political arena became competitive, it was possible to unveil the clientelistic tenet of party and governmental politics inherited from the military regime. On the other hand, previous conservative modernization practices were more effective here, and public resources comparatively more available than in São Paulo. This accounted for the slower process of awareness building, both within the local church and in the neighborhood movements at large.

Furthermore, it becomes clear that the resocialization process promoted by the CEBs goes hand in hand with similar processes taking place within the more dynamic sectors of the neighbourhood — in this case, the young people; in São Paulo, industrial workers. And both processes reacted to the practical experiences they had in their sociopolitical interactions — here, the 'voluntary work' promoted by City Hall; in São Paulo, real estate speculation. Finally, the network activity of the church also helped to link the neighborhood with other *bairros,* discussing priorities about values and aims, extending self-help initiatives to other areas, and creating collective resources and policies to influence the public arena. We now turn to a consideration of the internal processes of resocialization conducted by the CEBs.

CHURCH REFORM AND SOCIOPOLITICAL CHANGE: THREE EXAMPLES OF UNITY AND DIVERSITY

In another research project, some São Paulo CEBs were compared with CEBs in two other parts of the country. The aim was to understand the CEBs' actions within social and political contexts that varied according to region. The intention was to overcome some of the excessive generalizations that had been made about the CEBs in Brazil, due to a lack of local studies about religious reform in specific regional contexts. We chose to study the CEBs of the Diocese of Crateus, in the northeastern state of Ceará, and of the episcopal district (*prelazia*) of São Felix in the Araguaia region. The choice was based on the diversity of social context in which the CEBs acted in each case, and on the creativity and dynamism of their action, as nationally recognized by those who are knowledgeable about progressive church circles[17]. Group discussions and interviews were held with leaders of the most active church communities; we also conducted interviews with the bishops and some pastoral agents. In addition, we consulted archives and local publications of the CEBs and movements related to them; we also observed the CEBs' annual regional meetings. The data raised through these procedures made it possible to reach some conclusions, presented below in terms of similarities and differences[18].

SIMILARITIES: THE CHURCH'S INTERNAL REFORM AND ITS PROJECT FOR BRAZIL

A first set of results points to similarities found among the CEBs in the three regions. They have to do both with general trends of the progressive church in most parts of the country and with characteristics of religious reform everywhere. In the case of the Brazilian CEBs, these national and universal similarities reach a specific focus, in terms of a project for the church's internal democratization, and for the latter's diffusion within Brazilian society.

The first general trend that was observed in all three regions was the internal participation introduced by the CEBs' religious practices within the local structures of the church. Previous to the CEBs' existence, the church's prevalent strategy had been 'centralizing, vertical and pyramidal', in the words of the bishop of Crateus. Until the early 1970s, even progressive church sectors, which had a 'reformist and even revolutionary discourse'[19], 'excluded from the decisions the majority of participants' in the church. Furthermore, this approach 'neglected the local religious consciousness present in popular religiosity' — the cult of saints, processions, and pilgrimages. This 'imperialism of the spoken word', which imposed a 'competent, hierarchical discourse', was replaced in the CEBs by a 'democratic listening approach'. The latter was said 'to subvert the asymmetric relations within the local church' by permitting every person to 'learn to say his or her word', the bishop of São Felix said.

Of course, the language of liberation leaders and theologians tends to be optimistic. However, participant observation and interviews with local leaders support the hierarchy's assessment that there is a large and increasing participation of the grass roots in decision making. In the words of a pastoral agent in São Felix, 'Bishops, pastoral agents and people started to become a new kind of church - a democratic community in the full participatory sense, offering a sincere option for the poor'[20].

Moreover, in Crateus this emphasis on democratic participation has led to a 'necessary complementarity' between the mysticism that evolves from respecting and developing popular religiosity and the 'political-pastoral' line of support for CEB members' involvement with peasant unions and movements. In fact, the processions and demonstrations during the annual meeting of the CEBs in Crateus emphasized their dual emphasis on religious songs, prayers, and symbols, together with political and social slogans for land reform and human rights[21].

Although this trend toward internal participation in the CEBs takes different forms in the three regions, there is evidence everywhere of a resocialization process that skillfully combines references to religious themes and values with analysis and action in terms of the sociopolitical problems the participants face in their daily lives. One lay leader of a CEB on the outskirts of São Paulo said, for example,

> At the beginning I was ashamed, afraid even of being called a leader. Who is a leader? *Lula*[22] is a leader, I would think. Later on, I would think about the Gospel, observe the problems on my street, talk to people, hand out leaflets and invite people to meet. This is how our CEB started here. Nowadays we're all like one big family - everyone knows everyone else here.

A testimony like this shows the realization of a deliberate strategy started by the church when it created the CEBs. It was intent on encouraging a process of participatory resocialization, in which the alienation of personal relationships would be overcome in the 'horizontality' of the structures of the renewed church. The dual appeal of the CEBs to religious mysticism and social analysis allows it to combine the usual functions of community revival with an action group rationally oriented to social change. The CEBs thus tend to become a valuable asset both for the church and for society - restoring sharing, support, and solidarity in the midst of the oppression, individualism, and misery which plague the workers of this society.

Moreover, 'democratic listening' tends to promote a new style of leadership and the emergence of new community leaders - people who are sensitive to the problems around them and to a plurality of alternative possible solutions. This strategy of church reform tends therefore to project its influence on the 'horizontalization' of social relations outside the church, by arousing what Habermas (1984-7) calls communicative action. The same workers who 'learn to say their word' within the CEBs and vis-à-vis the church hierarchy tend also to overcome their traditional submission to secular authorities in their daily lives. Of course, active participation tends to challenge authority anywhere - particularly authority based on a traditional worldview[23]. This is why the process of communicative action unleashed by the CEBs often meets the resistance of conservative church sectors and other undemocratic sectors of society.

However, as far as the CEBs' political influence goes, Habermas (1973, 1975) also shows that it is important to make a careful distinction between the motivational and the legitimation orders - and between educational enlightenment and practical organization occurring in both spheres. The work done by the CEBs belongs at the level of values and motivations, while the appropriate institutional channels for a political and ideological manifestation in the sphere of legitimation go beyond the scope of the CEBs' action. The Brazilian Roman Catholic church always refused to support or create specific political parties, and the CEBs' strategy was essentially devised as a means of stimulating the laity's free exercise of their political and social choices.

Nevertheless, precisely because it acts in the motivational sphere, the religious resocialization promoted by the CEBs tends to produce effects on the participants' other activities. Ethical changes certainly have practical consequences in social and political behavior. The peasants of Crateus or São Felix, or the industrial workers of São Paulo, may not feel that they are on the same hierarchical level as their priests and bishops - as some of the latter would perhaps like to think. But when those workers and peasants have to face their bosses, it is good for them to know that they are not alone, that they have their unions and parties behind them, and farther behind yet their CEBs' support.

A second set of common results found in all three regions is the project for the liberalization of the state and society, proposed by the *Conferência Nacional dos Bispos do Brazil* (CNBB, 1977), the National Conference of Brazilian Bishops. This proposal is implemented by CEB members, using the alternative modes of participation which they find available or try to construct in their own regional contexts. The pluralistic project proposed by the CNBB as a way of liberalizing the political system (Mainwaring, 1986) takes on more radical connotations of direct or popular democracy at the grassroots level[24]. Here it can be seen that the process of religious resocialization promoted by the CEBs clashes with the traditional forms of political identity that characterized the political culture of authoritarianism. The bishop of São Felix considered this process of resocialization as an effort to 'form a new basis for a new church, a new society' - and therefore as a defined project, albeit for the long term. According to the bishop of

Crateus, its aim is to 'invert the pyramidal scheme of Brazilian politics', where 'the only space left for the ordinary people is a space in which they are outcasts and have no chance to express themselves'.

'Brazil turned upside down', was the expression used by one lay leader of São Felix to define this strategic aim. Thus generally stated, it sounds exactly like 'the world turned upside down' of England's 17th century chiliastic revolutionaries (Hill, 1972/1987). However, leaving aside mystical linguistic similarities, the historical situations are entirely different. The Brazilian situation is not revolutionary, but one of rather slow transition to democratic rule. The thrust of the CEBs' radical intent is clearly motivational, for it never takes on a precise meaning and program. Nicaragua was often mentioned as an example by liberation priests and theologians, in the 1980s, but no one pretended that popular liberation should evolve similarly in Brazil, by imitating this or any other example. Socialism is seldom mentioned in the interviews, perhaps for the same reasons: 'Every people must find its own paths' (*caminhada*). How to interpret, then, the radical thrust of this project? Perhaps it is possibile to say, using Habermas's (1984-7) categories, that this is a 'defensive' strategy, to protect a 'traditional life-world' (religion) from 'system colonization' by the state and marketplace?[25] Or is it mainly a form of resistance or reaction to the pyramid authoritarian enclaves of Brazilian political culture and institutions?

Basismo (grassroots-ism) has been stressed by the literature on popular movements as a defensive strategy to avoid political co-optation by state politics (Banck, 1989; Zermeño, 1987)[26]. But the Brazilian popular sectors have increasingly participated in institutional politics and in the greater union and electoral liberty of the 1980s and 1990s. In any case, the CEBs interpret their strategy of social and political influence by means of different tactics in the three regions studied. In some São Paulo CEBs, as noted above, the tactics involve the restructuring of sociopolitical identity through religious resocialization, by means of a dual pattern of interactions. Here the participatory practice of the community members is articulated with the asymmetric relations proper to the institutions that transcend the limits of the neighborhood. Other communities, where hierarchical control is stronger, use tactics that attain their strategic goals in different ways - both more directly, as in São Felix, where one lay leader observed that the CEBs 'tend to merge with unions and party', and more indirectly, through joint 'mystical-pastoral/political' influence, as in Crateus.

In all cases, there is a relationship to the CNBB's long-term strategy of supporting a liberal and democratic change of Brazilian society. In each place, this strategy takes on more or less radical connotations, and it is more or less controlled institutionally by the local hierarchy. These changes also relate to differences in the environment from one situation to another, and are discussed below.

Differences: Political Alternatives
and Socioeconomic Conditions

A factor that differentiates CEB activities in the regions studied has to do with the socieconomic and educational conditions of the populations. The bishop of Crateus said that the CEBs there 'were preceded by a discovery of *natural horizontal* communities of neighborliness and solidarity'. Because the CEBs reflect upon 'the social origins of misery', they strive to overcome 'cosmological fatalism' in popular culture - whereby the people's living conditions are attributed to divine will or to natural causes rather than to historical factors. These living conditions, however, vary greatly from one place to another. The *mutirão* (rural collective form of labor as self-help) in the northeastern countryside differs considerably from the squatters' resistance movement in the Araguaia region - and both differ from the neighbourhood associations that have grown up in São Paulo, or from the cooperative network in Florianopolis.

The new religious identity promoted by the CEBs tends to overcome 'cosmological fatalism' by means of a resocialization process that focuses on the historicity of religion itself. In this resocialization, 'theory and practice are brought together' as required by liberation theologians, and the participants 'learn to pronounce their own word of liberation'. This religious historicity consists of taking as a starting point the specific consciousness and stage of organization of the popular groups to which the CEBs are linked, in order to advance toward a new stage in their struggles. This 'theological/pastoral' orientation may take on a variety of practical forms and contents, according to the diversity of local conditions.

In the diocese of Crateus, where the church has a long-standing traditional presence in the midst of striking socioeconomic inequality, the CEBs 'begin with Bible-reading circles,' where the 'summons of the word illuminates the reality of misery,' said the bishop. In São Felix, the church established itself more recently. Here the poor were more homogeneous, dispersed, and unorganized. Religious identity was immediately linked to the conflict-ridden organizational practice of the peasant unions: 'The church is politically organized because all the people's organizations are political,' as one lay leader put it. In contrast, in the poor neighborhoods of São Paulo, with all their social heterogeneity, the lay leader of a CEB recognized pluralism as a necessary strategy of popular organization: 'A popular organization is like an orchestra, where each person plays a different instrument,' but where 'it is important to have a score and a conductor'- these were provided by the leaders, who often participated in the local CEB.

In all these examples, there is a relationship between religious resocialization and a historical commitment to changing socioeconomic and political conditions. But this relationship is neither univocal nor unilateral. The CEBs motivate their members to recognize their living conditions and thereby attempt to organize to change them. These conditions vary a great deal, however, and carry a considerable weight in the practical directions and ideological alternatives followed by CEB members. Thus the greater social heterogeneity of the São Paulo and Florianópolis neighborhoods leads to pluralist attitudes, with the possibility of cooperating with other churches, parties, and movements

- all of them within the 'popular arena', of course. In the Crateus region - and possibly in other rural areas where the big estates (*latifundios*) predominate - the tendency, by contrast, is to give priority to a long-term educational strategy, based on the mysticism contained in popular religion. And in the areas where land disputes are rife and popular movements previously unorganized — such as the Araguaia region in the mid-1980s — the church tends to merge with unions and parties through the actions of its members: 'If one is part of the rural community, one is part of this church,' said a pastoral agent there.

The CEBs also find different alternatives for political participation, from place to place. It was observed in São Paulo that some CEBs interact with a network of community movements and institutions, through the activity of those who live in these neighborhoods and who believe it is their duty - and lies within their power - to constitute an 'arena of popular organization.' These facts point to the simultaneous construction of a 'renovated' religious motivation in the CEBs and of the sociopolitical identity of the same militants in unions and party activities, neighborhood associations, and so forth. We also found that this interaction depends not only on the tactics and strategy followed by the church in the region, but also on the existing alternatives for sociopolitical participation and organization throughout the locality. These alternatives also differ greatly from one region of the country to another.

Crateus, for example, is marked by the extreme poverty of the peasants employed on the *latifundios* and by the highly exploitative character of work relations. In this context, church leaders make a careful distinction between the activities of the CEBs and the formation of peasant unions and political parties and movements. The bishop argues that 'the recognition of the social origin of misery' is achieved in the CEBs; the 'recognition of the partial nature of unions' leads to parties. In this case, the church is not seen as a surrogate for sociopolitical action, but an institution that supports and even 'prepares a democratic space, in anticipation of the new society of tomorrow.'

In the São Felix region, where most of the people are rural squatters (*posseiros*), small tenants are involved in dispute over the legal deeds to land. Where there is an absence of intermediate institutions, the local church tends to fill this gap. However, the bishop stressed that it is 'trying to leave aside some of this work as a political surrogate organization and take on its more specific role as a church, because popular organizations (unions and parties) are now springing up.'

In the outlying poor districts of São Paulo, the frustrating experiences of the past, involving both negotiations with the government and cooperation with left-wing parties, led church groups to be cautious about most forms of political participation by the mid-1980s. But, of course, the antigovernment attitude of many CEB members did not impede their frequent interactions, often involving conflict, with state agencies - when these CEB members took on leadership in sociopolitical organizations. To some extent, similar disillusionment could be seen in Crateus and Florianopolis, when the defeat of candidacies supported by CEB members was explained as a result of the 'pyramidal' character of Brazilian politics.

The skeptical treatment given to 'official' politics is therefore not a matter of principle but of method and tactics. The need for and the actual training of militants who can take on the tasks of 'being a Christian worker in the unions and parties' is a common thread in all the institutional relations in these situations. The CEBs provide the educational motivations for this kind of sociopolitical commitment. But the actions of these militants in the polity does not depend only on their church training or on the existence of a church strategy to 'release' them into union and party militancy. It depends fundamentally on the availability of viable social and political institutions at the local and regional level. In the absence of these, the CEBs would tend either to play a surrogate provisional role in the sociopolitical order, or to withdraw into internal activities linked to systematic opposition in the motivational order, while their members work for the unfolding of new sociopolitical opportunities.

Moreover, the changing sociopolitical alternatives of the country during the 1980s and 1990s have confirmed their importance as channels for different commitments of CEB members in the polity. We saw that differences in rural class relations and land tenure between Crateus and São Felix have produced a much denser political and organizational life in the former, and a more restricted role for the progressive church in the mid 1980s. As conflicts over land tenure became less prominent in São Felix during the decade, unions and parties became more institutionalized and independent from church influence, as the bishop himself had anticipated. We have also seen how CEB members learned later on to distinguish between community policies and party politics, in order to preserve the unity of the neighborhood movement in Florianopolis. Accordingly, the regulation on land and urban reform by the 1988 Constitution reoriented the communicative action of social movements linked to the CEBs in various parts of the country, to actively negotiate their newly acquired rights in the public arena. The successes and the high profile of the nationwide Rural Landless (*Sem Terras*) Movement is a case in point, since the mid - 1990s. Of course, this situation of greater democratic institutionalization does not preclude the existence of conflicts, strikes, land occupations, and so forth. But it provides the legal framework for a competitive public arena, where these differences may be negotiated and solved by the representative parties.

The CEBs have been described by liberation theologians as 'a new way of being the church' (L. Boff, 1977). This 'ecclesiogenesis' was devised as a national strategy for the religious reform of the church. In practice however, this common strategy tends to lead to a range of 'different ways of de-structuring/restructuring the Church,' as a São Felix lay leader put it. In all cases studied, the 'ecclesiogenesis' of the CEBs has interacted with the 'sociogenesis' of Brazilian democratic change, taking on different forms in different places. Defensive and adaptive as they may seem to be, the changes produced by the CEBs include hopes and expectations which are converging with other changes in Brazilian society: processes of social differentiation and institution-building; the search for new forms of life, ideological pluralism, and a representative party system; the tolerant recognition of the right of dissent, of the right of minorities to be different, and of majorities to a full and decent life. This is why it can be said that the reform of religious life cultivated by the CEBs is now part of the socio-cultural and political changes toward a new pluralist, democratic order whose construction has only begun in Brazil in the last decades.

REFERENCES

Azevedo, M. 1986. **Comunidades Eclesiais de Base e Enculturação da Fé.** São Paulo: Loyola.

Banck, G. and Koomings, K. (Eds.). 1988. **Social change in Contemporary Brazil: Politics, Class and Culture in a Decade of Transition.** Amsterdam: CEDLA.

Banck, G. 1989. **Local or Political Culture? Brazilian Neighborhood Movements in Anthropological Perspective.** American Anthropological Association, Washington, DC.

Bastián, J.-P.,1997. **La Mutación Religiosa en América Latina. Para una Sociología del Cambio Social en la Modernidad Periférica**, Mésico, D.F.: Fondo de Cultura Económica.

Betto, F. 1981. **Comunidade Eclesial de Base.** São Paulo: Brasiliense.

Boff, C. 1979. **Comunidade Eclesial, Comunidade Política.** Petrópolis: Vozes.

Boff, L. 1977. **Eclesiogênese: As Comunidades Eclesiais de Base Reinventam a Igreja.** Petrópolis: Vozes.

Bruneau, T. 1974. **The Political Transformation of the Brazilian Catholic Church.** New York: Cambridge University Press.

Bruneau, T. 1983. The Catholic Church and the Christian Basic Communities: A Case Study from the Brazilian Amazon. **Kellog Institute for International Studies.**

Camargo, C.P.F. 1971. **Igreja e Desenvolvimento.** São Paulo: CEBRAP.

Camargo, C.P.F. 1982. A Igreja do Povo. **Novos Estudos**, 1(2), 49-53.

Cardoso, F.H. 1982. Regime Político e Mudança Social. **Revista de Cultura e Política**, 3: 7-25.

Cardoso, R. 1982. Duas Faces de uma Experiência. **Novos Estudos**, 1(2), 53-58.

CNBB - Conferência Nacional dos Bispos do Brasil. 1977. **As Exigências Cristãs de uma Ordem Política.** São Paulo: Paulinas.

CNBB - Conferência Nacional dos Bispos do Brasil. 1979. **Comunidades Eclesiais de Base no Brasil.** São Paulo: Paulinas.

Della Cava, R. 1978. **Short-term Politics and Long-term Religion** Wilson Center Working Paper, 12. Washington, DC: Wilson Center.

_____. 1986. "A Igreja e a Abertura, 1974-1985". In Krischke, P. and Mainwaring, S. (Eds.). **A Igreja nas Bases em Tempo de Transição**, Porto Alegre: L&PM.

Doimo, A.M. 1986. "Os Rumos dos Movimentos Sociais nos Caminhos da Religiosidade". In Krischke P., and Mainwaring, S. (Eds.).O. Cit

Evers, T. 1982. "Os Movimentos Sociais Urbanos: O Caso do Movimento do Custo de Vida". In Moises, J.A. et. al. **Alternativas Populares da Democracia**, Petrópolis: Vozes.

Flisfisch, A. 1987. **La Politica como Compromiso Democrático.** Santiago: FLACSO.

Freire, P. 1970. **The Pedagogy of the Oppressed.** New York: Seabury Press.

Habermas, J. 1973. **Theory and Practice.** Boston: Beacon Press.

Habermas, J. 1975. **Legitimation Crisis.** Boston: Beacon Press.

Habermas, J. 1984-7. **Theory of Communicative Action** (2 vols.). Boston: Beacon Press.

Hartz, Louis (Ed.). 1964. **The Founding of New Societies**. New York: Harcourt, Brace and World, Inc.

Heller, A. and Feher, F. 1985. **Anatomia de la Izquierda Occidental**. Barcelona: Península.

Hewitt, W.E. 1986. "Strategies for social change employed by comunidades eclesiais de base (CEBs) in the archdiocese of São Paulo". **Journal for the Scientific Study of Religion**, 25 (1): 16-30.

Hill, C. 1972/1987. **The World Turned Upside Down: Radical Ideas during the English Revolution**. (Brazilian translation). São Paulo: Cia. das Letras.

Ireland, R. 1986. "Comunidades Eclesiais de Base, Grupos Espíritas, e a Democratização no Brasil". In Krischke, P. and Mainwaring, S. (Eds), O.Cit.

Krischke, P. 1983. Populism and the Catholic Church: The Crisis of Democracy in Brazil. Ph.D. Dissertation, **Graduate Programme in Political Science**, Toronto: York University.

_____. 1985. "The Role of the Church in a Political Crisis: Brazil, 1964." **Journal of Church and State**, 27 (3): 403-427.

_____, and Mainwaring, S. (Eds.). 1986. **A Igreja nas Bases em Tempo de Transição**. Porto Alegre: L&PM.

Lechner, N. 1988. **Los Patios Interiores de la Democracia. Subjetividad y Politica**. Santiago: FLACSO.

Levine, D. (Ed.). 1986. **Popular Religion, the Churches, and Political Conflict in Latin America**. North Carolina: Chapel Hill.

Macedo, C. 1986. **Tempo de gênesis: O Povo das Comunidades Eclesiais de Base**. São Paulo: Brasiliense.

Mainwaring, S. 1986. **The Catholic Church and Politics in Brazil, 1916-1985**. Stanford, C.A.: Stanford University Press.

Mainwaring, S. 1987. "Urban Popular Movements, Identity and Democratizacion in Brazil", **Comparative Political Studies**, 20: 131-159.

Mainwaring, S. and Viola, S. 1984. "New Social Movements, Political Culture and Democracy: Brazil and Argentina in the 1980s." *Telos*, 61: 17-54.

Marís, C. 1994. **Coping with Poverty. Pentecostals and Christian Base Communities in Brazil**, Philadelphia, PA: Temple University Press.

Matos Machado, S. 1989. **O Processo de Formalização Institucional dos Conselhos Comunitários em Florianópolis, 1975-1985**. Florianópolis, Brazil: Universidade Federal de Santa Catarina, (M.A. Thesis).

McCarthy, T. 1987. **La Teoría Crítica de Jürgen Habermas**. Madrid: Tecnos.

O'Donnel, G. 1988. "Hiatos, instituições e perspectivas democráticas". In. Reis, F. and O'Donnel, G. (Eds.), **A Democracia no Brasil: Dilemas e Perspectivas**. São Paulo: Vértice.

Paiva, V. 1985. "A Igreja Moderna no Brasil". In: Paiva, V.(Ed.), **Igreja e Questão Agrária**. São Paulo: Loyola.

Pierucci, A. F. and Prandi, R. 1996. **A Realidade Social das Religiões no Brasil:Religião, Sociedade e Política**, São Paulo: Hucitec.

_____, 2000. "Religious Diversity in Brazil. Numbers and Perspectives in a Sociological Evaluation", **International Sociology,** 14 (4): 629-39.

Sader, E. 1988. **Quando Novos Personagens Entraram em Cena.** Rio de Janeiro: Paz e Terra.

Slater, D. 1985. **New Social Movements and the State in Latin America.** Amsterdam: CEDLA.

Souza Lima, L.G. 1982. "Notas sobre as Comunidades Eclesiais de Base e a Organização Política". In: J. Moisés et al. **Alternativas Populares da Democracia.** Petrópolis: Vozes.

Telles, V.S. 1986. "Anos 70: Experiências e Práticas Cotidianas". In: Krischke, P. and Mainwaring, S. (Eds.), O.Cit.

Vasconcellos, E. and Krischke, P. 1984. "Igreja, Motivações e Organização dos Moradores em Loteamentos Clandestinos". In Krischke, P. (Ed.), **Terra de Habitação vs. Terra de Espoliação,** O. Cit.

Wanderley, L.E. 1981. "As Comunidades Eclesiais de Base e a Educação Popular". **Revista Eclesiástica Brasileira,** 41: 686-707.

Zermeño, S. 1987. "Hacia una Democracia como Identidad Restringida: Sociedade y Política en México". **Revista Mexicana de Sociología,** 49 (2): 57-88.

ENDNOTES

[1] Mainwaring and Viola (1984) proposed a reformulation of the concept of political culture, to include possible differences 'between verbal attitudes and practical behaviour' and their mutual influences. Our assumption here is that mutual influences between innovative values and behaviour may be observed in the CEBs' interactional strategies, as well as in those of the popular movements in which CEB members participate.

[2] It would be easy to present examples of optimistic overgeneralizations in the previous literature about the CEBs; for example, 'The CEBs and the pastoral organizations of the Church are the main force supporting the popular movements' (Souza Lima, 1982: 53). A more nuanced form of overgeneralization emphasized the CEBs' institutional limits:

> They constitute the Church in its most renovated form. The bureaucratic nature of the Church's power, based on the normativity of Canon Law, and the rationality of the Archdiocese's pastoral practice combine with the ethos of low-income groups to which the members of the CEBs belong.
> *(Camargo, 1982: 50).*

[3] Sader (1988) described this interaction in São Paulo's popular neighborhoods from a sociolinguistic perspective. (See Chapter 3).

[4] This distinction between the religious and the political dimensions of social identity is designed to introduce an heuristic focus, to observe the different relations that may occur between sociocultural and sociopolitical democratization (see Lechner, 1988, for a similar approach). It is an analytical distinction and does not deny that institutional party and union politics play an important role in the reorientation of lower class identities.

[5] Habermas (1975: 77) stresses the linkages between crises of legitimacy and their roots in the motivational order.

[6] In what follows, selected results of a research project are presented. For a fuller report, see Vasconcellos and Krischke (1984: 57-69). Eliane Vasconcellos, Dora Nogueira Porto, Thimoteo Camacho, and Airton Leite also worked on this project.

[7] The average *loteamento clandestino* was made up of 100 individual lots. It was developed by private initiative for low-income housing, in an area that did not comply with the official regulations for urban development, in terms of size of the lots, provision of basic facilities, zoning regulations, and so forth.

[8] The research was done by request of the movement's leadership, to support its internal evaluation of the movement's successes, difficulties, and future possibilities.

[9] There were references in the interviews to the professional activities of 130 neighborhood leaders linked to the movement, including 38 industrial workers, 24 manual service workers, 21 housewives, 17 salaried workers in nonmanual jobs, 14 workers in building or construction jobs, 12 self-employed service workers, and 4 unemployed workers.

[10] One interviewee said, 'This place is our life. We came here, worked and built this neighborhood. Nobody gave this place to us. We bought it and have created its value, living here, working here, and building it. Nobody will take it from us.'

[11] This dual pattern of interactions illustrates the local change in political culture, through actions and orientations which react against passivity and submissiveness to authoritarian rule.

[12] The resident of a *loteamento clandestino* had to deal individually with the real estate enterprise that sold him his piece of land through a private contract (not valid in public law). It was only when the residents organized themselves in the movement that they received public and legal recognition of their problem as a social problem.

[13] The interviewees reported many instances of what Habermas (1984-7) calls 'decentration' in the attitudes of the movements' leaders — namely, an ability to surpass ego-centered or sectorial self-interests to achieve a cooperative redefinition of aims, means, and norms among a plurality of actors. This more pluralistic focus was linked by some interviewees to the influence of the church. However, see notes 23 and 25 for a critical interpretation of religious worldviews from the perspective of communicative action.

[14] See Matos Machado (1989) for a preliminary appraisal of the community councils' strategy. Suzana Tornquist and Kathia T. Müller helped to obtain the data presented here, as part of a general research project on neighborhood movements in Florianópolis (see Chapter 4).

[15] In 1985 there were 1,975 people living in this *bairro*. The fact that 58% of the population was under 22 years of age explains the significance of education among community priorities, and also the importance of youth in its leadership. Many of the

neighbors were unemployed, some worked as public servants, and others were self-employed as street sellers (*biscateiros*). Many women worked as maids or did the laundry for middle-class households downtown. Most new migrants to the **bairro** were former fishermen and small farmers, bringing along their experiences of independent self-support and collective self-help.

[16] It is interesting to note that the 12 CEB neighborhoods were occasionally invited by City Hall to special consultation on the city's priorities and policies, in spite of the fact that they refused to participate in the citywide neighborhood confederation and have often demonstrated against public policies.

[17] Crateus is located in the arid hinterland (*sertão*) of the northeastern state of Ceará, where mystical religiosity is particularly strong among the peasants. The diocese of Crateus has gradually promoted reforms, establishing CEBs and other experiences of religious awakening, which attempted to redirect local mysticism to the practical aims of grassroots organization. São Felix is located in the Araguaia river region of central Brazil, in rural areas occupied by smallholders (*posseiros*). Conflicts over property and land titles are very common, and the church started its work in the area by supporting the peasant movements against the military regime - hence its highly politicized profile.

[18] Marcelo Nassif and Douglas Mansur helped in the fieldwork of this research.

[19] The 'pre-history' of the CEBs included a preliminary period of failed attempts at conservative modernization. For instance, the bishop of Crateus mentioned that 'one thousand catechists were trained by leaders in turn trained in Rio de Janeiro; but this 'pyramidal' model was a failure... because the people respond only to experience.'

[20] It is true that many problems persisted and were eventually mentioned by interviewees, such as a layperson who said that 'equality in speaking masks the fact that freedom to participate (within the church) is not conquered but conceded.' Or a pastoral agent who remarked that 'we are trained to question authorities but not those of the church.' Or worse still, 'We are trained to participate in work and organization but not in (final) decisions.' However, how could such questioning arise except as part of a conciousness-raising process, and one of 'horizontalizing structures' inside the church?

[21] The bishop of Crateus offered a dramatic account of how the 'democratic listening' approach was introduced in his diocese. When he arrived as the new bishop, he noticed that his preaching was not being understood by the people. Then, he started to visit every local community just to listen to what the people had to say about their daily lives. At that time, 'the people would complain that the bishop was not going there to teach but to learn.' But they understood the new approach as a 'new mode of being a church,' and the bishop could 'start speaking once again, but now as one of them, who could be understood by all.' Of course, this event was connected to Paulo Freire's (1970) approach to adult basic education.

[22] Luis Inácio *Lula* da Silva, gained prominence in the late 1970s as a leader of the São Bernardo metalworkers' union in the São Paulo metropolitan area. Since the early 1980s, he has been the chairman of the PT; he became a federal deputy in 1986; and the presidential candidate who came in second in the 1989, 1994 and 1998 elections.

[23] It is possible to discuss this point in Habermas's (1984-7) terms, suggesting that the strategy of the CEBs is 'defensive,' not simply because it protects 'traditional life-

worlds' against state and the marketplace, but because it is for the most part reactive and adaptive to changing historical conditions - no longer explainable or reducible to the terms of a religious wordview. See also Heller and Feher (1985) for a critical evaluation of these categories.

[24] The leadership of the 12 CEB neighborhoods in Florianópolis initially criticized the strategy of the citywide neighborhood confederation in 'proposing agreements from the top, among the boards of the community councils.' The strategy was said to 'neglect a long-term approach to creating unity through grass-roots participation.' (See chapter 4).

[25] The work of the CEBs in urban settings starts from what Habermas (1984-7) calls 'rationalized life-worlds, which experience new forms of existence and cooperation.' In this sense, to the extent that religious reform encourages members to adopt secular orientations and ideologies in the political arena, it may also undermine the cohesive functions of religion at the community level. The many trained CEB leaders who left the church when they took up leadership in social and political movements may serve as examples of this process of secularization.

[26] Early critical assessments of *basismo* were presented by F.H. Cardoso (1981) and R. Cardoso (1982). A more recent discussion was presented by Zermeño (1987). (See chapter 2).

Chapter 7

SOCIAL PARTICIPATION AND POLITICAL CULTURE[*]

This chapter reports on a study of popular participation in low income neighborhoods in the Southern state of Santa Catarina, Brazil[1]. The aim was to study the relationship between sociopolitical participation and democratic changes in Brazilian political culture. The first section of the chapter situates the problem of participation in the debate over change in political culture in Brazil, and in particular over the legacy of populist state-led mobilization and the demobilization promoted by the military authoritarian regime. The second section discusses data gathered in three low-income neighborhoods in Santa Catarina about sociopolitical participation, and local changes in the normative claims used by the residents, to justify participatory action. This discussion is based on previous studies of cognitive and moral development, using categories of Habermas' communicative action and Kohlberg's moral and cognitive development theories.

CONTINUITY AND CHANGE IN BRAZILIAN POLITICAL CULTURE

"Whoever controls the interpretation of the past in our professional history writing, has gone a long way toward controlling the future"
(Gabriel Almond, 1988:828).

Professional history in the area of Brazilian political culture studies is yet to be done. However, existing studies on Brazilian political culture can be divided in simple terms in two different trends: those that look at the data in terms of the past, and those that look at

[*] The fieldwork for this research was supported by the ***Conselho Nacional de Desenvolvimento Científico e Tecnológico (CNPq)***. The author is grateful to the Latin American Studies Center of Temple University, Philadephia, USA for its hospitality while this report was written. Benjamin Arditi, Rosario Espinal, Nancy Bermeo, Stephen Hellman, Judith Hellman, David Bell, Stephen Chilton, Luis Monteiro, Selvino Assman and Louise Lhullier presented helpful comments to the first draft of the report.

the same data in terms of the future. This simplification suggests that some emphasize the legacy of authoritarian demobilization under the military regime, and the patterns of state-led populist politics prior to 1964; while others focus on the electorate's potentials for learning and experiencing in the present context of democratization.

Colleagues at the **Universidade Federal do Rio Grande do Sul** have conducted surveys of political culture in Southern Brazil since 1968. They presented a longitudinal analysis of political culture and citizen participation, according to Almond and Verba's and other classic works in the literature (Baquero and Pra, 1992)[2]. The results indicated that "in the **gaucho** [as residents of the region are known] political culture the predominant subject-type attitudes contrast with those of participant political culture - which are considered necessary for an effective democratic consolidation" (1992:88). They added that "the lack of active participation in political action is a symptom of a society that has not yet established stable political structures that arouse interest among the citizens" (1992:109). Rather, the data portrayed "a transitional process from traditional political attitudes towards subject-type attitudes. The latter, in turn, provide the basis for the development of participatory attitudes - which, however, will depend on the direction taken by the process of democratic consolidation"[3] (1992:108).

This interpretation converged with other influential evaluations of Brazilian political culture, which emphasized the present legacies of past state-led populism and or authoritarian demobilization under the military regime (e.g. Banck, 1993; von Mettenheim, 1992; Guilhon Albuquerque, 1990). These conclusions in relation to Southern Brazil are also important, to demystify some common sense assumptions about civic traditions and levels of sociopolitical participation at the regional level, which are supposed to be higher vis-à-vis Brazilian standards.

In fact, the data presented by Baquero-Pra showed a relative continuity over time in some basic indicators of political awareness and participation in Porto Alegre (the capital of Rio Grande do Sul). These results are comparable both to the national data in 1989-90, and to data from the other Southern state (Santa Catarina, 1989) where I did my own research in low-income neighborhoods (1992).

Table I - Political Awareness and Participation in Southern Brazil
(Figures Denote %)

	Porto Alegre*					National		Santa Catarina	
	1968	1976	1982	1985	1986	1989	1990	1989	1992
1) Are you interested in politics?	67	56	51	60	-	63	77	55	59
2) Politics influences your life?	52	55	56	-	-	63	72	62	78
3) Reads or views political news	48	53	30	31	48	68	78	55	64
4) Participate in political campaigns	-	-	26	29	27	8	24	18	45

Notes - (*) Porto Alegre is the capital of the Southern state Rio Grande do Sul.
Sources - For 1968 until 1986: Baquero and Reis Pra (1992).
            For 1989 and 1990: Moisés (1992).
            For 1992: Krischke (1993).

However, this relative continuity with the past merits a closer scrutiny in terms of methodology and logitudinal analysis. For one thing, longitudinal analysis on the national level showed both a striking increase in some indicators (e.g. opposition to military involvement in politics) and remarkable stability in other aspects (e.g. divided opinions on support to political parties) during the transition and attempted consolidation of civilian rule (see Table II). The data for 1992 in Santa Catarina (Tables I, IV and V) were collected in only three low-income neighborhoods, which were assumed to be relatively more politicized. This assumption will be discussed below.

Table II - Opinion-Change in Brazil:
Democratic Institutions and Political Participation (as %)

Institutions	1972	1982	1989	1990
1) Favorable to military involvement in politics	79	52	46	36
2) Favorable to political parties	51	71*	50	56
3) Against government control over unions/strike activity	07	42	62	70
Participation				
4) Favorable to participation in elections	57	82*	66	71
5) Favorable of the right to vote for illiterates	38	60	59	56
6) Favorable to the idea that "people know how to vote"	50	47	52	-

Sources - Data for 1972 and 1982: Rochon and Mitchell (1987)
                    Data for 1989 and 1990: Moisés (1992).
(*) The first direct election for state governors since 1965 was held in 1982.

If Baquero-Pra's longitudinal analysis was valid for Porto Alegre and other cities in Southern Brazil, one must ask how "subject-oriented" deferential attitudes relate to the election of "Popular Front" left-center candidates for City Hall in 1992, in Porto Alegre (where the *PT* - Workers' Party was **reelected,** a result which was repeated in the municipal elections of 1996 and 2000) and in two of the cities studied in Santa Catarina (including the state capital, where the new 1992 mayor was a member of the Communist Party). Undoubtedly there must be an explanation that Baquero and Pra should be capable to present, in light of their long-term analysis. (See Baquero et al., 1995). To my mind this could have to do with the legacy of populist politics, which is especially strong in Rio Grande do Sul (though now relatively disconnected from Vargas and his heir Leonel Brizzola - who supported non-*PT* candidacies in the last four elections in Porto Alegre). This legacy is also present in S. Catarina, where Brizzola's party- *PDT (Partido Democrático Trabalhista)* Democratic Labor Party- joined in the different "Popular Fronts" that won in two of the cities studied below in 1992 (as well as in some other cities in the municipal elections of 1996 and 2000).

However, a fresh look at electoral change is being proposed by those studies of political culture, that emphasize the opportunities for learning and experiencing (the "future") now open to the Brazilian electorate. José Alvaro Moisés (1992) for example emphasized that in spite of the enduring demobilizing effects of the military regime, there were data about the electorate that included in the higher levels of political sophistication,

> "(...) not only the segments of the elite or groups close to it (because of inequalities of access to education) but also different segments among the mass public, which despite their lack of resources, feel the impact of politics in their lives, become interested in politics and experience the results of political resocialization (...) In countries like Brazil this comes partly from the mobilization and organization of the poorest sectors in pursuit of a less unequal distribution of resources (like education) (...) Political sophistication is much greater when the population is concentrated in middle-ranking and larger cities. The level of sophistication is connected with the variables that form the 'tripod' of political participation — income, education and occupation"[4]
> *(Moisés, 1992:15-17).*

Table III - Levels of Political Sophistication among Brazilian Voters by Size of Municipality, Income and Education (1989), and Support of Democracy (Figures Denote %)

	Brazil	Urban	Medium Cities	Income[1]			Education			Support of Democracy[3]
				0-5	5-10	More Than 10	Elemen-tary[2]	Secon-dary	Higher	
High	11	14	13	07	16	28	05	17	43	70
Medium	43	46	52	42	54	54	39	55	47	46
Low	46	40	35	51	30	18	56	28	10	30

Source: Moisés (1992).
Notes: (1) Income figures are given in multiples of minimum wage.
         (2) Elementary education includes illiterates.
         (3) Percentages in this column are on the totals for each level of sophistication.

Moisés adopted Neuman's (1986) "theory of the three publics", and created a scale to measure the differences in levels of sophistication of the Brazilian electorate. The scale correlated the usual indicators for political culture and socioeconomic resources - around such criteria as the mobilization of information, the salience of politics for the interviewees, and their capacity to conceptualize political life. He finally correlated these levels of sophistication with the interviewees' preference for democracy. He concluded that:

> "The most sophisticated tend to classify themselves preponderantly on the democratic end of the continuum; the least sophisticated at the authoritarian end (...) The public situated in the intermediate strata are divided almost equally among the three positions in the continuum (...)" (Hence the latter) "- nearly 50% of the electorate - is playing a crucial role in the consolidation of a democratic culture. It is composed of sectors that possess the minimal cognitive and informational resources required for public life to function. It therefore forms the core structure upon which any strategy to consolidate democracy for the long-term has to be based"
> *(Moisés, 1992:17-19).*

We have already noted that this "future-oriented" approach to change in the political culture relies on the same indicators of the literature that emphasizes the legacies of the past. However, it specifies methods of empirical analysis that underline the open-ended characteristics of political and cultural change. Other Brazilian studies oriented to the "future" (e.g. Lamounier and Souza, 1989; Figueiredo, 1990) may be less comparable (if at all) with the classic approach derived from Almond and Verba - for they rely on rational choice, adaptative or other theories of change. Moisés' proposal, however, may be compatible with the "subject-attitude" hypothesis advanced by Baquero and Pra — though he demonstrates that the range of situations of the general public is broader than the apparent homogeneity highlighted by the classic typological studies.

Moreover, the focus suggested by Moisés, on processes of resocialization, due to experience and learning in political and social life, has additional consequences for research: 1) It points to the need for studies on processes of **social** participation, to see whether they influence resocializations and thereby eventually effect political outcomes; 2) It also suggests that studies should be made about changes in the patterns of cognitive development, that are relatively independent from access to formal education and which relate to the learning experiences flowing from participation of low-income groups and organizations in society. The following section of this chapter draws on these two topics through an analysis of social and political participation in three low-income neighborhoods in Santa Catarina.

LOCAL STUDIES OF SOCIOPOLITICAL PARTICIPATION AND CULTURAL DEMOCRATIZATION

"By their very nature, cultural values are at best **candidates** for embodiment in norms that are designed to express a general interest. Participants can distance themselves from norms and normative systems that have been set off from the totality of social life, only to the extent necessary to assume a hypothetical attitude toward them...[that] covers only practical questions that can be debated rationally, i.e., those that hold out the prospect of consensus. It deals not with value preferences but with the normative validity of norms of action".
(Habermas, 1990:104, emphasis in the original).

There are many heated debates in the literature about political culture and sociopolitical participation, that are very far from settled, and whose general lines do not have to concern us here. The main point that guides the analysis below - of different cases of sociopolitical participation in low-income neighborhoods - is that respondents can best (in fact, can only – according to Habermas) interpret their actions through a reflexive evaluation of the normative validity of those actions - a reflection and validity shared with others (the interviewer included)[5].

A preliminary remark is in order here, to qualify the use below of the framework proposed by Habermas (derived from Kohlberg and Piaget) of "stages of moral and cognitive development". The framework does not assume that the process is linear or evolutionary, but rather that understanding change requires the use of a conceptual or analytical scale. For instance, we start below with the more complex situation of **Bairro** A, because it will enable us also to understand the less complex situations of **Bairros** B and C. Moreover, we are not therefore attempting to classify any of these **bairros** as being "superior" or "inferior" on the basis of its stage of "moral and cognitive develpment". We are rather attempting to assess their political cultures ("cognitive, affective and evaluative orientations") in the terms of the relative complexity of their shared normative validity.

A second methodological remark is that the data presented in the Tables about Santa Catarina (1992) was collected and organized using technical assumptions of survey research, i.e. they were considered as aggregate individual orientations that provide meaningful clusters for probability inferences. However, this data was not collected from a statistical representative sample of the state's population, but rather from 130 interviewees - a random sample of each of the three low-income neighborhoods. Our intention is not to make correlations among those data, but rather to see how these three local studies compare with the results of surveys of broader representative samples[6].

The main assumption of the following analysis is that the characteristics of the **bairros** are better interpreted through the shared visions and discourses of their own inhabitants[7]. For example, Sra. Alice[8] has lived in **Bairro** A since the late 1970s, when the neighborhood was settled. She migrated with her family from the surrounding countryside because her husband had lost his job due to the closing of a lumber factory — caused by indiscriminate deforestation. The couple and two children came to the **bairro** because they had heard that the municipal government was proposing to finance low-income housing neighborhoods, and the husband expected to work there as a carpenter. The local government financed the land and construction materials, through a long-term loan to the residents. The neighbors worked to build their own houses, under technical supervision from the municipality.

Sra. Alice said that those early days were very exciting, and "marked forever" the neighbors' ways of life and organization. Sra. Alice was then in her late forties and displayed a great vitality. Her husband had retired and received a very small pension; thus she supplemented family income with her work as a seamstress. Their two sons were already married and moved from the parents' house. Therefore she found enough time to participate in the board of the neighborhood association (where she has "always been active in the rank-and-file").

Sra. Alice said the neighbors were initially very pleased with the low payments they had to make for their houses when they moved in. Since the beginning they became organized in a voluntary association that held regular elections and tried to solve the problems of the **bairro**. Sra. Alice recognized "there were at times quarrels among the neighbors", and "different factions competed" in the yearly board elections. But they always "managed to reach an agreement", in which the contenders had "to sacrifice something in their positions", for the sake of "the welfare of all".

In fact this experience in participatory municipal government became well known in Brazil, as a showcase of civilian opposition to the military regime. However, during the next municipal election campaign, the candidate of the pro-military regime party visited

Bairro A. He promised to reduce the monthly installments paid by the neighbors, in "case they voted him in, and he promised even to cancel all the debt" if the whole neighborhood supported his candidacy. This candidate used a similar strategy with other sectors and groups in the city during his campaign, and he was therefore elected. But, as "the population was divided", and "the majority of *Bairro* A did not vote him in", the debt of the neighbors was not canceled, except for a few "*cabos eleitorais*" (electoral brokers). Nevertheless, the debt was gradually reduced and was finally canceled by the mayor, when the next election approached.

Meanwhile the neighbors' association searched for support from the state government, which was then in the hands of the party of the opposition to the regime (the same that had started the housing project in *Bairro* A, in the late 1970s). Even so, the conservative party won the next round of municipal elections again, though this time by a small percentage of the vote. Sra. Alice recalled that the neighbors pointed out at the time, that "any party that wanted majority support should unite with other parties and win popular support". For "popular division only favors those who oppress the people".

In the gubernatorial election in 1990, the residents of *Bairro* A faced the hard choice of either supporting their friends already in power, or (foreseeing their probable defeat) supporting the conservatives who occupied City Hall. The vote of *Bairro* A was again divided, with 51% supporting the conservatives. However, abstention was high (24%), and at the national level it was rampant (especially considering that voting is mandatory) reaching 52% including annulled votes. Sra. Alice explained: "when one goes to vote the cabin is closed and no one knows what the other does inside; parties and our association cannot and do not want to control anyone's vote; persons are free to chose what they want even when they are wrong". But after this doctrinal explanation she said the real problem was that "the parties of the center and the left did not arrive at a common platform and candidacy" for the state election.

When we did our fieldwork in early 1992, Sra. Alice was very convinced that neighbors from *Bairro* A would support a left-center candidacy, "because parties are forgetting their differences and preparing a common program to help the people, as they did in the late 1970s". In fact, as Table IV shows, 40% of the neighbors preferred politicians from the leftist parties, and 66% supported an eventual party coalition for the local government. The November municipal election confirmed this early prediction, which was repeated in 1996 (though the conservatives returned to power in the last municipal elections).

The life history of *Bairro* A and Sra. Alice is a history of awareness building, through social and political participation. In other *bairros* there are other life histories. For instance, Bert is a worker we interviewed in *Bairro* B, of the largest industrial city of the state. He is a typical local industrial laborer, from German ethnic background, who has a high school education and a technical manual job (trained by the *Escola Técnica*, a high school maintained by company and government grants). He migrated from a family farm nearby, and came to study in the city as a young man. He was 30 years old when interviewed and married to an industrial worker with whom he has a young child. He said they entered the housing project at *Bairro* B because they paid less here than the rent would be elsewhere, and could thus have a house of their own.

A fellow worker invited him to the municipal housing project, and his employer gave him a recommendation as a good worker with job stability. He had been working at this factory since 1983, and moved to the neighborhood in 1988. Bert said that "most people in the neighborhood liked very much being there", but "few participated in the meetings of the local association". These meetings were called by social workers and other municipal employees responsible for the housing project. The neighborhood was carefully planned, organized and controlled by these municipal officials.

Bert said that the neighbors' participation was done through "voting in the assemblies, on proposals presented by the officials". They neither had ("nor needed", he said) an elected board: "the officials are good, and take care of everything, avoiding conflicts and differences among the neighbors". In fact, the *bairro* even had its own police post, "which watches over everything". The only problem Bert saw in this model-process of social organization was that "the government sometime forgets, or does not pay attention" to demands made locally, and "does things in the *bairro* without telling anybody what is going to happen"[9].

Considering the satisfaction of the neighbors with the local government, it is not surprising that the conservative parties that have been in power in this city for so long always received a majority vote. However, the 1992 municipal elections were very competitive, for all parties ran separately and no coalition was formed. In fact, a runoff election had to be held, and conservatives won by joining forces, against the center-left parties that remained divided. The neighborhood's prospective voting pattern was similar: right wing parties and politicians received the largest support and the people were not in favor of forming a coalition. However, the party of the center (*PMDB*) won the municipal elections of 1996 and 2000, when the Left led by the *PT* (the Workers' Party) also gained considerable support.

The relatively high electoral participation of *Bairro* B in 1992 contrasted with the lower social participation of the neighbors in their association. Hence it is clear that this model of participation tends to demobilize the population and that social demobilization was part of a "conservative-modernization" strategy of the right coalition to remain in power. This strategy, implemented by local and state authorities, was earlier conceived at state level — as a response to and a cooptation of, the participatory experiences (such as that of *Bairro* A)[10], formerly promoted in the late 1970s by the parties of the left-center opposition to the military regime.

Let us look now at our last case. Carlos is a street vendor who makes a living in the central square of the capital of Santa Catarina. For 12 years he continuously struggled to defend his house in *Bairro* C where he lived with his wife and 4 children in a two-room wooden shack. This *bairro* was a group of 50 shacks along two streets, without sidewalks, pavement, sewers or any kind of services. They only obtained electricity and running water three years before the 1992 elections, by joining the "*Sem Tetos*" (Homeless) movement, which was sponsored by church sectors and the *PT* (Workers' Party). Due to this organized political support, *Bairro* C managed to have the authorities issue documents legally recognizing their land ownership and residential status as part of the urban area.[11]

Since its beginning, Carlos' life history is one of conflict and hardship, when these neighbors first invaded public ground in the center of the city in the early 1980s, and settled there as squatters. There followed a long decade of fear and uncertainty, when these people were first misled by various politicians, and by promises of the administration; they then faced attempts at removal by force, and brutal police repression. For over a decade, these residents were: once "removed from the center of the city into its outskirts": three times "threatened with eviction to another place" both by city authorities and private groups competing for their land; twice were "surrounded by police forces armed with machine guns, dogs, and horses"; and several times had to suffer "gunfire in the neighborhood, involving competing drug dealers and policemen". The question immediately arises: why did they stay there? And Carlos' answer is very straightforward: "Where should we go? The government first said we should come here, so we stayed...".

That is why he also said: "In this neighborhood we don't believe in anybody, everyone comes here as a liar and our enemy. The only ones I trust are my own family, because my wife and children depend on me". After saying this he reconsidered and added: "Well, Sister X and Dr. Y" (the nun and the lawyer who supported them in the "Homeless" movement) "are different: they are good and tell us how to claim our rights and become organized".

The characteristics of these three neighborhoods fit quite well into Habermas/ Kohlberg's categories for cognitive and moral development. These categories analyze cognitive structures and social perspectives around three basic types of action: preconventional, conventional and postconventional.[12]

Postconventional action-discourses rely on principles for testing the validity of norms, and they are the highest stage of cognitive and moral development present in contemporary societies. For they compare existing social validity norms to ideal standards or principles, in the interactions of daily life. The basic motivation of postconventional types of action is the affirmation of group and individual autonomy, around perspectives oriented by principles of justice. We saw above how *Bairro* A sustained its neighborhood association through consensual norms, where an ideal standard of well-being prevailed over divisive tendencies and sociopolitical changes. Its autonomy was affirmed in the criticism of parties and politicians, through a careful distinction between different strategies of action, and the ultimate aims of building a society free from oppression.

The high levels of sociopolitical participation and party identification of this community were thus oriented to building up a coalition in the city at large, in order to oust the conservatives from government. This neighborhood certainly included neighbors who supported populist or conservative politicians - indeed a minority in *Bairro* A. But they participated in cognitive and organizational experiences conducive to a higher stage of moral development: that which strives for justice as an end in itself, and they struggled to adjust the course of their daily life to this aim (even when they did not achieve electoral success - as it happened in the last municipal elections)

By contrast, **conventional** types of action focus on role behavior, structured in group-wide generalization of social roles. Their conceptualization of authority is based on loyalty to supraindividual will. The motivation of conventional actors is to make duty prevail over personal inclination, and duty is internalized from a primary-group perspective in conformity to prevailing social roles. This seems to be the basic situation of conservative and populist attitudes of loyalty and deference.

Bairro B was an example of this conformity to prevailing social roles - though in this case the dominant note was not a populist charismatic allegiance, but a conformity to "conservative modernization" parties and policies. This stage 3 of moral development is usually incapable of accomodating differences and dissent through the legitimacy of a system of norms for action (in fact the latter only emerges in the normatively grounded interactions of moral judgement).

However, dissent may arise all the same, for there is already a cognitive coordination between observer and participant perspectives, and the confrontations between duty and inclination may generate divergencies - as we observed in the data on minority vote. Therefore, there were also dissident minorities in *Bairro* B, who would prefer the left-center politicians and/or competition among party coalitions - over the then prevailing domination on the basis of a conformity to roles. Incidentally, data from the next elections illustrated the growth of the opposition in this city as well as in several other cities of the state. For instance, the dissident minorities of this *bairro* helped to elect the centrist *PMDB* candidate to City Hall, in the 1986 and in the 2000 elections, as well as opposition canditates to City Council, to the State legislature and the National Congress (including from *PT*).

Finally, **preconventional** types of action are either based on self-interest or controlled by authority. Their cognitive structures interlock submissive perspectives and particularist behavior, where authority is externally imposed via reference persons. Adherence to these persons is based on reward and punishment motivations, from an egocentric perspective. The conceptualization of justice may be either a complementarity between order and obedience (stage 1 of moral judgement) or symmetry of compensations (stage 2). *Bairro* C seemed to be in a transition between these two stages of preconventional action and moral judgement.

For one thing, their action had been oriented by self-interest from the beginning; but it was then controlled by the authority of external leaders. The reward and punishment motivations were formerly applied to a complementarity between order and obedience, in relation to the government. They were later on used in a symmetry of compensations with their current external referents - in this case, church and *PT* militants.

It is striking to see that, despite the high levels of demobilization, apathy and alienation of *Bairro* C (Table IV), these neighbors may have supported the candidacy of the center/left coalition that won the municipal elections of 1992. This may be related also to the fact that a Communist mayor was elected, alongside a majority of conservative council members (who have a strong patronage system in many low-income neighborhoods). (See Chapter 4). Therefore, these voters may easily change their minds if they do not find immediate rewards – according to their conceptualization of justice as "symmetry of compensations". Perhaps this is one of the reasons why the Popular Front lost the municipal elections in 1996, which were won by the conservatives, who also remained in office in the last elections.

In conclusion, this summary use of Habermas/Kholberg's categories covers a considerable proportion of the internal variations one may find, looking closely at the apparently homogeneous indexes of sociopolitical participation of these three neighborhoods. The group with the longest and most successful life-history among these neighborhoods is ***Bairro*** A - which also presents the highest stage of cognitive/moral development.

Table IV - Political preferences before the municipal elections in Santa Catarina (1992). (As %)

	1) Has party preference	2) In 1990 voted in:			3) Favorite politician:			4) Favors party coalition:		
		Right	Left	Abstained/ Don't know	Right	Left	Don't know	Yes	No	Don't know
Community A	75	51	24	25	29	40	31	66	27	07
Community B	52	42	10	48	21	28	51	36	49	15
Community C	33	33	-	67	29	17	54	58	21	21
All Communities	57	43	14	34	26	32	42	54	34	12

Source: Krischke (1993).

Both ***Bairros*** B and C, in turn, indicate the vulnerability of low-income neighborhoods to state-led and populist manipulation. They provide additional evidence to Baquero-Pra's assertion that a "subject" type of orientation tends to prevail in Southern Brazil. On the other hand, the case of **Bairro** A is surely exceptional, because it arose out of the party program of the civilian opposition to the previous authoritarian regime. The latter's experience can (and should) certainly be extended to other places, as the national study by Moisés on popular sophistication has suggested. This potential is illustrated by the apparent homogeneity of the neighborhoods, in the right column of Table V.

Table V - Social and political participation in Brazil and Santa Catarina (Figures denote %)

	Brazil		Santa Catarina	
	1989	1990	1989	1992
1) Politics influences your life	63	72	62	78
2) Read or view political news	68	78	55	64
3) Talk to others about politics	44	51	29	30
4) Try to convince others how to vote	31	53	29	32
5) Go to meetings and associations	23	25	31	67
6) Participate in electoral campaigns	08	24	18	45
7) Has party preference	44	48	33	57

Sources - 1989 (Brazil and S. Catarina); 1990: Moisés (1992)
          1992: Krischke (1993).

However, there is a long and sad history of co-optation of participatory politics in Brazil. The comparison above, among three local studies of neighborhood sociopolitical participation in Santa Catarina is an obvious case in point. The experience of *Bairro* A is to this day a "showcase" of the possible results of participatory democratic mobilization. But instead of stimulating other experiences, it has served as a warning for the rightist parties to implement their "conservative modernization" strategies (e.g., *Bairro* B), and also for their overt repression and manipulative domination of popular protest (e.g., *Bairro* C).

These local studies underline the central role of the party leadership and the local administrations in stimulating the learning of a democratic culture by the electorate. This learning of a democratic culture is implemented through the interactions between government policies (here low-income housing policies) and the demands and orientations of the citizens. Citizens may elaborate, clarify and normatively ground their orientations, as their array of choices is sharpened and instituted within the polity.

It remains to be seen whether the left-center forces in Brazilian politics will be able to learn from their experiences, and in turn propose a coalition program and strategy to educate the electorate politically. For as Moisés has emphasized there is a crucial 50% of the population who have moderate political sophistication, and may either support a democratic program, or turn to some "conservative modernizer" - or even to a populist demagogue, in any future election (as happened, for instance, in the Presidential election of Fernando Collor de Mello, in 1989).

Therefore, if both Baquero-Pra and Moisés are right, the point is how to strike a balance for a party coalition and a government program - and not only for a successful electoral campaign. Such a program and coalition would have to confront the legacy of conservative and state-led politics with an active strategy of democratic education and sociopolitical participation - one that would be applicable to different segments of the population, their representative parties and leadership. For such a combination could be the only way to consolidate a democratic regime and national political culture in Brazil.

REFERENCES

Almond, G. and Verba, S. 1963. **The Civic Culture**. Princeton, NJ, Princeton University Press.

Almond, G. 1988. "Separate Tables". *Political Science and Politics*, 21: 828-841.

Andrade, E. 1991. "Cultura Política e Democracia. A Experiência do Bairro Habitação, Lages 1977-83". MA Thesis, **Graduate Program in Political Sociology**, UFSC.

Baierle, S.G. 1998. "The Explosion of Experience: The Emergence of a New Ethico-Political Principle in Popular Movements in Porto Alegre", Brazil", in Alvarez, S. et al., **Cultural Politics and Politics of Culture. Re-visioning Social Movements in Latin America,** Boulder, CO: Westview Press.

Bank, G. A. 1993. "Cultura Política Brasileira: Que Tradição é essa?" *Revista Brasileira de Estudos Políticos*, 76:41-54.

Baquero, M. and Pra, J. R. 1992. "Cultura Política e Cidadania no Brasil: uma Análise Longitudinal". *Estudos Leopoldenses*, 28: 87-110.

Baquero, M.*et al.*, 1995. "A Dimensão Direita-Esquerda na Definição do Voto: O Caso das Eleições em Pôrto Alegre", **Seminario Nacional sobre Comportamento Político,** Florianópolis.

Canella, F. 1992. "A UFECO e o Movimento dos Sem Teto: Práticas Instituintes nos Espaços Políticos da Cidade", MA thesis, **Graduate Program in Political Sociology,** UFSC.

Chilton, S. 1991. **Grounding Political Development**. Boulder, CO: Lynne Rienner Publishers.

Figueiredo, M. 1991. **A Decisão do Voto,** ANPOCS-IDESP. Ed. Sumaré, São Paulo.

Guilhon Albuquerque, J. A. 1990. "Atitudes Políticas e Tipologia do Eleitorado Brasileiro". **Departamento de Política,** Universidade de São Paulo, Typescript.

Habermas, J. 1990. **Moral Consciousness and Communicative Action**, Cambridge, Mass: MIT Press.

Inglehart, R. 1988. "The Renaissance of Political Culture". *American Political Science Review*, 82:1203-1230.

Kohlberg, L. 1981-1984. **Essays on Moral Development**. San Francisco: Harper and Row, 2 Vols..

Krischke, P. J. 1993. "Participação Municipal e Democratização da Cultura Política: Estudos de Caso em Santa Catarina". Research Report presented to the **Conselho Nacional de Desenvolvimento Científico e Tecnológico** (CNPq).

_____, 1997. "Cultura Política e Escolha Racional na América Latina: Interfaces nos Estudos da Democratização", **Revista Brasileira de Informação Bibliográfica em Ciências Sociais. BIB,** 43: 103-27.

Lane, R. 1992. "Political Culture. Residual Category or General Theory?" *Comparative Political Studies*, 25 (3): 362-387.

Mettenheim, K. V. 1992. "Democratic Theory and Public Opinion in Latin America", **LASA Congress,** Los Angeles, September.

Moisés, J. A. 1992. "Democratization and Mass Political Culture in Brazil", **Annual Meeting of the American Political Science Association,** Chicago 3-9 September.

Moser, L. 1991. "O Cotidiano dos Moradores de Mangue em Joinville: Modo de Vida e Relações de Poder". MA Thesis, **Graduate Program in Political Sociology,** UFSC.

Neuman, R.W. 1986. **The Paradox of Mass Politics**. Boston, MA: Harvard University Press.

Pateman, C. 1979. "The Civic Culture: A Philosophic Critique", in Almond, G. and Verba, S. (Eds.) **The Civic Culture Revisited**, Boston: Little, Brown & Co.

Pinto, C.R. 1997. "Das Formas de Fazer Política. As Eleições Municipais de Porto Alegre, 1996", **Cadernos de Ciência Política**, 7, Porto Alegre: UFRGS.

Rochon, T.R. and Mitchell, M.J. 1987. "The Withering Away of the Authoritarian State - Social Bases of the Transition to Democracy in Brasil", **Western Political Science Association**.

Souza, A. and Lamounier, B. 1989. "A Feitura de Nova Constituição: Um Reexame da Cultura Política Brasileira", *Planejamento e Políticas Públicas*, 2:17-38.

Welch, S. 1993. **The Concept of Political Culture**, New York: St. Martin's Press.

ENDNOTES

[1] I must express my gratitude to the students and colleagues, at the **Universidade Federal de Santa Catarina** who supported this project. And especially to Liliane Moser, Edinara Andrade and Francisco Canella, who have written their M.A. theses on each of the neighborhoods we study below. Ligia Luchmann helped to conduct the fieldwork.

[2] The classic study by Almond and Verba on the "Civic Culture" (1963) suggests that a stable democratic polity requires a "balanced" political culture (the "civic culture"), which combines both a participatory and a deferential attitude toward politics. This combination of participatory and "subject" orientations may vary (as illustrated by the cases of American and British cultures). But it contrasts with other "unbalanced" cultural "blends", which combine various levels of commitment and involvement in political life, and do not provide stability for democratic politics. (See the various appraisals and criticisms of this approach in Almond and Verba [Eds.], 1983.

[3] Baquero/Pra's study showed that there was a "growing dissatisfaction, apathy and a feeling of inefficacy of the citizens toward politics, the political parties and the dilemmas of the political transition" (1992:95). "Parochial participation may emerge and blend with a parochial alienation, resulting in various dissenting subcultures" (1992:97). In short, "subject orientations must precede participatory orientations" (1992:98). Otherwise "passive, modern (...) or alienated parochialism, plus other deviant subcultures" may emerge (p.102) and impede the consolidation of a democratic culture. Nevertheless, the study shows that we are in a "transitional situation, that extends from the traditional to the subject types of orientation"(p.108) - "though we are far from a political culture characterized by participatory attitudes." This situation of political culture in Porto Alegre has probably changed considerably, after 12 years of **PT** administration in that city. (See Pinto, 1997; Baierle, 1998; Baquero [Ed.], 1997).

[4] Moisés adds: "Although not a causal phenomenon, it shows that starting from the assumption that sophistication precedes commitment to values, we can reach the conclusion that the degree of heterogeneity in sophistication encountered in middle groups is closely associated with their differentiation in terms of commitment to political values" (Moisés, 1992:17).

[5] In the last decades there has been a "renaissance of political culture" studies (Inglehart, 1988), which revived earlier criticisms of Almond and Verba (e.g. Pateman, 1979), together with new debates on the actual transformation of the concept - into what was considered by some as a "residual variable" (Lane, 1992; Welch, 1993). In this chapter I have adopted a different definition of political culture, in terms of "moral reasoning development". This definition was derived by Stephen Chilton (1991:68), from Habermas' and Kohlberg's approaches, as a cultural "way of relating 'shared' only if it is **publicly common** within the collectivity". This means that this cultural "way of relating shares" validity claims for norms of action that are "common" and "public" among participants in interactions, for they are (a) understood by most in that culture (a **common** understanding); and (b) in fact used by them to orient one another on sociopolitical matters (the **public** focus of orientation).

[6] This is certainly a powerful claim that corrects (but does not invalidate) the usual aim of survey research on political culture — that of inferring the general characteristics of value-systems from aggregate individual responses to questionnaires. The correction goes in the direction of affirming the probabilistic limits of survey research — provided that overgeneralization of value inferences be avoided, and a new emphasis be focused on the normative validation by respondents of sociopolitical actions. On the other hand, survey research should be always accompanied with local studies of subcultures and historical analysis, in order to substantiate value inferences (i.e. to test whether they can in fact be substantiated). See Krischke, 1997 and Welch, 1993.

[7] The three low-income neighborhoods were chosen on the assumption that they represented different forms of sociopolitical organization, participation and normative orientation - as in fact was shown to be the case. The main preliminary criterion for selection was that these *bairros* were all involved in government negotiations and social struggles over policies concerning low-income housing. The benchmark for the contrasting situations was the situation of *Bairro* A - a long-established experience of sociopolitical participation that had an impact on the housing policies (as well as on other social policies) in the state. They were also selected because these neighborhoods were formed on three different occasions, over the last decades, and under different local and state governments. An additional sociogeographic criterion was that the local studies were located in different regions of the state of Santa Catarina: *Bairro* A in a medium-size city in the cattle-growing and lumber region of the *planalto*; *Bairro* B in the largest and most industrialized city of the state; *Bairro* C in the capital, - which is primarily a center of public administration, tourism and commerce.

[8] The names and personalities of the interviewees are fictional. Their life-histories were constructed from the "shared" experiences and responses of various respondents in each neighborhood. I thank Rodrigo Baño for his assistance in formulating this procedure.

[9] See the MA thesis of Liliane Moser (1991).

[10] See the MA thesis of Edinara Andrade (1991).

[11] See the MA thesis of Francisco Canella (1992).

[12] What follows is an analysis of the data based on Habermas (1990:116-196).

Chapter 8

THE CHILEAN PATHWAY TO DEMOCRACY[*]

The current debate on the judicial charges raised (nationally in Chile and internationally since the arrest of Pinochet in Britain) against the military accused of human rights violations during the previous authoritarian regime, often disregards the social and political changes which are happening in that country since the start of the transition to democracy in the late 1980s. Several recent studies (e.g. Frank, 2000; Weeks, 2000; Policzer, 2000; Garretón, 1999; Moulián, 1999) have pointed to the fact that the strengthening of Chilean democracy depends not only on the reconstruction (or re-consolidation) of its previous institutions, but also on the development of social and cultural changes that are having a great impact on the country's polity. From this perspective, the Chilean transition to democracy may be seen as a 'benchmark' from which other Latin American cases of democratization could be assessed. This chapter of the book focuses on the first stages of Chilean democratization, in order to highlight its contributions to so-called 'new democracies', in Chile and elsewhere.

The plebiscite that derailed the Pinochet regime and also the elections that re-established the country's formal democracy in the late 1980s, have called attention to the antecedents and preconditions of the process of democratization. Studies carried out by *FLACSO* researchers in Chile shed light on this issue by providing a wealth of information about the transformations in Chilean society during the past decades and also about the role and self-definition of intellectuals in the context of democratization. This chapter will discuss these two dimensions of Chilean democratization in five books published by *FLACSO (Facultad Latinoamericana de Ciencias Sociales*, supported by UNESCO and OAS). The focus adopted here of distinguishing between social democratization and political democracy was suggested by the books themselves, which all differentiate the two dimensions carefully (although they consider various relations between the two). As will be shown, it makes sense to distinguish between democratization in the social sphere (in terms of values and orientations, modernization

---

[*] Parts of this chapter were included in a review essay, translated by Sharon Kellum for *The Latin America Research Review*. Norbert Lechner and José-Joaquin Brunner made insightful comments on the earlier draft, which were taken into account for the present version.

of behavior, access to socioeconomic equality, and related aspects) versus transformation of the political regime in the sense of democratic institutionalization. This chapter will first address the transformations in Chilean society and then consider the proposals for political democratization and the role of Chilean intellectuals.

TRANSFORMATIONS IN CHILEAN SOCIETY

As presented in these studies, Chile displays one facet of striking continuities with the past and another of great discontinuities generated under the military regime. One facet consists of the sociopolitical identities that have persisted remarkably (in terms of cultural traditions, party symbols, and collective memory) under repressive and clandestine conditions. They have nevertheless suffered progressive differentiation due to forced reorganization in the public arenas emerging as alternatives to the old institutional channels and also due to new cultural influences. The discontinuities include divisions in social classes, sectoral and corporative struggles to appropriate income and property, and socioeconomic inequalities maintained and exacerbated under the exclusionary regime.

Rodrigo Baño's *Lo Social y lo Político: Un Dilema Clave del Movimiento Popular* (Baño, 1985) rigorously mapped the evolution of urban popular movements in the unions and neighborhoods (*poblaciones*). He demonstrated how social and economic demands since the mid-1980s led to a rapid politicization of distributive conflicts in the absense of legitimate institutional channels under the military regime. Baño presented impressive data, like his figures on growth in unemployment and the decline in real salaries over the decade, and he also described various strategies adopted by labor and other popular movements for confronting the problems of deteriorating living conditions. Baño believes that the 'objective politicization' of the social movements *vis-à-vis* the state has not been accompanied by a 'subjective politicization' that would have led these movements to unity of action and projects of transformation.

Baño employed the classic dichotomy between community and society to highlight the differences between objective and subjective politicization of the union movements as compared with the neighborhood movements, on the one hand, and between the entire social movement and the political parties in an authoritarian context, on the other. He concluded that the 'split between the social and the political spheres translates into a separation between parties and social movement' (Baño, 1985:184). But according to Alain Touraine, historical reconstruction coming from the trajectory of social movements centers around characterization of various conflicts that organize these actors into new 'popular subjects' oriented toward an 'alternative popular project', however incipient under the authoritarian regime. Baño explains, 'A union movement [is] defined by the contradiction between capital and labor as manifested in the particular relations of production of any given firm [whereas] a movement encompassing neighborhoods is not defined by the capital-labor relationship. In the end, the issue is fundamentally political, which may not be obvious in an era of "institutional normalcy" but reflects the characteristics of domination also present' (Baño, 1985:186).

We will see subsequently how these outcomes relate to party politics and proposals for democratization. But the tasks of reorganizing the public sphere could be perceived here, from the beginning of the decade (and more dramatically with the 'pot-bangings' and national protests of the mid 1980s), as demands emerging from changes in Chilean society (mainly in terms of objective and subjective politicization). Or perhaps the socioeconomic and political problems left unresolved since the coup in 1973 led the popular sectors to demand real solutions unlike those proposed in the past.

José Joaquín Brunner, in *Un Espejo Trizado: Ensayos sobre Cultura y Políticas Culturales*, (Brunner, 1988) linked these transformations to relations currently existing between a heterogeneous culture and society:

> Cultural heterogeneity means, after all, something quite distinct from diverse cultures or subcultures of ethnic groups, classes, or regions, something more than the mere overlay of cultures, whether or not they have found a form of synthesis. Cultural heterogeneity actually means segmented and varying participation in an international market of messages that "penetrate" the local framework of culture from all sides in unexpected ways, leading to a veritable implosion of the meanings consumed, produced, or reproduced and to a consequent destructuring of collective representations, failures in identity, longings for identification, confusions of temporal horizons, paralysis of creative imagination, loss of utopias, fragmentation of local memory, and obsolescence of traditions.
> *(Brunner, 1988 : 218)*

Hence comes Brunner's metaphor of the 'cracked mirror', in which the identifying-rationalist logic of modernity is negated by the 'anomie' of actors constantly divided by the pre- and postmodern logics of their contradictory constitution. In the Chilean case (and with possible extension to other democratization processes in Latin America), Brunner perceives in this heterogeneity the confrontation between what he describes as two communication modalities (*regímenes comunicativos*):

> One modality structured around the military government operates through the combined effect of repression, the market, and television. The other modality, which is weaker, more scattered, less institutionalized, and has a variable local range, is structured around opposition organizations and initiatives. The former develops from the top down and is controlled in a rather centralized manner. The latter rises from below, has multiple centers of articulation, and operates in the spaces it manages to create or in gaps in the official system. The official communication modality is necessarily antipolitical and abhors the tumult of collective voices, while the opposition communication modality stimulates politics and promotes representation of collective expressions.
> *(Brunner,1988: 74)*

In this context, Brunner observed, "daily reality is experienced as a strange amalgam of judgments and interpretations competing for individuals' attention and seeking to legitimize themselves according to their pertinence to opposing systems of communication... The country survives on its own as an implosion of images, none of them having enough force to establish meaning that can be generalized and shared. A special kind of *anomie* rules day-to-day events" (Brunner, 1988: 75).

Thus Baño's initial diagnosis of a split between the social and political spheres took on more drastic overtones when Brunner incorporated the effects of cultural heterogeneity into the analysis. The issue transcends the impasses of the social movements' incomplete politicization when faced with the exclusionary political regime to consider the dilemmas faced until today by democratic sectors in trying to broaden the coherence and inclusiveness of their 'communication modality'.

Angel Flisfisch's *La Política como Compromiso Democrático* (Flisfisch, 1987) made normative and institutional proposals for fulfilling and consolidating the processes of democratization. He also retraced the emergence in authoritarian regimes of the Southern Cone of a 'new democratic ideology', which he viewed as 'defensive forms' of political action by contemporary social movements in Chile - the feminist movement, sectors of the Left, and the church (Flisfisch, 1987: 98-100). The author perceived in these actions the rise of three 'human models' - the 'liberated person', the dissident, and the individual with human rights. He characterized them as 'three orienting figures' that 'represent regulating principles, thus forming an ethics of politics' based on four dimensions: 'First, the idea of self-government. Second, the idea of expanding the areas subject to personal control. Third, the idea of a necessary dispersing or socializing of power. Fourth, the idea of restoring to the collectivity (and simultaneously superseding) the personal capacities and potentials lost in the interplay of social structures, which had become autonomous of the women and men who endured them'(Flisfisch, 1987: 100).

This emerging democratic ideology embodied a 'reinforcement of civil society' by valuing the ethical contents of democracy as well as expressive and participatory forms of political action - in 'anti-statist' counterpoint to what Flisfisch characterizes as 'the Napoleonic conception', which traditionally considered the state and the government as holding the monopoly on political rationality. Flisfisch did not minimize constitutionalist and democratic-institutional traditions as part of the political legacy to be restored in Chile. But in the context of authoritarian regimes, the combined violation of human rights, negation of public values of citizenship, and forced privatization in a fragmented daily life have all made the ethical contents of democracy a priority for countering the exclusionary logics of the state and the market.

Flisfisch's approach thus underlined the ethical-normative dimension as fundamental to appreciating the transformations of Chilean society under the Pinochet regime. To get beyond the socioeconomic and political dilemmas of the popular movements (as discussed by Baño) or even the 'anomic' cultural fragmentation of the population (as outlined by Brunner), one must recognize the new values emerging in society in opposition to authoritarianism. Adding to the situation are the problems of overcoming 'Napoleonic' forms of equating politics strictly with the state or political society in the narrow sense of the political party system.The democratization process that succeeds will be the one capable of including the new actors emerging - new social movements, sectors of the churches, and dissidents of various kinds who can verbalize the 'voice of the voiceless' to defend values, individual and minority rights, and all those marginalized and dominated in Chilean society.

Of course, this antistatist orientation had to be modified in a progressive proposal for building democratic institutions. But its ethical standards revealed a broad reformulation in Chilean daily life that was not necessarily antipolitical. This topic was the main focus of Norbert Lechner's essays in *Los Patios Interiores de la Democracia: Subjetividad y Política*, (Lechner, 1988) which attempted to 'look beyond [institutional] politics'. Lechner asserted, 'In order to carry out political reform, we must above all undertake a reform of politics' in which 'the inquiry turns toward less tangible aspects generally neglected by democracy', such as 'the daily experience of the people, their hopes and fears'. According to Lechner, 'democracy, which depends so much on public scrutiny for its development, also hides backyards', corners representing 'the cognitive-affective substrate of democracy'. Lechner proposed to explore these hidden areas in order to 'get a different perspective on politics' (Lechner, 1988: 18-19).

In discussing daily life under the Pinochet regime, Lechner focused on Chilean 'discontent with the usual ways of conducting politics':

> Even when the old party loyalties survive the military regime, the common people find it difficult to objectify in the parties the sense of social setting and collective belonging. To the extent that the political organizations, which are increasingly specialized (bureaucratized) and remote from the daily life of the common people, no longer believe in nor assure collective identities, such identities must reorganize around the edges and in opposition to the institutions. Also weakened are spheres of informal sociability (like the neighborhood, the soccer club, or the university itself), where emotions and passions, memories and dreams are shared and where collective referents are formed.
> *(Lechner, 1988: 52)*

On this basis, Lechner considered the 'culture of fear' generated under the military regime as deriving from the foundations of 'a violated order': 'Fear, above all, of a life without meaning, stripped of roots, deprived of any future. These kinds of hidden fears, the price every Chilean has had to pay to survive, support the exercise of authoritarian power' (Lechner, 1988: 97). The author continues, 'By producing the loss of collective referents, the deconstruction of future horizons, the erosion of social criteria about what is normal, possible, and desirable, authoritarianism whets the vital need for order and presents itself as the only solution' (Lechner, 1988: 98). Dictatorships continually create new fears: 'they profoundly disrupt routines and social habits by making even daily life untenable. As normalcy disappears, the sense of helplessness grows, [and]... a moral apathy develops... Discontent with the existing state of things becomes narcissistic, self-complacent, and finally self-destructive... Thus authoritarianism's tendency to disrupt collective identities ends up undermining its own basis for legitimacy. The promise to bring order turns out to be an excruciating experience of disorder' (Lechner, 1988: 100-101).

For this reason, according to Lechner, the democratic project must 'assume our fears and insecurities' to prevent authoritarian manipulation and must contain them acceptably within the construct of a feasible future. Like Brunner, Lechner related sociocultural heterogeneity to the emergence of 'postmodernity' or 'incomplete modernization' (to use Habermas's phrase). He also related it to the need for collective referents offering a minimum of security and shared values assuring an emerging democratic ethos in society (as noted by Flisfisch). Without neglecting the institutional aspects of democratization's future, Lechner's diagnosis underscored the generalized nature of the search for collective referents, its strategic importance in confronting authoritarianism, and its extra-institutional relevance for creating a new democratic order: 'In sum, to take on the uncertainty of a history without a subject or goals is a disillusioning experience, necessary but insufficient. We develop a disenchanted vision only if we take seriously the demands of enchantment. Political realism justly must make us see that uncertainty brings with it the search for certainty. *If democracy is born out of uncertainty, does it not arise precisely to respond to that uncertainty?* (Lechner, 1988: 137)[1].

Manuel Antonio Garretón's *La Posibilidad Democrática en Chile* (Garretón, 1989, written after the opposition victory in 1988), diagnosed the decade's transformation by focusing mainly on the institutional sphere: 'In Chile... democratization has occurred only via political democracy' as a *sine qua non*. Garretón therefore considers it appropriate to postpone the ethical-cultural and socioeconomic demands for democratization until the consolidation phase of the democratic transition because 'in political democracies, the ones who create democratization are the political majorities' (Garretón, 1989: 14-15). This interpretation of the long-term Chilean experience explains for Garretón why the opposition transformed 'its social majority into a political majority... and the latter into an electoral majority' in the plebiscite called by the military regime (Garretón, 1989: 29).

In Garretón's view, this victory was only possible after overcoming 'the obstacles that had held the opposition back since it gained access to the public arena in the mid-1980s with the national protests' (Garretón, 1989: 46). These obstacles resulted from the opposition's inability to formulate a proposal for 'democratic transition from below': 'This social force did not become a political force in a horizontal sense, or perhaps for historical or functional reasons did not envision a unifying formula for transition until February 1988', when an accord was reached on participating in the October plebiscite (Garretón, 1989: 23-24).

Moreover,

> this social force did not become a political force in a vertical sense. Basically, what developed was a social mobilization of multiple meanings that involved repairing the social fabric and favored agitation. Above all, this movement possessed symbolic and expressive value in its affirmation of identity, belonging, dignity, and rejection of subjugation... The inability to transform the social force into the political force for transition is partly explained... by the transformations experienced over the past fifteen years, which gave rise to a type of society and a type of "mass situation". It was well expressed in the form of the protests, for example. They, however, were not tied to any political formula but rather to expressing a hope or positive wishes (like "Democracy Now"), which completely skipped over the institutional issue of *how to achieve that goal*.
> *(Garretón, 1989: 24-25)*

According to Garretón, the passage from social mobilization to political transition (and on to 'consolidation of democracy') involved creating new political actors: 'If one factor can be associated with founding, restoring, and consolidating democracy, it is the *desirability* of democracy by the various significant actors. This desire for a democratic regime organizes the *democratic actors* by converting structural factors or conditions into categories of historical action' (Garreón, 1989: 64).

The answer was not to discard preexisting political identities, even under repression, but to support their reorganization into democratic political actors that could inject themselves into the public arena in a unified manner with a transition project relevant to the historical moment.

PROPOSALS FOR DEMOCRATIZATION AND THE ROLE OF CHILEAN INTELLECTUALS

The five works under review presented a critical vision and varying proposals for transforming the Chilean political scene in a democratic direction. Baño, for example, devoted an entire section to discussing the 'urban popular movement from the perspective of political tendencies', which led him to emphasize 'the split between the social and the political spheres, [which] translates into a separation between parties and social movement. Yet this schism implies not a lack of relations but relations between leaderships (which are interchangeable at times) because in circumstances where no individual space exists for citizens, the social movement seems to be the condition for the party's existence' (Baño, 1985: 184).

As we have seen, this statement represents Baño's critique in underlining the alternative character of the 'popular project' emerging from the social movements and also denouncing the primarily 'statist' orientation of party politics:

> The statist character of party politics impedes the development of sectoral politics and national politics... The party invokes the abstract nation, the entire society, which it claims to represent or direct as a whole without integrating the existing social movements... If we add the dominance of the intellectual as political subject, we have the bases for understanding why this splintering of political parties is accompanied by discourse as a style of conducting politics. Discourse is the mechanism for bringing together the anonymous and fragmented people. It reveals that the social situation is taken to be a 'mass situation', before which the leader (the party) projects itself as a subject that the mass will begin to recognize as the start of its own identity.
> *(Baño, 1985: 178-79)*

Although Baño recognized the historic precedent established by the 'moment of party politics' beginning with the protests in the 1980s, he emphasized its weaknesses, mainly the lack of incorporation or any solution to the main dilemma - the 'split between the social and the political spheres'. Baño attributed many of these weaknesses to the political and intellectual sectors of the Left (despite the renewal they were going through under the dictatorship):

> The most novel concept, which was formulated by 'renovated' socialism in the 1970s, is closely linked to the modern preoccupation with social movements. This concept does not seem to have been developed far enough theoretically, nor has it been shaped

effectively in the so-called sociopolitical movements... Most of the intellectuals who
subscribe to this tendency (strongly influenced by Touraine and the European critique of
existing socialisms) ended up separating social movements from parties again,
emphasizing the [split between the] demand-making ability of social movements and the
democratic institutional arena of parties.
(Baño, 1985: 181)

Although Baño has probably reformulated his critique in light of later developments,
the radical meaning of his diagnosis remains clear. In the mid-1980s, political
democratization arose mainly as a threat of returning to the institutional problems
existing before the coup in 1973, now swollen by social demands and an alternative
'popular project' that did not seem compatible with a democratic transition. Implicit in
Baño's diagnosis was the demand for a new kind of democratic political actor, one
capable of overcoming the 'split between the social and political spheres' and eventually
representing the new 'alternative popular project' emerging from the social movements.

Brunner's political appraisal takes another drastic step in proposing an institutional
exit toward democratization. His 'cracked mirror' reflects the social and party
fragmentation of the 'mass society'. But it also reflects the cultural diversity achieved in
Chile (and Latin America) as a pluralist value of the modern era (however stunted and
incomplete in countries on the ' periphery'), a value to be deepened and reoriented during
political democratization. Brunner goes on to suggest, 'It may be that democracy is
effectively the only setting in which this cultural mix, this heterogeneity, these cognitive
and affective dissonances of perceptions and languages can manifest themselves without
each component demanding the others' elimination as a condition for existence, thus
insisting on exclusion in one of its thousand contemporary forms' (Brunner, 1987: 256).

Following an extensive discussion of the 'models of cultural politics' and their
application to party proposals in Chile, Brunner concluded that *'democratic* cultural
policies should be considered and designed primarily according to a liberal or
Toquevillean model, which features the combined presence of private and public agents
regulated by the market, the government, and the community. And when attempting to
implement these policies, they can be considered as issuing from *civil society* (not from
the state) under a Gramscian model, or a model of hegemonic competition' (Brunner,
1987:377).

In the Latin American context, particularly during transitions to democracy, cultural
politics will undoubtedly have to be revised, as will the role of intellectuals. According to
Brunner,

In a country like ours, after the experience of the last twenty years or so, intellectuals
evidently find themselves deprived of certainties... The theories they embraced, their
'paradigms' or 'grand pronouncements' on history have been cracked or hopelessly
shattered... It is late to be talking about the *responsilility of the intellectual*, but it surely
has to do with the uncertainties of history - especially in a democracy, where decisions
must be made in circumstances that render outcomes uncertain. Moreover, the very
exercise of thinking and speaking, supposedly the irreducible core of the intellectual task,
is subject to this uncertainty about effects, to the constant back and forth between
inconclusive arguments, between words and things, between meanings that do not hold

up - in short, subject to the natural uncertainty that follows when one never again claims to be in the position of having the last word.
(Brunner, 1987: 470-71)

Here Brunner criticized the 'statism' of the politics of democratization in terms of strategic analysis (or the 'interdependent decision' of the actors, according to Adam Przeworski, whom he cites). Brunner was trying to 'de-dramatize' politics by unburdening it of the 'ideological inflation' (to employ Albert Hirschman's phrase) characteristic of traditional political actors. This approach assumed that it could be more faithful to the cultural heterogeneity of the modern 'society of masses', respecting the differing contents and individual and sectoral values emerging in it while delimiting the range of feasible and necessary accords - from democratic institutionalization to a 'cold' (uncontroversial) core of durable procedures of political coexistence, which is considered valuable in itself.

Of the five authors, Flisfisch took this perspective to the greatest extreme (drawing mainly on the ideas of Jon Elster, another 'analytic Marxist'). Because Flisfisch emphasized the 'reinforcement of civilian society' in light of the new 'democratic ideology' emerging in social movements against authoritarianism, he could speak of 'politics as a democratic agreement' that neither sacrifices nor trades off these values and ideals but rather protects and orients them:

> By definition, the style inherent in the contractual elaboration of order issuing from political society implies a modality of *deliberate* internalization of the crisis... [A] reasonably authentic strategy is being unfolded here, not by a monolithic state actor but by a coalition of actors maintaining cooperative relations among themselves... The style of conducting politics implied makes alliances and coalitions a major political issue. In this scenario, politics is viewed in terms of a coalitional arrangement: the political chances themselves (electoral or other), whose maximization is the basic goal of the parties' traditional behavior, is subordinated to the goal of achieving broadly inclusive sociopolitical alliances. Politics now attempts to maximize this goal. A related requirement is a political society completely open to civil society, with full representation of the *world of the excluded*. A political society run by an oligarchy, which would not make room for this world, would be identical to the model of unilateral imposition by the state and would therefore face all the insoluble problems already analyzed.
> *(Flisfisch, 1988: 324-25)*

Clearly, it is impossible to retrace every step in the five analyses, but their points of convergence permitted gradual clarifying of the strategies for overcoming authoritarianism and building democracy. Among their common emphases was the necessity of reexamining the formulas of traditional politics, Flisfisch's 'Napoleonic conception of politics'. In this traditional 'statist' conception, the intellectual's role would be 'advisor to the prince', according to the Machiavellian model. Flisfisch explained, 'In the contemporary period, this idea has been associated with an equivalent social figure: the *technocrat*. Since the modernization model was displaced by the development paradigm, the relation between the social sciences and reality - civil and political society

society versus the state - has been interpreted according to this kind of instrumental logic' (Flisfisch, 1988: 20).

Flisfisch's study criticized this instrumental view of the 'paradigm of the prince', which he associated with the 'philosophy of history' and its legitimizing intellectual functions within the 'Napoleonic' statist model of politics:

> Its first and basic function lies in identifying several ends that are objectively assignable to the course of history. The supposition that one is dealing with genuine ends, besides reinforcing the expert's partial knowledge, allows one to resolve the general problem of legitimacy seeking justification when employing the coercive resources of the state. This philosophy of history also identifies an agent or agents, historically privileged, who are summoned to fulfill the tasks of development implied by the identifiable ultimate ends in history. This historic privilege allows not only justifying fixed positions in society - property owners, the party and its functionaries, and so on - but devaluing society's resistance to state and governmental action: such resistance is wrongheaded and therefore irrational; furthermore, its protagonists are condemned by history itself. Consequently, to repress them is to act in harmony with history, clearing its path by eradicating useless outgrowths. Finally, this philosophy of history claims to possess wisdom or knowledge of the future. Beyond its scientific pretensions or other kinds of guarantees (such as religious faith expressed in a wish for life after death), this supposed knowledge has the virtue of removing politics from the contemporary world where it is being wielded by displacing its meaning to a space and time that are definitely not worldly..., thus desecularizing politics by transcendentalizing it.
> *(Flisfisch, 1987: 284-85)*

Flisfisch counters this model and paradigm with the idea of the institutional accord, but he distinguishes it carefully from the simple 'compromise state' or the 'political marketplace' because

> the latter conceptualization rests on an image of society differing in no way from that of Hobbes... Such a society basically consists of clashes of interests - not necessarily individual interests but perhaps group interests, corporate interests corresponding to various sectors, or more encompassing interests imputable to larger conglomerations like classes. Yet Hobbes's state of nature does not vary. Possessive individualism must yield to possessive corporativism and so on, with the main feature continuing to be the clash of interests.
> *(Flisfisch, 1987: 287)*

According to Flisfisch, just as the 'Napoleonic model' errs in desecularizing politics, the model of the political marketplace or the compromise state oversecularizes politics: 'The risk of oversecularization derives from the essentially instrumental nature attributed to politics, a common characterization in these two conceptual models. To avoid this risk, this instrumental nature must be relegated to a secondary role in order to higlight the presence in political activity of certain values that only politics can consummate. This requirement involves seeking an ethical basis for politics that is inherent in it, some essential dimension of its definition that permits rejecting the legitimation of politics on any basis external to it, as happens when a philosophy of history is invoked' (Flisfisch, 1987: 291-92).

In reaching an accord on the values inherent in politics, the role of intellectuals was redefined as combining 'critical reason with invention', 'invention being understood as identifying the plausible or possible state of the facts on a rational basis. Then the social scientist is neither the academic nor the advisor to princes nor the prophet but the producer of inventions' (Flisfisch, 1987: 23).

For such inventions to become effective social innovations during democratization, they must meet two general criteria according to Flisfisch:

> First, the path from invention to innovation should be a complex chain of mediations strongly anchored in civil and political society. If democracy means... the opportunity for the people and the lawful majorities to intervene, this complex demand for mediation is an obligation. Also central to this path is the idea that critical and positive knowledge must be transformed into mass common sense to be effective. From this perspective, the social scientist is also an educator, an intellectual functioning in the classic Gramscian sense, on behalf not of the individual or collective prince but of liberating critical reason and national mass culture.
> *(Flisfisch, 1987: 24)*

Lechner, consistent with his appraisal of daily life and the extra-institutional dimension of politics, stressed the ethical-evaluative element (or 'precontractual' element) of the democratic accord:

> I think of the possibility of pacifying our fears of the other, that strange and different being, and of assuming this uncertainty as a condition for the other's freedom. Because democracy means more than mere tolerance. It means recognizing the other as a participant in producing a shared future. A democratic process, unlike an authoritarian regime, allows - and demands - that we discover the future as an intersubjective elaboration and the otherness of the other as that of an "alter ego". Viewed thus, the other's freedom, his or her unfathomableness, ceases to be a threat to one's own identity and becomes the condition for one's own development.
> *(Lechner, 1988: 107)*

Adopting this ethical referent (transcendent-processual, in John Rawls's approach) of a shared future breathes life into initiatives of interaction that could challenge the rest of society to establish mutual trust and overcome their fear and daily isolation. Lechner explained, 'Trust is not something that can be demanded from another; it begins by being given to another. Trust is bestowed by signaling to the other certain expectations of oneself, with the promise of fulfilling them... Trust is therefore a risky act of anticipation: one pledges oneself to specific future conduct without knowing whether the other person will respond to it. It is a voluntary offer; the other can accept the show of trust or not... But once the other person responds to the trust offered, the other pledges himself or herself' (Lechner, 1988: 83).

Lechner admitted the necessity of going beyond intersubjectivity in establishing the normative assumptions of legitimacy and democractic legality. But he insisted that he would not focus on 'the reciprocity of expectations based on legal order, although it is the most important. From the realist perspective, the prelegal field holds more interest as the diffuse sphere where social and moral obligations are created that allow hope that the other will fulfill legal prescriptions effectively... Being realists, we refer more to what other *can do* and not to what he or she should or should not do' (Lechner, 1988:80).

In this interactive context of ethical realism arises the significance of a new kind of secularized democratic intellectual. According to Lechner, 'Today the complex social differentiation in South America no longer allows one to conceive of the struggle for liberty and equality in essentialist terms... The use of Marx has lost its quasi-religious connotation... [in] a kind of settling of accounts with 'the Marxisms' and simultaneous efforts to actualize that tradition as *a point of departure* for thinking about the democratic transformation of society" (Lechner, 1988: 31). He continued, 'What would seem to demand a secularized conception [of politics] is renouncing utopia as an achievable goal, but without abandoning utopia as the referent by which we conceive of what is real and determine what is possible. A major task of democratization is thus established: changing the political culture' (Lechner, 1988: 40).

In Lechner's view, this change had already been partially achieved: 'Largely because of intellectuals of the Left, democracy has been determined to be the main task of society. Constructing the social order is [now] conceived of as the *democratic transformation of the society*' (Lechner, 1988: 41). This outcome resulted partly from the new way in which intellectuals have reoriented their activities: 'The analysis of the *social* scientist will always be an *interpretation* whose validity depends not only on the conventions within the scientific community but equally on the intersubjective recognition of those who were studied... Society is not only the "material" but simultaneously the "interpreter" of that material' (Lechner, 1988: 59). Lechner concluded, 'To reform society is to discern the competing logics and reinforce those tendencies we think are best. The result will not be a pure and definitive social order. On the contrary, our societies will continue to be as contradictory and precarious as life itself - and for that very reason, they will be creative processes' (Lechner, 1988: 189).

Certainly, the ethical intersubjectivity emerging in the new democratic political culture required the institutionalization of a new political and legal order that could provide the historical referent of normative stability. This passage from 'intervention' to democratic 'innovation' (using Flisfisch's terms) must penetrate to the core of the authoritarian regime, tipping the strategic significance of the November 1988 plebiscite in favor of democracy. Such a 'moment of the political parties' (in Baño's anticipatory phrase) presupposed as a condition for democracy's success a 'de-sacralization' of the traditional ideological 'overload', allowing reentry into the political arena according to a strategic calculation and thus the meaningful reorganization of a competitive institutional setting as an end in itself.

Garretón's *La Posibilidad Democrática en Chile* (1989) described the institutional emergence of democracy, which had to take place within the space defined by the institutions of the Chilean military regime:

> If the [institutional] space were neutral and provided equal guarantees to the regime and the opposition, we would not be living under a dictatorship... Under a dictatorship, everyone always plays by the regime's rules of the game unless they are ignored, and then

the most probable outcome is only a mobilized population or perhaps a revolution if an opposing military power exists, but there is no transition. A transition presumes a space for resolving conflict, and under a dictatorship, this space must be one defined by the regime... In Chile, for example, no consensual formula was developed by the opposition for conducting a transition until 1988. The opposition never said in unison, "Look, either a constitutional reform or a plebiscite now", when the people were in the streets in 1983... Now the opposition's problem is whether it can propose or impose its own space.
(Garretón, 1989: 18-19)

Garretón analyzed the impasses in legitimizing and institutionalizing the authoritarian regime in terms of its dual nature (unique in the Southern Cone) as a personal dictatorship and a military regime. The contradictions inherent in this situation, as well as the legality assumed by the regime in the 1980 plebiscite, opened opportunities in 1988 for the democratic opposition to confront Pinochet's attempts to legitimize his staying in power. Garretón maintains that in this context, the 1988 plebiscite 'unleashed a dynamic of transition, regardless of the alternatives' (Garretón, 1989: 28).

The government of transition elected in December 1989 was charged with completing the institutional tasks of transition to democracy, trying to overcome the authoritarian enclaves. Garretón refered to these enclaves as 'constitutional aspects, the political power of the armed forces, possible political exclusions, unresolved human rights problems, the absence of democratization of local and state power, etc' (Garretón, 1989: 31). The second large undertaking of the transition government was 'to initiate the tasks of overall democratization that will assure... consolidation of a democratic regime' (Garretón, 1989: 32). Garretón conceived of this democratization as 'growing equalization of opportunities, incorporation into modern social life, participation and creation of collective subjects and actors, all of which implies envisioning a complete change' (Garretón, 1989: 36).

Undoubtedly, the breadth of these objectives would lead to setbacks and to difficult negotiations with the dominant political actors of the military regime. The democratic project would seek to involve many of them (mainly the political parties of the Right) in its institutionalization or to politically neutralize others (the armed forces and the business associations) via the majoritarian legitimacy of the democratic alternative. Garretón specified step-by-step what the priorities of the transition government should be in moving toward democratic consolidation, and he discussed the institutions, actors, and symbols of the authoritarian enclaves in terms of overcoming them gradually by consensual means (Garretón, 1989: 51- 63). Incidentally, Garretón (1999) has pointed out recently that current struggles in Chile surrounding the judicial process against Pinochet have much to do with the delayed and incomplete tasks of the country's democratization, in regard to the "authoritarian enclaves" that survived in the new regime (see also McCoy, 2000).

But the basic premise of the opposition project was the existence (and expansion) of the 'democratic subject' that won in the 1988 plebiscite: the unity of democratic political forces that succeeded in transforming their 'social majority' into a 'political and electoral majority'. As Garretón elaborated,

166 Paulo J. Krischke

One condition for consolidating a successful transition is configuring a coalition of the Center and the Left, initially led by the Center but with the possibility of change in leadership. The problem here is the old theme of the relations of the Christian Democrats with the Communist party and of the Socialists with the Communists. In this regard, a unified and renewed Socialist force can play a significant role in organizing the coalition, which should maintain basic continuity with the one that won the plebiscite, thus changing the traditional balance within the Left.
(Garretón, 1989: 62-63)

It would be difficult for the outside observer to understand how much this proposal differed from previous attempts at democratic coalition-building in Chile without considering the sociocultural transformations and political settings analyzed by the other four authors. This capacity for strategic analysis also illustrated the repositioning of Chilean intellectuals during democratization, which was summarized perceptively by Garretón in defining the collective 'democratic subject': 'There are no social and political actors that are "essentially" democratic. In other words, what can be called the "democratic subject" is not incarnated unequivocally in any particular actor but contradictorily among diverse actors, who may change position constantly with regard to this subject... Here I am discussing the democratic project in the sense of regime, as a subject or principle of historical action that requires actors to be implemented' (Garretón, 1989: 64, 72, n.12).

If any further conclusion can be added, it is that democracy in Chile became possible to the extent that the majority of Chileans wanted it and to the degree that important political and social leaders (the *FLACSO* researchers among them) began to agree on the unconditional 'desirability' of democracy. The encouraging aspect of these *FLACSO* studies is their demonstration that an authoritarian regime is undermined by its internal (or international) contradictions but also by new democratizing actors capable of reexamining their past experiences, mistakes, and divisions for the sake of building a common future.

REFERENCES

Baño, R. 1985. **Lo Social y lo Político: Un Dilema del Movimiento Popular**, Santiago: FLACSO.

Brunner, J.-J. 1988. **Un Espejo Trizado. Ensayos sobre Cultura y Políticas Culturales**, Santiago: FLACSO.

Elster, J. 1979. **Ulysses and the Sirens.: Studies in Rationality and Irrationality**. Cambridge: Cambridge University Press.

Flisfisch, A. 1987. **La Política como Compromiso Democrático**, Santiago: FLACSO.

Funk, R.L. 2000. "The Pinochet Affair: A Crisis of Transition", **LASA Congress**. Miami, March, 16-18.

Garretón, M.A. 1989. **La Posibilidad Democrática en Chile**, Santiago: FLACSO.

_____. 1999. "Chile 1997-1998: The Revenge of Incomplete Democratization", *International Affairs*, 75 (2): 259-267.

Gauchet, M. 1985. **Le Désenchantement du Monde**. Paris: Gallimard.

Habermas, J. 1984/7. **The Theory of Communicative Action**. 2 vols., Boston, MA: Beacon Press.

Habermas, J. 1985b. "La modernidad, un proyecto incompleto". In: **La Posmodernidad**, in Foster, H. (Ed.). Barcelona: Kairós.

Hirschman, A. 1970. **Exit, Voice, and Loyalty: Responses to Decline in Firms, Organizations, and States**. Cambridge, Mass.: Harvard University Press.

Lechner, N. 1988. **Los Patios Interiores de la Democracia, Subjetividad y Política**, Santiago: FLACSO.

Levine, Andrew, Sober, Elliot and Wright, Erik Olin. "Marxism and Methodological Individualism". **New Left Review**, 162.

Luhmann, N. 1979. **Trust and Power: Two Works**. Edited by Tom Burns and Gianfranco Poggi, translated by Howard Davis et al. New York: John Wiley and Sons.

Moulián, T. 1999. "The Arrest and its Aftermath", **NACLA Repport on the Americas**, 32 (6): 12-17.

Pizzorno, A. 1986. "Sobre la racionalidad de la opción democrática". In: Germani, Gino et al. **Los límites de la democracia**, vol. 2, Buenos Aires: CLACSO.

Policzer, P. 2000. "The Paradox of Truth vs. Justice: Trials for State Crime in Chile and Argentina", **LASA Congress**, Miami, March 16-18.

Przeworski, A. 1984. "Ama a incerteza e serás democrático". **Novos Estudos CEBRAP 9**, São Paulo.

Rawls, J. 1971. **A Theory of Justice**. Cambridge, MA.: Harvard University Press.

Touraine, A. 1984. **Le Retour de l'acteur**. Paris: Fayard.

Weeks, G. 2000. "Waiting for Cincinnatus: The Role of Pinochet in Postauthoritarian Chile", **LASA Congress**, Miami, March 16-18.

ENDNOTES

[1] Emphasis in the original in this and all other citations.

CONCLUSIONS

We may now return to the questions raised in the introduction, for a discussion in the light of the findings of the book. In the introduction we asked, for instance, about the constitution and change of social actors, and their capacities to become political actors. What do the chapters of this book indicate about these points, and, more specifically, how do social and political actors learn a democratic culture? What can be said about the objections to a former union leader (Lula) becoming Brazil's president, and eventually doing a good job as the top political authority of the country?

We have seen in chapter 1 that two of the more inffluential approaches to the study of democratization in Latin America offered competitive and insufficient explanations about political change, for they were unable to account for political, social and personal learning as comprehensive and historically comparative processes. Both approaches have surely identified the resilience of the authoritarian culture of oligarchic rule as one of the main - perhaps the strongest- impediment to Latin American democratization.

Nevertheless, these alternative approaches failed to analyze comparatively the actors and processes that could overcome this problem. They simply restated the antinomy of classic theories between 'minimalist' vs. 'maximalist', or representative vs. participatory democracy. Their different emphases on either culture or institutions present what appear to be insurmountable challenges to the processes of democratization. For instance, they argue that the individual rational actor among the political elites, or democratic 'collective citizens' among the population at large – are the only agents of democratization.

I have suggested that Habermas's approach to 'cognitive-moral development' could be seen as a solution to this dilemma. For his theory is pluri-dimensional, including a cognitive dimension (development of worldviews), a normative dimension (moral-legal development), and a subjective dimension (increasingly complex identities and personality structures). Both an extensive theoretical discussion and considerable empirical demonstration would be necessary, in order to support this alternative approach to the study of democratization. Such ambitious tasks are beyond the aims of this book - and they would need a research team to compare some national cases in Latin America. What was done in the book was a presentation of some historical evidence from a few local and national situations, arguing that they sustain the likelihood of this proposal.

For instance, we discovered in Chapter 2 that, as soon as a process of open negotiation of basic needs and interests began to take place among some social actors, it began to influence the opening up of the local polity. This is not an argument about what comes first in political liberalization; rather it is an emphasis on the interactive character of all historical events. Thus, case studies and survey research among participants of some social groups in Brazil (in contrast to Mexican cases studied earlier) showed that their actions and orientations had cumulative effects on social demands and public policies (and even on electoral trends at the municipal level). The 'background culture of hierarchical legitimacy' (Rawls)[1] - which in this case is authoritarian and oligarchic - was thus gradually challenged by the emergence of new social groups and organizations. These experiences introduced new strategies, values and orientations among the people (specifically among mobilized sectors of the people), with some impact on the political leadership as well.

Chapter 3 stressed in turn the importance of institution-building at the national and regional (provincial) levels, in order to guarantee an appropriate legal and political framework for democratic transition and consolidation. It emphasized that social actors necessarily achieved certain capabilities, in order to enter the public arena, and to contribute to the constitutionalization of the country. Specifically, social actors oriented to democratic participation underwent some stages of learning and cooperation - which included a capacity to link their demands for the satisfaction of basic needs, on the one hand, with an ability to build coalitions with different sectors which wanted to reform the institutions, on the other hand - in order to assure a process of democratic institutionalization.

This process of institution building and consolidation is still unfinished in Brazil. The reasons advanced for the interpretation of this flaw (which will be expanded below) point both to an insufficient decentration of sociopolitical actors, and to an incomplete juridicization of social relations. But this is not to be seen as a circular argument for institution-building, because it locates the bottlenecks that hinder democratization within the difficult learning of political competence by sociopolitical actors. Therefore, Chapters 2 and 3 developed the theoretical debate of Chapter 1 (cultural vs. institutional change) showing how grassroots organizational activities interacted with institutional democratization. Chapter 3 developed the contrast proposed earlier with Mexico (Chapter 2) showing that in Brazil there are also traditional actors and institutions which oppose and delay the democratization process.

Nevertheless, Chapter 4 also indicated that the access of social actors to the public sphere expressed different and opposing trends that emerged in society, and became gradually displayed in the polity. Therefore, this passage of social actors to political representation was only the beginning of a public negotiation among contradictory interests which were previously concealed (and/or repressed) under authoritarian rule. Thus, institutional representation publicly portrayed divergent social trends and cultural orientations that were more or less attuned with the ideals and practices of tolerance, pluralism and the open resolution of social disputes. In short, the inauguration of a competitive public arena - in this case at the local municipal level - manifested the existence of conservative, progressive and radical trends that could now compete for political support and the allegiance of the electorate. The details of the political process showed how the grassroots and the pluralist-representative groups confronted the conservative forces that opposed democratization.

Moreover, the chapter emphasized the important legacy of authoritarian and oligarchic rule, which impregnated to a large extent the actions and orientations of individuals and social groups - though openly conservative groups had to compete in an enlarged public arena with other (pluralist or radical democratic) orientations. This was seen as a process of political learning among social groups and political leaders (in the City Council, City Hall, government bureaucrats and new political representatives). These diverse negotiations and conflicts among opposing cultural and political trends were mutually influential. For social and political actors gradually learned from each other, reelaborating their own programs and identities, in the search for alternative cooperative or competitive solutions to the problems of their daily lives. Significantly, they started to learn also how to distinguish between their own sectoral and special interests, on the one hand, and their common need for an expansive public arena to negotiate their differences, on the other hand. This arena was to be the place where general goals and a joint vision of the future could eventually be formed or agreed upon.[2]

The fifth chapter of the book is a proposal to extend this historical evaluation to Latin America as a whole. It indicates that one may assess the increasing changes among social and political actors as the signs of a new form of democracy, previously unknown in most of the Latin American countries. The changes go beyond economic constraints and institutional legacies, for they manifest the behavior and orientations of social actors as an interactive learning process - which aims to build a new democratic way of life. Thus, strategic orientations are helping to expand the polity, through cooperative and competitive (sometimes conflictive) attempts at public representation and institutional negotiation of divergent demands and interests. Traditional oligarchies, new representative parties, and radical social groups and movements are learning to openly negotiate their different orientations and interests in the public sphere.

New and diverse forms of identity and expressive symbolism are also assumed by sociopolitical actors. They evolved from a reflexive reelaboration of the traditions and new universalistic orientations, which may adopt multiple identifications, and may both converge or diverge in the public sphere. The "postmodern" traits of the internationalized media, and the communicative trends that interplay within local societies, expand the possibilities of mutual recognition and agreement on the polity. The 'politics of life' (Giddens, 1990) also shows daily life and politics as a public 'spectacle', where people are called upon to participate, in their desire for a new and better life. A new civil society is thus emerging in Latin America, from the mixture of contradictory symbols, identifications and messages displayed in the "cultural market", under the inflence of globalization.

Finally, the increasing normative transformation within society confers legitimacy on the democratic regime during the attempts to reconcile divergent strategies and identifications through a permanent revision and a growing consolidation of the institutions. The demands of the poor and of the large majorities for a full and decent life, as well as the claims of minorities for their right to be different and recognized as such by others, also suppose a consolidated political regime and an expansive democratic culture.[3] From this perspective, social and political actors are seen through their abilities to promote such changes in their daily lives, and to reflexively introduce the effects of this transformation into the polity.

This cultural reorientation began by restoring self-respect and solidarity within primary relations - family life, friends and colleagues at the workplace, and neighborly relations at the grassroots of society. Chapter 6 showed that such cultural changes in daily life motivated both leaders and members of local associations to tolerate dissent and to respect the right to difference - and thus introduced an initial pluralism into public negotiations. In fact, these changes were not as smooth or peaceful as they look in retrospect - for they resulted from many forceful struggles and conflicts, both among social groups and in the interactions between the latter and the established parties and interests within the polity.

The point here is that cultural resocialization initiated at the grassroots of society (by religious and other associations) had important effects on the abilities of individual and social actors to influence the opening of the polity in a democratic direction. This means that there is an analytical distinction between the motivational and the legitimacy spheres, but also that there is in fact a continuity between social and political democratization, whenever the latter is capable to unfold.

But one has to look more closely at the processes of learning of the democratic political culture, and the results of the case studies of Chapter 6 are supported by a quantitative study in Chapter 7. This chapter reports the results of survey and local studies in Southern Brazil, which relate to electoral changes at the municipal level. These changes occurred during President Collor's administration inaugurated in 1990, and fieldwork for this research was done eight months before the November 1992 municipal elections. Therefore, this report helps to interpret the changes in the Brazilian political culture that supported the mass demonstrations for the impeachment of Pres. Collor in August 1992, and the ensuing electoral trends in the municipal elections. Incidentally, these changes were also confirmed at the 1996 elections, in the same cities – and expanded to many other cities of the country at the municipal elections in the year 2000.

The results of the research show an increasing dissatisfaction with government policies, and also different orientations towards the alternative solutions available within the party system. These different orientations derived from the diverse experiences of the voters with municipal administrations, public policies and the party leadership. Thus, the voters of one location had a decentered ('postconventional') autonomous relation with the polity, whereas participants in two other low income housing projects (in different cities) manifested different degrees of subordination ('conventional' and 'preconventional' orientations) to the traditional culture of oligarchic legitimacy. Postconventional orientations were seen as the outcome of progressive municipal policies that encouraged and challenged the residents toward self-organization. The other two locations reacted to either 'conservative modernization' policies of the right-wing parties, or radical conflicts and confrontations led by sectors of the church and the Workers' Party against the local oligarchy.

These results indicate that the learning of a democratic political culture is an interactive process between the electorate and the party leadership, which is continuously renewed (and which may also deadlock and/or regress). Political learning thus results from a public negotiation between social demands and orientations on the one hand, and government responses and policies on the other - where the latter are aimed at satisfying the former. Therefore, these evolutionary dynamics of politico-cultural democratization depend mainly on the programs and policies of the party leadership - which may (or may not) encourage people to overcome the patronage relations inherited from authoritarian/oligarchic rule.

Political leaders may emerge from society and participate in its daily life, looking for solutions to the priority problems chosen by the electorate. Thus, they may be more (or less) responsive to the new demands and orientations for democratic participation and self-organization. In turn, voters may select new leaders among themselves, who express their capacity for self-organization and autonomous relations with the polity. In short, the permeability of the institutions and the party-system to the public emergence of new accountable political actors is a key test to assure the consolidation of a democratic regime, to strengthen the competence of social actors and to expand cultural democratization within society. We have seen that this change of political actors and institutions is still unfinished in Brazil.

The flaws of political democratization in Brazil can be enlightened by a comparison with the successful transition to democracy in Chile (Chapter 8). The point here is that a successful democratic transition requires both an efficient institution-building, however incomplete, *and* a democratic cultural reorientation of major sociopolitical actors. This may sound trivial, especially considering that both the Brazilian and the Chilean transitions started within the institutional setting of military regimes. But the Chilean case had some characteristics that are worth considering. The transition in Chile occurred within the institutional framework of Pinochet's dictatorship, which was sanctioned by the 1980 plebiscite. The actors who wanted democracy in Chile had to deal openly, from the beginning of the transition, with the conservative sectors of the electorate (and their political leaders) - who would rather support again (at the 1988 referendum) the continuity of authoritarian rule. The focus of the opposition was thus on how to attract majority **electoral** (plebiscitary) support for a non-conservative orientation: how was it to be achieved?

The answer offered, in different ways, by the studies reviewed in this chapter, is that the capabilities required of social actors to negotiate their needs in the public sphere complemented their competence to expand and reform the polity. It is certain that at times this complementarity was not achieved (as has been the case in Brazil) but it was achieved in Chile and Uruguay (and apparently also in Argentina, after the collapse of the military regime).[4] The point is that political competence can be learned - or reelaborated from the country's democratic traditions. In short, the studies of the Chilean experience found a convergence among sociopolitical actors in the search for electoral democratic solutions to the problems of their daily lives.

Moreover, the aim here was not only to achieve majority **electoral** support for a democratic transition and institutionalization, because an electoral majority could easily lapse into a plebiscitarian 'catastrophic equilibrium' (Gramsci)[5] - as had happened before in Chile (1970-3) and could also happen in the future in Brazil and elsewhere in Latin America. There is thus a need to understand how conservative, progressive and radical actors who emerge in society may learn to conceive the democratic way of life as an end and a value in itself - continuously reelaborating their actions and orientations to achieve this goal. The Habermasian focus on normative decentration helps us to see how changes in the political culture may occur during democratic transition and institutionalization.

For instance, it shows that specific social demands can be satisfactorily negotiated in the public arena, when rational choices about particular benefits are balanced by both normative considerations (e.g., the willingness to recognize the rights of others to their own claims) and demands for veracity among the social actors (e.g., about their mutual trust). Therefore, it is not enough from this perspective to achieve **majority** support (electorally or otherwise) for democratic institutionalization, unless a reasonable guarantee of survival and satisfaction is extended to the **minorities** (conservatives, radicals, or any other sectors) within the polity. We must note that this is not a "game-theory" analysis of institution building (which may also be useful)[6] but an understanding of the achievement of normative and cultural decentration - namely the recognition of the right of others to be different, in the search for inclusiveness, through a plural and reflexive interaction, considered as a more just and efficient process of deliberation.

The test of this emphasis on communicative action in the Brazilian case (Chapter 3) indicated that gradual normative decentration played a crucial role in the access of new social actors to the public sphere - as they attempted to achieve and exercise their citizenship rights during the constitutionalization of the country. It also stressed in many cases the institutional and legal impediments that hindered Brazilian citizens in reaching their aims - mainly due to the incipient juridicization of social relations, the lack of sanctions and regulations to guarantee their rights, and related problems. In turn, such legal and institutional blockages were initially circumscribed in the Chilean case, where sociopolitical actors of every persuasion reached an agreement on the strategic, symbolical and normative requirements for the democratic political transition.

This is why the emergence of Lula - a former union leader and chairman of the Workers' Party - as presidential candidate (in the first direct presidential elections in 1989, again in 1994 and 1998, and possibly also in 2002) created such a tremendous challenge to the established patterns of authoritarian and oligarchic rule in Brazil. The unfinished liberal and democratic transition of the 1980s and 1990s instituted a legal and political framework which is noted for its frailty - and is therefore unable to process institutionally the demands emerging from the transformation within society. Among other problems, the feebleness of the party system created the opportunity for charismatic candidates (as in the case of Collor in 1989) to manipulate the basic needs and orientations of the electorate (in this case with large support from the oligarchies and the mass media). On the other hand, the representatives of organized sectors of society (such as Lula's Workers' Party) have great difficulty in finding interlocutors within the polity and in working out coalition strategies to advance their goals of democratization.[7]

Therefore, the threat mentioned above of an electoral 'catastrophic equilibrium' has been quite serious in Brazil. The solution to this problem will in part depend on the ability of the political leadership to introduce the necessary legal and institutional reforms in the polity. The present government of Fernando H. Cardoso has been striving to negotiate at least part of these reforms, without much success. (Schwartzman, 2000; Korzeniewsky and Macías, 1998). But the real solution to this problem will mostly depend on the capacity of the leadership to address the needs for participation and self-organization that exist in society. For, otherwise, these needs will continue to be manipulated by opportunistic candidates outside (or within) the party system. These challenges pose therefore gigantic tasks for the political leadership. But they are conceivable as part of the current changes of Brazilian political culture, where the demands for democratic participation and the conquest of citizenship rights have increased and expanded in the last decade.

It is certain that the reform of the institutions and the competence (and willingness) of the political leadership are fundamental to the consolidation of the democratic regime and the democratization of the political culture. It is also certain that the 'authoritarian enclaves' and the legacy of traditional oligarchic rule exercise most of the heavy load of their influence within the institutional setting of the new democratic regimes. Therefore, the studies that are being conducted on the elites and the political leadership (especially the conservative parties, the media and the business sectors)[8] are extremely important for an understanding of the trends that may limit democratic consolidation. Moreover, the studies on institution-building and coalition policies will clarify and evaluate the prospects, the strategies and procedures, and the legal and political rules needed to guarantee and strenghten democratic institutionalization in Latin America.[9]

A case in point is the current debate within the *PT* regarding the process to appoint the party's candidate for Presidential elections in 2002. Some currents of the party demand an internal referendum to choose the best candidate to attract coalition support, and to overcome the usual prejudices of the establishment (and in large sectors of the electorate) against Lula's candidacy, as a former member of the working class. Regardless of the results of this debate, it is certain that this Presidential election will present a new test for the democratization of Brazilian institutions, the country's political elites, and the political culture of the electorate.

But this book has stressed another, and hopefully brighter, dimension of sociopolitical change in Latin America: namely that this change expressed the demands and orientations of individuals and social actors who are striving, at the grassroots of society, to become full citizens and competent political actors. They may often fail and suffer severe losses and defeats in facing stronger privileged opponents. But they continue to challenge oligarchic rule, through a communicative/reflexive reelaboration of their own traditions, a process which is gradually undermining the traditional culture of authoritarian legitimacy. Therefore, social and political actors are learning from their own past and present struggles, in order to establish and expand political democracy in Latin America. Social scientists are also learning their new role in society, as they contribute to the study of the relations between political and cultural democratization.

REFERENCES

De La Torre, C. 1998. "Populist Redemption and the Unfinished Democratization of Latin America", *Constellations*, 5(1): 85-95.

Elster, J. 1993. "Majority Rule and Individual Rights". In: Shute, S. and Hurley, S. (Eds.). **On Human Rights**. New York: Basic Books, 1993.

Geddes, B. 1994. "Uses and Limitations of Rational Choice in the Study of Politics in Developing Countries". In: Smith, P. (Ed.), **Comparative Perspectives in Latin America: Methods and Analysis**, Boulder: Westview.

Giddens, A. 1990. **Consequences of Modernity**. Stanford: Stanford University Press.

Gramsci, A. 1971. **Selections from the Prison Notebooks**. Ed. by Q. Hoare & G. Nowell-Smith, New York: International Publishers.

Inglehart, R. 1997. **Modernization and Postmodernization. Cultural, Economic and Political Change in 43 Sotieties**, New Jersey: Princeton University Press.

Keck, M. 1990. **The Workers' Party and Democratization in Brazil**. New Haven: Yale University Press.

Korzeniewscz, M. and Macías, T. 1998. "Economy and Society in Brazil: Cardoso's Presidency and its Possibilities", *Latin American Research Review*, 33(1): 226-238.

Kowarick, L. (Ed.) 1994. **Social Struggles in the City: the Case of São Paulo**. New York: Monthly Review Press.

Limongi, F. and Figueiredo, A.C. 1995. "Mudança Constitucional, Desempenho do Legislativo e Consolidação Institucional", *Revista Brasileira de Ciências Sociais*, 29: 175-200.

Linz, J. 1993. "The Future of an Authoritarian Situation or the Institutionalization of an Authoritarian Regime". In: Alfred Stepan (Ed.). **Authoritarian Brazil**, New Haven: Yale University Press.

Mainwaring, S. et al. 1999. "Conservative Parties, Democracy, and Economic Reforms in Brazil", **Kellogg Institute Working Papers**, 264.

McCoy, J. (Ed.). 2000. **Political Learning and Redemocratization in LatinAmerica: Do Politicians Learn from Crisis?** Coral Gables, FL: North-South Center.

Minella, A. 1998. "Elites Financeiras, Sistema Financeiro e Governo FHC", in Rampinelli, W. and Ouriques, N. (Eds.) **No Fio da Navalha. Crítica das Reformas Neoliberais de FHC**, São Paulo: Ed. Xaman.

Rawls, J. 1985 "Justice as Fairness: Political not Metaphysical". **Philosophy and Public Affairs**, 14(3):223-51.

_____, 1993. "The Law of Peoples". In: Schute, S. and Hurley, S. (Eds.). **On Human Rights**, New York: Basic Books.

_____, 1999. **The Law of Peoples**, Cambridge, MS: Harvard University Press.

Selbin, E. 1993. "Whither Socialism in Latin America and the Caribbean: the Continuing Relevance of Non-revolutionary Progressive Politics". **Washington: APSA Annual Meeting**, Sept. 2/5.

ENDNOTES

[1] See Rawls (1993) for a seminal discussion of legitimacy in "hierarchical"societies. However, his later work on this topic (Rawls, 1999) does not provide a theoretical approach to analyze the transition from a "hierarchical" into a democratic society. I have tried to demonstate in this book that Habermas's approach to social and political democratization addresses the "evolutionary dynamics" of political transition.

[2] Rawls (1985) provides the initial focus for a dynamic interpretation of the democratic policy, further developed later in his book on "Political Liberalism" (Rawls, 1993).

[3] In this non-deterministic context, the findings of Inglehart (1997) make suggestive indications for research on the "new political culture".

[4] See on this point the comparative approaches proposed by Selbin (1993) and Moreira (2000).

[5] Gramsci (1971:201) describes the situation where "hegemony" is not achieved by either of the contending parties, and there is thus a political stalemate. My point here, however, is not that there should (or could) be any sort of "hegemony" (whatever its definition) in Latin American countries. The point is that a political stalemate may result from a lack of decentration of sociopolitical actors – e.g. their attempt to impose on others their own point of view (even when backed by an electoral majority). See also De la Torre (1998) on the recurring threats of populist politics, and Linz (1993) on the deficit of institutionalization in "authoritarian situations".

[6] See Elster (1993).

[7] Electoral support for the Workers' Party steadily increased since it was founded in 1980 (Keck, 1990). Thus, it managed to win (through "popular front"coalitions) municipal elections in many cities – including two of the three locations studied in Chapter 7. The appraisal of earlier administrations in other cities (elected in the 1980s) showed mixed results. Cultural innovations, participatory policies and public accountability were recognized as some of their positive contributions. But there were also criticisms about their inexperience in relations with City Councils, lack of long-term political and economic policies, and little publicity to debate and disseminate priorities among the electorate. In any case, the *PT* has been reelected in various of these locations during the 1990s, and won also in several others in 2000. (On the Workers' Party São Paulo 1988-92 administration, see Kowarick, Ed., 1994. On the present increase of electoral support to the *PT* see Moreira, 2000).

[8] e,g., Minella, 1998; McCoy (Ed.), 2000; Mainwaring et al., 1999.

[9] e.g., Geddes, 1994; Limongi and Figueiredo, 1995.

INDEX